A long-overdue gift (a small one) to a great public servant. — Many thanks for all you've done to advance the goals and to preserve the flexibility perhaps the most significant reforms social security will have ever seen. There is so much more to do and our presence in the process is a great comfort to all who have followed the reform effort and who know you were a part of thanks for the opportunity to be a part of it all

— Chuck 3/../01

REFORMING SOCIAL SECURITY

For Ourselves and Our Posterity

Charles P. Blahous III

Foreword by Senator Alan K. Simpson

Published in cooperation with the
Center for Strategic and International Studies
Washington, D.C.

Westport, Connecticut
London

Library of Congress Cataloging-in-Publication Data

Blahous, Charles P., 1963–
     Reforming social security for ourselves and our posterity / Charles P. Blahous III.
          p.   cm.
     Includes bibliographical references and index.
     ISBN 0–275–97044–2 (alk. paper)
     1. Social security—United States.   2. Social security—United States—Finance.   I. Title.
     HD7125.B55   2000
     368.4'3'00973—dc21   00–035968

British Library Cataloguing in Publication Data is available.

Library of Congress Catalog Card Number: 00–035968
ISBN: 0–275–97044–2

First published in 2000

Praeger Publishers, 88 Post Road West, Westport, CT 06881
An imprint of Greenwood Publishing Group, Inc.
www.praeger.com

Printed in the United States of America

The paper used in this book complies with the
Permanent Paper Standard issued by the National
Information Standards Organization (Z39.48–1984).

10 9 8 7 6 5 4 3 2 1

If we could first know where we are, and whither we are tending, we could then better judge what to do, and how to do it.

—Abraham Lincoln
Springfield, Illinois
June 16, 1858

Contents

Contents

Illustrations

TABLES

Illustrations

FIGURE

Foreword

When I first met a fine young man named Chuck Blahous in 1989, I was not supposed to know him for long. He joined up with my "outfit" for a one-year hitch as a Congressional Science Fellow. We would just take a few weeks or months to get him up to speed, he'd pinch-hit for my legislative staff on an issue here and there, and then be on his way.

When I retired from the United States Senate after 18 years of service in 1996, Chuck Blahous was my legislative director, as well as a trusted confidant, a magnificent researcher and fact gatherer, a gifted writer . . . and a special friend.

The story you are about to read is a remarkable one, written by a persistent, steady and extremely thoughtful man. There's no other issue in American political discourse that calls forth so many heavy combat troops. Chuck and I went through these wars together—on the Kerrey-Danforth Entitlement Commission where Chuck staffed my work, on our subcommittee's review of the operations of the American Association of Retired Persons (AARP), and on so many other tasks.

On this issue, Chuck has done it all, and he has seen it all, too. He has been deeply involved with most every credible bipartisan effort to try to shore up Social Security in recent years—from the Entitlement Commission right on through CSIS's National Commission on Retirement Policy. In every instance, he quickly earned the respect and admiration of his colleagues for his knowledge and his fairness.

Early on in Chuck's tenure, I learned to rely on him for lucid memoranda that would cut through the usual smoke and mirrors and present the facts in a concise way. Whether the issue was the human rights situation in East Timor or baseball's antitrust exemption, Chuck hit all of the salient features in a memo of two pages or less. And I could always trust him to lay out the facts that I needed to know, whether they were pleasant or not. The issues that really test the mettle of staff, though, are the programs that deliver entitlement benefits to America's seniors, like Social Security.

Until recent years, few knew the truth about how well these programs were working, and fewer others, Democrat or Republican, really wanted to actually find out. As a legislator, you have to know not only what is happening in the federal government but also why it's happening. Here in these pages Chuck performs the same service for you that he often did for me—laying out an issue in stark detail, not just the facts but the players, the perceptions, the history, everything that goes into making the current Social Security debate the tangled web it is.

If you never read another book on Social Security, you surely ought to read this one. There is probably no other issue on the national agenda that slices so directly to the core of what this nation is about: what our values are, whether we are capable of honestly leveling with each other in political discourse, and whether we value the interests of all Americans or just those who organize the phone banks.

I can certainly tell you this based on 18 years of experience serving as a U.S. senator. My schedule would be crammed full with meetings each and every day, and each time that door would swing open, someone would come through it asking for money. In one meeting, a constituent would want a government grant. In another, a cabinet official would insist that their department needed more money. No one would ever come through that door and offer to give more to the government, or give something back, or to take less the next time. And getting the "straight story" from someone who has an obvious self-interest is a tough thing to do.

Nor is it any easier to get the straight story from the individuals who are employed to tell the Congress, the public, and the press just what is happening on policy issues. Every night on the talk shows, the press sets up a shouting match between one think tank "expert" and another. It's not news, and it's not policy; it's entertainment. The folks who work for those think tanks may be fine people, but they're no more objective than any other set of hired hands when it comes to talking about a subject. They are there to represent a particular position at one extreme or than other, and then make up reasons to support it as they go along.

This does not even begin to touch on the influence and character of the various interest groups that try to influence Washington every day—from the AARP to the National Committee to Preserve Social Security and Medicare. These organizations are about one thing and one thing only—making money—and they get it either directly from the federal government, or by scaring it right out of the pockets of senior citizens. So in the final analysis, there aren't many places that a senator can turn to get an objective source of information on a subject. Staffers try, but there are usually too few of them to have enough time to dig very deeply into an issue. And there is too often a peculiar strain of staff mentality that sets in, inducing them to tell the boss only what they believe is in his political interest to hear, even if he is earnestly trying to weigh the issues that are greater than his own political fate.

This is why Chuck was so valuable to me, and why he was quite unusual in Washington. He wasn't "of the culture" when he came in. He had a life, and a good one, outside of politics. And I learned that he always had much more to offer to me than the usual sources. If "politics" is one's only passion in life it can be a barbaric experience. Chuck always had a larger perspective and a truly remarkable range of interests: history, classical music, piano, baseball, humor, chess, and more. I learned that he always had much more to offer to me than did the "usual sources."

What the usual sources won't tell you is that the social security issue is one that Americans had better figure out, and fast. It needn't affect today's seniors. It doesn't affect me. No, this one is about the future. These pages lay it all out. Chuck is by no means the first to have comprehended the big picture here. Thoughtful legislators and citizen groups on both sides of the aisle—Paul Tsongas, Pete Peterson, Bob Kerrey, Warren Rudman, Pat Moynihan, The Concord Coalition, Third Millennium—understand and appreciate much of the larger question already.

But what they don't have, and what this book offers, is the expertise to sift through all of the standard arguments on the subject with a fine-toothed comb. Every day somewhere there's a conference or a rally on this subject, and someone will say, "There wouldn't be a problem if Congress would just stop raiding the Trust Fund!" Or, "I'm a notch baby, and I'm tired of being ripped off!" Or, "Won't this problem go away if the economy just grows a little bit faster?"

After you finish reading this book, you'll know the real story behind those myths, because it presents the hard information and then lets you figure it out for yourself. And better yet, you'll also know why so many self-interested parties say the things they do about this issue.

The book begins by describing the political history of the Social Security issue as it is felt and seen by public servants on both sides of the aisle. I was there on the Senate floor the night we wheeled Pete Wilson of California in on a gurney to cast a deciding vote for a tough budget in 1985. I was also there when the election returns came in that tossed seven Republicans right out of the Senate, and cost us the Senate majority. I saw the ads: "This is the bum who voted to cut your Social Security!" And, if you want to understand how this subject is dealt with, you have to understand that fear mentality in Washington, the way that legislators are deathly afraid of the seniors' groups.

Foreword

This book relates not only the history of Social Security, but also gives a taste of the pungent flavor of interest-group politics. There's a brief chapter in here dedicated to the phenomenon of the AARP—30 million individuals bound together by a common love of airline discounts. This group is ever lobbying happily for increased spending every chance they get—usually without the knowledge of, or approval by, their members. No one can understand anything about Social Security politics until they see how the seniors groups weigh in on it, even though long-term reform doesn't affect their members in any way.

The real meat of the book presents the coming costs of the Social Security system and the burden it will lay on the shoulders of future wage earners unless we do "something." All of the standard manipulation and emotional crunching of the numbers by interest groups, politicians, and think tanks is deftly refuted here.

Whenever I criticize something the press does, they respond that this will have a "chilling effect" on free press and free speech. What malarkey. The First Amendment is for me, too, and I surely intend to keep exercising it!

This book is written in that spirit. It does not attempt to muzzle the propagandists, but it fights fire with facts. Right now there are plenty of Social Security plans in which it seems that no one will to have to "pay anything" to get the Social Security system back on track. Half of the presidential candidates are telling Americans that they're going to get everything that has been promised to them, but that no one will have to pay to fulfill these promises.

This book should make it absolutely clear to you what that rhetoric amounts to. After reading it, you'll know that there is a lot more to the story than is given in those vapid reassurances. You'll not only understand the full and complete cost of every reform approach, but you'll also see what happens when political operatives get a strangle hold of policy issues. It isn't pretty.

Just before I left the Senate, I told Chuck of my plans to retire. He too had been giving some thought to leaving Washington and was pondering whether he should return to the academic ranks, or even start another career altogether. He had received expressions of interest from a number of other senators, and he sought my good counsel. One of those members seeking him was Senator Judd Gregg of New Hampshire. My advice to Chuck was: "You know when the time comes to leave Washington. It'll be when they're trying to stick you on the eighth floor of the Hart Building in a broom closet. It won't be when we're in the majority, when people are interested in issues you care about, when you have the respect of your peers, and when a Senator like Judd Gregg wants you to work for him." Chuck had overtures from other senators, but I knew that Judd's was the one that he ought to accept, because unlike some of the others, Gregg had no political "fear streak." It would have driven Chuck goofy to have a boss who would continually disregard policy advice for political considerations. Judd Gregg is one skilled politician, but he doesn't harbor political queasiness. And Chuck would learn a lot from him, the thing he loves most to do.

I've long known that great things were in store for Chuck, and I am so very pleased that his work for Senator Gregg has enabled him to serve the public ever more vigorously. This book may not be the last word on Social Security—but I can hope and pray that it won't be the last word from Chuck Blahous either.

Senator Alan K. Simpson

Acknowledgments

This book could not have been written without the generous assistance of many contributors. Of necessity, this brief section lists only a small fraction of the people to whom I owe a tremendous debt.

Whoever first said, "Actions speak louder than words," must have been from New England. The person to whom I owe the greatest thanks for making this book possible, Senator Judd Gregg, embodies this aphorism and has shown his generosity towards me in countless silent but significant ways. These include his granting me permission to taken a period of part-time and part-salary to compose this work, as well as his constant willingness to share public credit with his staff, even to the point of allowing one to publish under his own name on a controversial political subject. Working for Senator Gregg is a refreshing antidote to the norms of a profession where virtues are sometimes extolled rather than practiced or, when practiced, are publicly displayed to political advantage.

Thanks also belong to the Center for Strategic and International Studies (CSIS), the sponsor of this volume, whose convening of the National Commission on Retirement Policy (NCRP) was the genesis of the book. At CSIS, Brad Belt's constant support, counsel, and tireless advocacy of the project were indispensable, as was the work done by Jim Dunton and Pamela Mills to transform my drafts into a presentable work.

Among the many who helped with editorial suggestions, I must single out two: Carrie Lips labored on every aspect of this project, embraced it as she would her own, and put up with a lot of me in the process, for which I am so grateful. Syl Schieber contributed important suggestions as well as

Acknowledgments

the benefit of his expertise. Daniel Sarewitz, Richard Thau, James Hamilton, and Michael Tongour also provided helpful edits of earlier drafts.

At this point, I must apologize to the many others whom I cannot name despite all that they have done for me. I trust that my family and friends are already well aware of my gratitude for their patient support. Others, whom I can only list in group form, include the Washington offices of Senators Alan Simpson and Judd Gregg, the senators, congressmen, experts, and staff associated with the National Commission on Retirement Policy, Steve Goss and the Office of the Social Security Actuary, the staff of the Senate and House bipartisan coalitions, and last but far from least, the "Friday Group."

An additional word of clarification may be helpful to the reader. The proposal developed by the National Commission on Retirement Policy is often referred to as the NCRP plan, the CSIS plan (after its sponsoring organization), or the GBKS plan (after Gregg-Breaux-Kolbe-Stenholm, the four members of Congress who first introduced it as legislation). It is intended here to use the NCRP name consistently, but the reader would be well advised to treat any string of four initials as referring to the same proposal.

1

The View from the Future

Imagine that you are the president of the United States in the year 2027, grappling with a Social Security program on the verge of bankruptcy.

Imagine, too, that in order to pay the benefits that have been promised from the system, you would need to propose and to enact an immediate increase of nearly 50 percent in the Social Security payroll tax, from its current rate of 12.4 percent to nearly 18 percent.

Imagine, further, that the political and economic climate of the time is riven with discord and discontent, that "stagflation" has afflicted the country for years, that federal deficits are out of control despite record levels of taxation, that economic growth is down, and that unemployment is up.

What do you do?

Do you cut Social Security benefits drastically, sending more seniors directly into poverty? Or do you impose even higher tax rates, weakening the economy still further and creating more poverty through increased unemployment?

In just a few decades, it may not require imagination to perceive the essence of such choices. The current-law path of Social Security may mandate this course of events.

I present this alarmist scenario, not in the belief that we will travel down the path to ruin, but to elucidate the full extent of the crisis that could await if we do not act to avert it. It is not a pretty picture.

In the 1990s, America has enjoyed a time of comparative peace and prosperity. Inflation has been low, so too unemployment. A surge of national productivity enabled a Congress, otherwise wracked with partisan divisions, to pass a balanced budget agreement. In 1998, for the first time in more than a generation, total annual revenues of the federal government exceeded total annual outlays.

To a degree, this surplus in the "unified budget" is illusory. Only the Social Security program runs a surplus, whereas the rest of the budget until recently showed a deficit. Moreover, Social Security clearly needs all the savings that its surplus can provide, in order to cover future benefit payments. But though the long-term fiscal challenges remain very real, the short-term budgetary picture looks better now than it has for decades.

It had been expected that 1999 would be a year of action on Social Security, when Congress and the president would work together to enact reforms that would eliminate the program's projected insolvency. It didn't happen. Republicans and Democrats could not agree on a means of using our surplus resources now to limit the future liabilities of the program.

By contrast, Republicans and Democrats spent more time considering the wholly irresponsible: creating new spending obligations, through additional entitlement programs external to Social Security, doing nothing to reduce the long-term tax burdens latent in the current system, or simply camouflaging the whole challenge with a series of confusing accounting maneuvers.

What would be the result of taking either course? In 2008, things would begin to change radically. The annual cash surplus in Social Security, long having offset the imbalance in the rest of the budget, will begin to decline. If the economy is still essentially healthy, no more than some minor belt-tightening might be required to keep the fiscal house in order. We might have to cut back on a few expenditures in education, transportation, and defense—or roll back a few recently enacted tax cuts—but we could make these choices without undue harm to the economy at large.

In the year 2014, however, things would change again. The Social Security system will have obligations that year of $929 billion—more than twice the level of 2002. Total revenues from the payroll tax and from benefit taxation would together be only $917 billion. In other words, enough won't be being collected to issue all of the checks on which beneficiaries rely.

From this point forward, payments to the Social Security Trust Fund will be anything but an abstract accounting concern. For the first time in three decades, the federal government will have to make real payments to the Trust Fund immediately, in cash—or else someone's Social Security check won't be sent.

This $12 billion outlay in 2014 is not likely to appear very large at first, but the gap between Social Security's revenues and its spending obligations will expand drastically in the next few years, topping $100 billion annually by 2018. Simultaneous with Social Security's new claims on the

2

Treasury, spending on Medicare will accelerate briskly because of the wave of retirements of the baby-boom generation.

These would be the early sparks in what would eventually become a fiscal conflagration. Cash imbalances within Social Security would continue to grow (passing $200 billion in 2021), because we would not have addressed them directly other than simply to raise the general taxes necessary to pay Trust Fund obligations.

Faced with such pressures on the general budget, Congress would face the unpleasant choices of increasing taxes, cutting all appropriations to the bone, or resuming a spree of federal borrowing. In all likelihood, it would have to do a little bit of all three, simply because the payments required from the general treasury to Social Security would become so large that neither tax increases nor spending reductions alone could possibly accommodate them.

Ultimately, this pressure would cause the economy to cry "uncle." Hiking taxes perpetually to maintain these payments would reduce both personal and corporate income growth. To the extent that the enormous expansion in new federal deficits stimulates inflation, the Federal Reserve would be under tremendous pressure to keep the money supply under control, stifling the economy. If the Fed relaxed its grip on the money supply in order to give national productivity a boost, increased inflation would likely result.

One result of this series of events would be a popular resurrection of the term "misery index," coined in the late 1970s to describe the simultaneous existence of both high inflation and high unemployment. Another would be that higher inflation would mean higher COLA (cost of living allowance) payments within Social Security, worsening its fiscal balance and threatening its solvency.

Under current law, the gap between Social Security's revenues and its outlays in the year 2023 is scheduled to be a cool $327 billion. That is too big a gap in one year to fill with tax increases alone, and by then there would be no more meaningful room left within appropriations for further spending cuts. This in turn would mean more borrowing, thus more inflation, and thus greater deterioration in the balance of Social Security.

At such a point, Congress might have to look for ways to bring the program into line on an emergency basis. Perhaps full COLAs could not be given to everyone, and upper-income beneficiaries would have to do without them. Perhaps a politically treacherous Social Security rescue package could be passed if the public fully comprehended, and thus supported, the need for drastic action.

Perhaps. But there are a lot of unforeseen variables in the future. Will the twenty-first century be a century of peace, or of war? Will there be unforeseen expenses on the military? Could there be a recession in the early years of the twenty-first century that makes the economic picture worse than we can currently foretell? If any of these takes place, then even these predictable fiscal crises would be far more severe than just enumerated.

It does not take much in the way of variance from projected expenses to imagine annual imbalances within the Social Security system of more than $1 trillion per year before the year 2035. If all goes as expected, the cash shortfall will be more than $850 billion in the year 2034. If inflation does not, in fact, turn out to be only 3.3 percent, as the actuaries assume, then the pressure on the economy will be substantially worse.

This is not a hypothetical, nightmare scenario. Under current law, though the Social Security system is projected to be "solvent" through the year 2034, we are banking on making annual cash payments from general revenues to pay off the Social Security Trust Fund, of hundreds of billions of dollars in most years.

Remember where we are today. We have been unable until recently to fully balance the federal budget even *with* enormous surpluses from Social Security. Imagine that this situation turned around and that we were responsible for making payments of hundreds of billions of dollars *to* Social Security each year. What is the likelihood then that we could keep the budget balanced? What is the likelihood then that we can avoid a massive increase in federal borrowing that would lead to higher inflation and to all of the increased problems that this would create for Social Security?

Even were we to manage these tasks, the Social Security system would become insolvent anyway in the year 2034, or perhaps before. In other words, current law assumes that we will somehow find the cash to make a $861 billion payment from general revenues to Social Security in the year 2034 and that we will have been able to budget for more than $7 trillion of such payments in the years from 2014 through 2034. After we succeed in doing that, the program becomes insolvent anyway.

It should be apparent that the process of coming up with an additional $7 trillion in new payments to the system from 2014 to 2034 will create adverse economic consequences far beyond our capacity to imagine at this time. What kind of shape we would be in, in the year 2034, for finding a good way to get the system back on track is not a pleasant prospect.

I do not believe that the preceding scenario will ever happen, for the simple reason that our democracy will not permit it to happen. Although cynicism about our form of government is rampant, the American people do not, as a rule, elect individuals who are so venal or so shortsighted that when they possess advance notice of a crisis they refuse absolutely to address it.

Our government indeed has its blemishes, the occasional scoundrel in public office. As is the case with any profession, there will be a certain number of crooks and ne'er-do-wells elected to Congress. But the blasé cynicism expressed by so many Americans about those who represent them in Washington is not validated by my observation.

4

Consequently, I disdain alarmist scenarios as a general rule. This is not to say that such projections are necessarily wrong, but rather that the worst effects predicted are often delayed, if not eliminated, by willful resourcefulness, especially when expressed through democratic action. Malthusian projections of irreversible trends towards mass starvation underrated our capacity to increase agricultural production. Alarmist environmental scenarios have underrated our capacity to manage natural resources.

Though we will always blunder in our management of the environment and of food supplies, we take constructive action as well. We are not mute and impotent observers watching disaster play itself out. Those who ignore human will and creativity as key elements of the equation often wind up looking terribly silly a few decades later. I thus hesitate to describe the worst of what could happen, so confident am I that reality will take a different course.

But the fact remains that these problems will not fix themselves. We have put ingredients into current law that bear devastating implications if we do not move to change them. We can change them, and we must change them if America is to prosper—and I believe that we ultimately will.

Foolish is the man or the society that reacts to each crisis only as it comes and does not strive to create the best possible range of choices for the future. Similarly, the economic choices facing America in 2030 will in large part be a consequence of decisions made in 1999. We must bear the appropriate awareness and the appropriate humility not only to use the wisdom and knowledge that we have but also to recognize their limits. We know enough to recognize that we will, under current law, deprive posterity of the wherewithal to make choices as to the allocation of its resources, because we will have forced much of our chosen allocation upon them. We should, more humbly, retreat from requiring them to pay the consequences of our attempting to outbid each other to demonstrate who cares most about the seniors of 2025. We ought to have some faith that future generations will make such provision for the needs of their elderly if we provide them with the opportunity to do so. But what we absolutely must not do is to bequeath them a structure that we know cannot work effectively toward this end.

President Clinton declared that 1998 would be a year of national discussion about Social Security. Like many other public servants, the president has been aware for some time of the looming crisis inherent in the nation's Social Security program. However, better than most of them, the president understands the need for political preparation of decisive action. And so he requested that the American Association of Retired Persons and the Concord Coalition—two organizations representing, respectively, the interests of senior citizens and of fiscal responsibility—hold a series of forums around the country to discuss the future path of Social Security. The goals were twofold: not only to hear from the American public regarding various proposals for reform but also to better acquaint the public with the vast extent of the existing problems.

The introduction to this book represents a different attempt to acquaint the public with the full scope of the challenges facing the Social Security program. Despite all of the sound and fury already unleashed in public discussions of Social Security, I believe that the program is still widely misunderstood and is conceived of in ways that too often reflect the prejudices of the observer, rather than the realities of the program.

The year 1999 could have been, and should have been, a time of action to strengthen the Social Security program, to enable it to withstand the retirement of the baby-boom generation and to remain strong and viable throughout the twenty-first century. Presently, America is at peace. Our economy is sound. Inflation is low. Unemployment is low.

But this era may instead prove to be a season of missed opportunity, when Americans tended only to their short-term wants and chose to ignore the hard information that they possessed.

This book reflects a firm belief that it is not selfishness but ignorance that would cause Americans to continue the latter course. If the nuts and bolts of the Social Security program and the consequences of allowing current law to play itself out are laid before the public, it will support the reforms necessary to avert a crisis and to build a retirement income system that will increase the security and prosperity of Americans in their retirement years.

To do this, it is necessary to discuss where we are, both politically and substantively, how we got here, and whither we are tending. This requires looking beyond the superficial descriptions of the Social Security program as they are often given in press accounts and beyond reflexive reactions to the issues that are raised. To say that we care for senior citizens and for fiscal responsibility is not enough; we must develop the resources to provide retirement income in a fiscally realistic manner.

This is also a time of danger, as well as opportunity. We can, for lack of a better phrase, screw this up and make things even worse. Every challenge brings with it a range of possible tough choices, and every tough choice brings with it a temptation to ease it in some way. To the degree that we decide to make things easier for ourselves, someone else may pay for those decisions. We must be diligent in reviewing how the burdens of our decisions are shared by different generations of Americans and not be blind to elements of those burdens that we find discomfiting to peruse.

There is, within the Senate and the House of Representatives, a bipartisan core of legislators willing to act. What is needed is the active engagement of the president and a willingness for leaders of both parties to step forward responsibly. Neither of these two elements will be added unless there is a perception that it is politically safe to do so. These judgments of political safety will inevitably be influenced by the organizations that actively lobby the federal government on this issue.

The View from the Future

Throughout this process will be heard the voices of self-interested lobbying organizations, groups that will have every incentive to be shrill, first because they raise money for themselves by capitalizing on the political risks taken by any legislator and second because they fear reform, for the reason that the cries of alarm through which they earn their living will be heard with less credulity once the Social Security system is secured. These groups will do everything in their power to drown out reasoned and informed deliberations about Social Security and will try to whip legislators and their staffs into positions of partisan intractability.

As vaccination helps us to ward off disease, so too does education make us less susceptible to demagoguery. This book, therefore, attempts to broaden readers' understanding of the Social Security program and the political currents that buffet it, even though many of these readers might disagree with some of the policy recommendations that it contains.

What is at stake? Nothing less than the standard of living of future generations of American seniors and working wage earners alike. This is our chance to do for posterity what previous generations did for us: to give them the opportunity to chart their own course and to pursue the American dream in their own way, unbound to our necessarily limited visions.

The power to tax and to spend, to borrow, and to commit to the payment of taxpayer-financed benefits is an awesome power of the federal government that must be used with humility. We literally have it within our power, if we so choose, to bankrupt this nation before the next century is half over, if we simply choose to accelerate our spending and eventually our debt. But we also have it within our power, if we are guided by our consciences and by our intellectual integrity, to take our place among many previous generations of Americans in giving posterity a reason to look back and to congratulate us for a job well done.

2

Challenges to the Culture of Entitlement

In 1993, newly elected President William Jefferson Clinton pursued two significant, and somewhat inconsistent, initial fiscal packages. One was a $13 billion "stimulus package" of targeted federal spending, ostensibly designed to "jump start" an economy mired in a mild recession. The other was a deficit-reduction plan. Republicans, as a party, opposed both, the first on the basis that deficit spending was the cause, not the cure, of our fiscal woes, and the latter on the basis that the president's deficit reduction was to be achieved through tax increases, rather than by addressing the spending patterns that had led to our current budget predicament.

Special rules in the Senate protect budget legislation from being obstructed by a minority. Accordingly, though Republicans were able to defeat the supplemental appropriations package, they could not stop the budget plan if it retained sufficient support from the Democratic majority. The supplemental appropriations package was the first item presented by President Clinton that really riled up the Republicans. Though a more public controversy raged around "gays in the military," it was the stimulus package that was the first overtly partisan legislative confrontation. The Democratic majority attempted to pass the package without opening it to any amendments, using restrictive floor procedures. This unified the Republicans behind filibustering the package. At one particularly raucous Republican conference, my boss, Senator Alan Simpson (R-WY), said that he would "sleep on a cot in his office" during the next few nights if that was what it took to stop the appropriations bill. In retrospect, Republicans did the president a favor by stopping it. Passing a large additional spending bill would have set back the goal of balancing the budget, which became a singular political asset for the president a few years later.

When it came time to consider the budget package, one Democrat who was in a serious quandary was Senator Robert Kerrey of Nebraska. His complaints with the president's budget concerned not so much the actions taken, but rather the opportunities missed. The deficit-reduction plan seemed to address the budget with a sort of temporal myopia, avoiding the issues that governed the long-term course of federal spending. Specifically, this meant the mandatory growth of such entitlement programs as Social Security, Medicare, and Medicaid. Kerrey ruminated for some time, until it became clear that his would be the swing vote that would pass or defeat the president's budget.

Ultimately, Kerrey decided that, however unsatisfactory he found the president's budget, he did not desire to hand the president a major defeat on his first significant domestic initiative. Moreover, the president assured Kerrey that he would take concrete steps to address entitlement spending trends, just as he had similarly assured Congresswoman Marjorie Margolies-Mezvinsky (D-PA) when she cast a similarly decisive vote in the House. Press accounts portrayed the eventual establishment of the Kerrey-Danforth Entitlement Commission as the fulfillment of the president's promise to Kerrey.

Though Kerrey was indeed the leading Senate player in the establishment of the commission, it would be a simplification not to note various other efforts within Congress. Kerrey was one of a number of senators who were pushing for a heightened collective determination to take action to address entitlement programs.

When I first joined Senator Simpson, he wasn't known primarily as a budgetarian. When asked for his committee assignment preferences upon arriving in Washington in 1978, he effectively said, "Give me everything that nobody else wants." In 1978, this meant nuclear power issues and immigration issues. Nobody else in the Senate wished to touch either of these with a ten-foot pole. Simpson soon found that it served him well to be seen grappling with the toughest of issues in a responsible, bipartisan, statesmanlike way. This gutsiness, combined with a folksy demeanor and a sense of humor rare in Washington—or anywhere else—made him one of the city's most popular public figures, and he was soon elected to the position of Assistant Republican Leader.

Though I had never heard Senator Simpson cited publicly for his positions on budgetary issues, I noticed in private meetings that whenever he spoke about the future course of Social Security or Medicare, he became as impassioned as with any other issue. His eyes would glisten, his arm would reach up for emphasis, and he would gesture dramatically to demonstrate to his listeners where the country was headed. He would describe how Social Security would be in "deep drawdown" in a couple of decades, and how all of this spending would spiral to extremity, without so much as a single further congressional vote being necessary.

Back then it was rarely acknowledged in public discussion that "entitlement" spending was the principal force driving federal deficits. Members ran for office pledging that they would cut congressional "pork"—meaning wasteful appropriated spending—and citing the need for a line-item veto—presumably, to rein the pork in. At the same time, the wise politician would pledge to defend every penny of projected Social Security and Medicare benefits, even though the latter had much more to do with spiraling spending than did appropriations.

These rhetorical trends changed in a hurry in the early 1990s. By mid-decade, a fashion of decrying increases in "entitlement" spending had essentially played itself out, and discussants were willing at last to address programs by their specific names: Social Security, Medicare, Medicaid. Al Simpson had much to do with that change. He started by using the term "entitlements" as well, but as he sensed that his audiences were still in denial about what he was talking about, he would spell it out: Social Security, Medicare, Medicaid.

In 1963, all such entitlements had accounted for 22.7 percent of federal spending. The share of national spending that was taken up by entitlements had more than doubled by 1993, to 47.3 percent of the budget. In practice, this meant that the nation was gradually losing control over its ability to prioritize national spending. Each year, a shrinking share of national resources could be allocated according to the will of the country. Each year, an increasing share was paid out automatically. This spending required no new congressional vote and no signature by the president. It continued on its own unless the law was changed.

President Clinton's 1992 election was a personal loss for Al Simpson—the defeat of his dear friend, George Bush. But the senator was never one to let personal disappointment interfere with his conception of his duties. During early meetings with the new president, he spoke passionately about the need for leadership to address entitlements and promised to cast whatever tough votes the president might request.

The president made no such requests. His 1993 budget submission was a mix of short-term revenue raisers and lesser restrictions on spending, leaving untouched the long-term structural factors that threatened to produce a long-term fiscal crisis. Both parties exaggerated the effects of this budget. Many Democrats claimed that it was a bold and decisive step to rein in federal deficits. Too many Republicans claimed that the tax increases would plunge the nation further into a deep recession and would actually swell the deficit. Democrat Bob Kerrey saw the budget for what it was: modest in its concentration on short-term aims. He ultimately consented to vote for it only after concluding that the budget's defeat would do more harm than its passage.

Still, 1993 showed that there was a leadership vacuum that had to be filled. The lion's share of public servants were still determined to take the path of least resistance. It was imperative to more fully demonstrate the reality of the fiscal situation to the American public and to make it more difficult to hide the facts of such spending behind the perceptions peddled for political purposes.

Senator Simpson and I looked for ways to make the realities of entitlement spending more vivid for other senators. We felt that a great barrier lay in the popular perception that entitlement programs mainly represented transfers of income from wealthy taxpayers, who could afford to yield the resources, to individuals of greater need. But this perception was unsupported by data. The vast majority of federal spending, entitlement spending, took place without Congress having much of an idea from whom it was taking and to whom it was giving. This was a set of social policies being conducted almost entirely in the dark.

Since then, analysis both within Congress and at various think tanks has significantly illuminated the treatment of different demographic groups by the various federal entitlement programs. In 1993, however, it almost seemed as though Congress was in a state of willful ignorance as to how wealth was being redistributed in these most massive of federal projects.

With Senator Simpson's blessing, I determined to find out. On October 6, we sent a letter, signed by a bipartisan group of senators, requesting that the Congressional Budget Office complete a study of which income groups were benefiting from federal entitlement programs, and to what extent. Those signing the letter included Senators Simpson, Nunn (D-GA), Boren (D-OK), Cohen (R-ME), Campbell (D-CO), Domenici (R-NM), Bradley (D-NJ), Danforth (R-MO), and Durenberger (R-MN). CBO promised to do what they could to put the data together and to let us know to whom these hundreds of billions in annual federal spending were going.

Of course, much of the data this effort generated is not really news anymore. But there had once been a strong predilection in all electoral contests to act as though these programs were, in the main, the essential protections against poverty for the most vulnerable among us. We found quite the opposite; taken collectively, they constituted a nebulous and chaotic redistribution of money from middle-income people to other middle-income people and did not add up to much of a policy at all.

Following are 1990 figures, and thus all will have grown since the data was collected. They are nonetheless illuminating. More Social Security benefits were being paid to individuals with non–Social Security incomes above $50,000 than below $10,000. In other words, people who would have had more than adequate income in retirement anyway were actually taking more from the system than those who, without Social Security, would face destitution. More was being paid in military pensions to those above $75,000 than to those below $20,000. Adding it up, there was very little reason to suppose that entitlement benefits were predominantly channeled to those who needed them or represented any sort of net "poverty protection."

Defenders of the current structure of entitlement programs—including Social Security—often cite the numbers of seniors whom the program allegedly "keeps out of poverty." These figures are produced with the most mindless of calculations, simply subtracting Social Security income from the person's total income and looking at nothing else. Such studies do nothing to answer the question of what would have happened had Social Security not existed (as Al Simpson would say during an irreverent speech, "Now, don't hurl your dinner rolls"—I'm not advocating this!), because they shed no light on what would otherwise have happened to the money that individuals were forced to pay into Social Security. When one looks closely at the vast total structure of entitlement programs, one has a difficult time proving that they are lifting more people out of poverty with benefits than they are pushing people into poverty with tax burdens. We can choose to believe it intuitively, but it's pretty hard to *prove*.

About this time, Pete Peterson (former secretary of commerce) released his book, *Facing Up*. Though he cannot be singly credited for drawing public attention to the troublesome long-term consequences of the structure of entitlement spending, Pete Peterson certainly did as much as any other private citizen to educate the public. In 1992, Peterson joined with former senators Warren Rudman and Paul Tsongas to form the Concord Coalition, an educational organization that fought for balanced budgets and sought to expose and explain the factors that threatened the future solvency of the federal government. Peterson's book crystallized many of the complex issues surrounding federal spending and presented them as stark, easily comprehensible trends. He showed how entitlement programs were skyrocketing as a fraction of overall spending, how they would gradually extinguish the nation's ability to prioritize spending on other vital national interests, and not least of all, how the autopilot nature of federal spending was systematically diverting resources away from the young and towards the elderly, with the predictable result of rising poverty rates among the former.

This was the state of play by the end of 1993. The critical mass of senators—both liberals and conservatives—still stood ready to defend the current spending structures and to take political advantage of anyone who offered proposals to turn from the path embodied in then-current law. But information was being gathered, programs were being rethought, and a small but growing band of legislators were busily at work to improve the information available to both policymakers and the public. The formats for doing so were still in the form of informal groups, but the work was ongoing, and would soon be transformed into a more concrete arena for education and action.

The announcement of the President's Commission on Entitlement and Tax Reform was greeted with what can gently be termed suspicion by Republicans, who had not yet seen any evidence that the president was willing to confront the issue of spiraling entitlement spending. Our party leader, Senator Bob Dole (R-KS), was displeased that he had not received more advance warning of the commission's formation and had not been consulted as to Senator John Danforth's being named the Republican cochair of it. The commission, as announced, would include five senators from each party. By Dole's reasoning, Danforth was the president's appointment, not his own, and he insisted on the right to appoint five Republican senators, not four plus Danforth.

More fundamental, however, was the open question of whether Republicans should participate at all. We already were making progress in putting together something of an informal, bipartisan Senate task force, that was looking into these issues. Why surrender leadership of it to a president of uncertain commitment?

The answer: because it was nonetheless an inevitable fact that the prominence and visibility of the presidency was something that no group of senators could match. Whether we liked it or not, the President's Commission on Entitlement and Tax Reform would now be treated by the press as the major-league game in town, and if we didn't participate, we would consign ourselves to a subordinate, spectator role. We would need to reorient our efforts and to jump on the president's new bandwagon, or become irrelevant.

Senator Simpson argued to Senator Dole that Republicans should participate and further, that he himself wanted to be one of the appointees. After many negotiations with the president, during which time Senator Dole's willingness to constitute the commission vacillated frequently, a structure was finally established. There would be 32 members, including cochairs Bob Kerrey and John Danforth, 5 House Republicans, 5 Senate Republicans, 5 House Democrats, 5 Senate Democrats, and 10 participants from outside of Capitol Hill. To prevent the president from producing a 20-to-10 Democratic majority, the president's 10 appointees from off the Hill would be reviewed by Senator Dole before any final agreement was made.

Senator Dole gave careful thought to his appointments. Senator Judd Gregg (R-NH) was named, bringing with him such assets as his status as a freshman member, his personal relationship with Dole, and his commitment to fiscal responsibility. Senator Malcolm Wallop (R-WY) met Senator Dole's goal of including a member of the Senate Finance Committee, as well as a senator of impeccable conservative credentials. Senator Domenici's stature as the ranking Republican on the Senate Budget Committee ensured him an appointment. Senator Thad Cochran (R-MS), chairman of the Republican Conference and a Dole loyalist, was also included.

It soon became apparent that Senator Simpson's appointment was the duplicative one. Dole already had a member of the leadership (Cochran) and even another senator from Wyoming (Wallop). No obvious political goal was served by also appointing Simpson, only the goal of representing his passionate attachment to the issue. Dole asked Senator Simpson to step down so that he could make a different appointment.

Senator Simpson resisted, explaining to Dole that his staff had passed over another job opportunity largely based on the expectation of staffing him on the commission. Needless to say, it was not standard practice for Senator Simpson to resist any request from the Majority Leader.

Had that conversation gone a different way, the Entitlement Commission would have had different appointees, and I would have had no possible reason to blame Senator Simpson. It was only because Chief Counsel Mike Tongour tipped me off to the fact of the discussion that I became aware of it. Senator Simpson never mentioned it to me.

That's the sort of man Al Simpson was to work for. And it's that sort of person—willing to make the honest and considerate call when no one else is looking—we will all need to be if we are to do right by posterity, as we review the challenge of fixing Social Security. Future Americans may not be in the negotiating room with us, but we must remain forever cognizant of how what we choose to do will affect others.

3

The Political Inheritance of Social Security

Well before the early 1990s, Social Security had established its reputation as the "third rail" of U.S. politics. "Touch it, and you die." It was prevailing Republican political wisdom that fiscal conservatism had to check itself at the door so far as Social Security was concerned, whether the program was growing by leaps and bounds or whether the program was insolvent over the long haul. Republicans had taken something of a vow of silence about the program because, in the eyes of the public, it was untouchable, unassailable, and popular. Moreover, Democrats were only too glad to leap onto any perception that Republicans were less than committed to the program or, worse yet, hoped to dismantle it. The 1998 election provided several reminders that this tried and true tactic is still a favorite.

From the early 1980s to the 1990s, the nation faced a mounting federal deficit and repeated attempts to get it under control. Every few years, a deficit-reduction package seemed to be required. In 1990, President Bush reneged on his "no new taxes" pledge to reach a deal with congressional Democrats—a deal that the conservatives in his party rejected and that contributed to Bush's defeat in 1992. In 1993, President Clinton and a Democratic majority enacted another deficit-reduction package that contained further tax increases. Only in 1997 was an agreement reached between President Clinton and a Republican Congress that actually succeeded in balancing the budget.

In almost every instance, actions taken to right the federal budget balance did not touch Social Security. There were several reasons, one being the quite appropriate recognition that in the short term, Social Security was more than paying its way, however temporary the Social Security surpluses might be. A separate accounting was kept of Social Security's revenues and outlays, part of the political legacy of President Franklin Delano Roosevelt. In the current political environment, this surplus virtually ensured that Social Security planning would be shortsighted, because the program's long-term difficulties lacked the political force of its short-term status of being in the black.

The exception to this political rule occurred in 1985 and 1986 and created a political legacy that weighed heavily in the minds of politicians, Republicans especially, for years afterward—right up through today.

In 1985, Republicans brought to the Senate floor a budget package that would have taken decisive action against the federal deficits that had begun to spiral upward in the early 1980s. It would have eliminated 13 domestic programs, held defense spending to the rate of inflation, and eliminated one year of the Social Security cost of living adjustment (COLA). The COLA was a relatively new feature of Social Security and had not been part of the original structure of Social Security benefits before it was added in the mid 1970s. Republicans were to find out just how quickly such a benefit expansion becomes construed as being part of the inviolate core of the program.[1]

Budget negotiations in 1985 had been difficult every step of the way. President Ronald Reagan's submitted budget, like many of his previous ones, had been declared "dead on arrival." There were several failed attempts by Republican leaders to draft an alternative budget before Republican Leader Robert Dole and Budget Committee Chairman Pete Domenici crafted a plan. The issue went down to the wire, with more than the usual amount of arm-twisting to prevent an embarrassing floor defeat. The climax came when Senator Pete Wilson (R-CA) was carried onto the Senate floor from his hospital bed, dramatically casting the vote that would create a 49-to-49 tie—which tie was broken by Vice President Bush's "aye." Dole had worked hard to get the administration to sign off and to support the package and to salvage apparent victory from the jaws of failure.

House Speaker Tip O'Neill knew a wedge issue when he saw one. The Democratic House developed a package that Republicans felt had comparatively little in the way of meaningful deficit reduction and most especially did not go near Social Security, allowing Democrats to contrast their position with Republicans. House Republicans had no appetite for joining the Senate Republicans on the firing line. Minority Whip Trent Lott (R-MS) took to the floor to state that House Republicans favored getting back to the conference table and for holding the line against the COLA freeze passed by the Senate. He and other House Republicans were determined that Social Security not become an issue that would divide Democrats and Republicans.

The Political Inheritance of Social Security

There are a number of problems. Not enough cuts in domestic spending; too many cuts in defense; and the Social Security freeze. To get the conference going, the Social Security freeze should be eliminated. The chairman of the Senate Budget Committee does not speak for House Republicans. A great majority of House Republicans have voted several times against the Social Security freeze. Eliminate the Social Security freeze from the conference, get back to work, and bring us a budget that will provide $50 billion in real cuts without tampering with Social Security.[2]

President Ronald Reagan, who had allowed Senate Republicans to believe that he would stand behind the deficit-reduction package, flinched. Standing up to the "evil empire" was one thing; standing up to the AARP was another matter altogether. House Democrats were poised to attack Republicans over the issue. House Republicans did not want to defend a COLA freeze. The president had to choose either to stick by his earlier representations that he would back the Senate or to leave the Senate Republicans hanging out to dry.

President Reagan was willing to stand up and to take his lumps on many issues, but his experience with Social Security politics had been disastrous. Prior to the formation of the 1983 Greenspan Commission, bold plans to avert Social Security insolvency had been the subject of a unanimous condemnation by the Senate. Now there stood the menacing likelihood that standing by the Senate would subject both the presidency and the House Republicans to a merciless set of new attacks. So he bailed out, leaving Senate Republicans alone to bear the brunt of the political disaster.

On July 9, 1985,[3] the president agreed with Speaker Tip O'Neill to oppose the Senate's COLA freeze, in return for which the House would join the Senate in allowing defense spending to grow with inflation. Basically they compromised in the time-honored Washington tradition, by going to the higher-spending side on both issues. Senate Budget Committee Chairman Pete Domenici, who had worked so hard to bring the Senate together, was not invited to the Reagan–O'Neill discussion.

When the smoke cleared after the autumn election day, the Senate had passed from the control of the Republicans. Seven Republican incumbents were defeated—Jeremiah Denton, Paula Hawkins, Mack Mattingly, James Broyhill, Mark Andrews, James Abdnor, and Slade Gorton. House Republicans held their ground.

The message was unmistakable, and it was seared into the consciousness of the Republican Party: Social Security is the one area of spending that you must not touch, no matter what.

The political fallout from the 1985–1986 elections affects Republican thinking to this day. Even the most conservative, free-market-oriented advocates of personal accounts within Social Security accept the notion that current benefit promises, even if wholly untenable, must not be tampered with. Consequently, Republicans on the right often join Democrats on the left in their unwillingness to restrain the untenable cost growth projected for the Social Security system. Republicans have been resolved never to allow Social Security to be a wedge issue again.

Consequently, calls for fiscal responsibility tend to come from a small band of ideological centrists from both sides of the aisle, deficit hawks who are skeptical of the prescriptions spelled out by the parties' ideological wings, which wings hold that lofty benefit promises can be met if the preferred mechanisms are put in place to stimulate economic growth. Even today, any negotiations on Social Security will be affected by the 1986 election results and by the belief inculcated, especially in House Republicans, that cost restraints are the road to political disaster. Again, it is the Senate that is more likely to travel down the road of restraining cost growth, induced in part by iconoclastic Democrats such as Bob Kerrey and Pat Moynihan (NY) and a new breed of conservative Senate Republicans, such as Rick Santorum (PA), who believe that the electorate has sufficiently changed since the mid-1980s to permit acceptance of reform.

Ironically, this political debacle occurred on the heels of a significant Social Security event that many consider to have been a rousing success, an example of government working together at its bipartisan finest. Since the implementation of the recommendations of the 1983 Greenspan Commission, many analysts, including many members of the commission itself, have become disillusioned with the results of the commission's work. But this example of how a solution can be crafted with bipartisan backing can serve as a political model, if not a policy one.

It bears recollection that in the early 1980s, partisanship was as endemic as it is now. Newly elected President Ronald Reagan was an authentic conservative, the first president who could be categorized as such since before the Great Depression. The other Republicans who had held the office during that long period had themselves made significant intellectual concessions to principles held dear by the American left. Eisenhower viewed himself as cut from a different, centrist cloth than the conservative Taft-led main body of the Republican Party. Even Richard Nixon, for all of the partisan antagonisms that he facilitated, was far from conservative in his domestic agenda, expanding a number of federal housing and welfare programs and imposing wage and price controls on the economy.

Reagan was something different, and the mainstream press reacted to him with a mixture of excitement and fear. Partisan opposition to him sought to strip away his image as a genial and avuncular leader and to sow suspicions that he was extreme or even wacky behind that smile, away from the control of his political handlers. Reagan's willingness on occasion to challenge the basic premises of various government programs, including Social Security, added fuel to such attacks.

But at the same time, bipartisan action on Social Security was clearly required. There was an immediate threat of bankruptcy in the Social Security program, driven in no small part by the inflation indexing provisions created in the 1970s. Prospects of such cooperation between House Speaker Tip O'Neill and President Reagan did not look promising. President Reagan had entered office musing out loud about the contradictions within Social Security and implying that he might be willing to act decisively to address the program's spending growth as a means of averting bankruptcy. Though he was quickly steered away from such utterances, they provided fodder for Democrats for some time afterward, meaning that the president would face fierce opposition were he to personally lead a Social Security rescue. The best he could do was to set up a bipartisan commission, charged with making recommendations at arm's length from the president.

History is littered with the corpses of failed commissions. The Greenspan Commission too, sputtered and stalled before a small subset of the commission's membership, a negotiating group, took responsibility for the process. Critical to its operations was the active participation of a team directly representing the president. The negotiating group ultimately developed recommendations that were sold respectively to O'Neill and Reagan. O'Neill was promised that the changes would protect Social Security for the long haul. President Reagan was assured that they would avoid Social Security's insolvency for as far as the eye could see and thus end his partisan peril over the issue. The recommendations of the commission were signed into law with broad bipartisan support, and congratulations were distributed all around.

The political moral of this story was understood to be this: Legislators, and particularly Republicans, could not directly engage in comprehensive Social Security reform, but needed cover from a commission. This idea remains strong today, especially in the House of Representatives. In 1998, the Republican Senate and the Republican House took very different paths on Social Security. Various Republican Senators advanced bold and politically risky plans to shore up the program. House Republicans remembered not only the bitter electoral experience of 1985–1986, but also the near disaster averted through the Greenspan Commission in 1982–1983. Accordingly, House Republicans sought to appoint a commission to make Social Security recommendations. Senators felt that this would relinquish control over the ideational process and exclude many Republicans who felt a strong personal interest in participating in a solution.

Another lesson was that nothing of significance could happen on Social Security without direct presidential involvement. This principle has only gained in force since that time, because of President Clinton's strong political backing from seniors and from low-income groups who are historically more dependent upon Social Security income. Republicans do not have the political credibility to take on a rescue of the program on their own, something that could only be provided by the office and offices of President Clinton.

Reforming Social Security

One of the few exceptions to Republican silence on Social Security was New Hampshire Senator Warren Rudman. Perhaps because he did not particularly care about having a long political career or perhaps because he had a natural pugnacity, Senator Rudman refused to be cowed by the prevailing view that senators should keep their heads down and not speak the truths about spiraling entitlement spending. Rudman's reaction to such sentiments was usually to respond with loud indignation. During conferences of the Republican caucus, Rudman would demand to know why either party would tacitly accept the idea that the wealthiest citizens in the United States should have 75 percent of their Medicare premiums paid for by average-income taxpayers. Once after a Senate debate concerning the imposition of entitlement spending caps, Rudman decried how the defeat of the measure had been facilitated by scare mailings sent around by political operatives. He punctuated his floor speech by crumpling such a mailing and tossing it to the Senate floor. His anger was no act.

Not only Rudman and my boss, Senator Simpson, were directly involved with sounding the alarm on the fiscal implications of entitlement spending growth. The Senate Budget Committee's ranking member, Senator Pete Domenici, repeatedly tried to force Congress to inject budget discipline into entitlements, in the way that the Gramm-Rudman act had done for appropriations. Gramm-Rudman required across-the-board cuts in appropriations whenever Congress failed to hold spending within established caps. It had received something of a disdainful reception from the nation's press, which noted that deficits had been going up even while Gramm-Rudman had been in effect.

In reality the problem was not that Gramm-Rudman was ineffective where it operated, but that its reach was limited to appropriations spending only, whereas entitlement spending continued to mushroom. By the late 1990s, it was clear that appropriations spending caps could and did have some positive effect on the government's fiscal balance. But a decade before, Senator Domenici and others were noting that little could be done to ultimately keep the fiscal ship afloat if entitlement spending remained unaddressed. Even Domenici, however, tended to exclude Social Security from his attempts to rein in entitlement spending growth, a concession to the political power of the program as much as it was to policy.

Not only Republicans were reading ominous handwriting on the wall. The ever independent Democratic Senator from New York, Daniel Patrick Moynihan, jolted the body politic with a proposal to cut the Social Security payroll tax by 2 percent early in the Bush presidency. Cut by 2 percent? At first glance, it seemed a perverse suggestion in an age of spiraling federal deficits.

But as was often the case, Moynihan was an intellectual step ahead of the body politic. He perceived that the buildup of enormous Social Security surpluses, followed by long-term annual deficits within the program, far from financing future benefits, was actually useless to Social Security.

There was no real sense in which short-term surpluses were being "saved." Instead, they were simply a cover for other federal spending. The surplus Social Security money enabled the federal government to reduce the amount of borrowing that it would otherwise have to do. By decades-old Social Security law, all surplus Social Security taxes were required to be invested in Treasury bills. These can only be redeemed with the tax dollars of future taxpayers. Thus, significant excess contributions were being taken from working Americans, masking non–Social Security deficit spending, and none of this extra taxation was meaningfully financing the future obligations of the program.

Discussions with staff associated with the Greenspan Commission reveal that they never believed that building up a huge Social Security surplus would actually help to finance future benefits. Doing so served two purely tactical goals: first, to allow for the promise of long-term actuarial solvency, and second, to reduce near-term deficits in the short run with the infusion of surplus Social Security revenue. The Reagan administration had as much to gain from the second factor as from the first, as this would reduce the pressure to increase income taxes. It was Moynihan who blew the whistle on the setup later in the decade.

Yes, the assets building in the Social Security Trust Fund were real—but they were real liabilities of future taxpayers to the exact extent that they were real assets to Social Security. We may as well simply run Social Security on a pay-as-you-go basis, raising payroll taxes as necessary to fill the need, if we were simply going to pass the tax burdens onto future generations indirectly through general taxes collected to redeem the Trust Fund.

So, Moynihan said, let's cut the payroll tax. Let's stop burdening working Americans with the extra load, let's stop telling everyone that this money is going to finance future retirement benefits, and let's stop allowing government to disguise the size of the non–Social Security deficit. Indirectly, it was clear, Moynihan hoped to force the government to do more to balance its own books.

Moynihan's proposal went down in a firestorm of controversy, in no small part because federal finances were so badly out of balance and because surplus payroll taxes were a significant factor in preventing a rapid acceleration in federal borrowing. Moynihan's proposal was criticized as "weakening Social Security" because it would have eliminated much of the projected buildup of the Social Security Trust Fund. In truth, though it would indeed have worsened the *reported* near-term balance of the Social Security program, too few fully realized then how nonsensical were the current-law financing plans for the program, which could not in a literal sense be damaged by what Moynihan was proposing.

Reforming Social Security

It's interesting to reflect that our current task would be much easier had we been willing, back when Senator Moynihan made his proposal, to cut the payroll tax and to put that money instead into funded accounts. But Moynihan was ahead of his time.

Part of the reason that Moynihan's bold proposal could not be enacted was that there simply was no room in the Social Security discussion for boldness at that point. The fact that now there is even a possibility of decisive action is testimony to the tireless work of modern-day Paul Reveres, people like Pete Peterson, Paul Tsongas, Bob Kerrey, and Al Simpson, who determined to jolt politics out of its somnolence and confront it with the approaching threats.

Social Security traveled a long way to reach its eventual status as a government icon, powered forward by a self-perpetuating momentum, ultimately gaining strength to overcome the political resources of anyone seeking to divert it into a different channel. The approach of the program's inherent difficulties could be accelerated—for example, by the decision to add COLAs in the mid-1970s—and occasionally was. But no one, for decades, could oppose or even question it and prevail in a political contest.

It is not as though Social Security entered the world with ease. Franklin D. Roosevelt had to apply all of his political brilliance not only to establish the system but also to provide it with every possible political safeguard. Though we have come to accept such programs as Social Security and Medicare as part of the fabric of government, such innovations were fairly original in the United States of the 1930s. The prevailing intellectual and political climate then was more adventurous and experimental than our own, borrowing design parameters for these programs from a diversity of nations around the globe. This was not because policymakers then were fundamentally more creative than they are now, but rather because policymakers today see the resources of government committed through the choices made in previous decades—largely through programs such as Social Security and Medicare—in a way that did not constrain the policymakers of the 1930s.

It is difficult at a distance to conjure up today the genuine uncertainty that intellectuals and politicians felt in the 1930s about U.S. economic institutions. The Great Depression had brought many previous shibboleths into question, and the discredited outgoing administration of Herbert Hoover had been castigated for indifference and stand-pattism, when experimentation and initiative seemed to be required. And it was not only in the 1930s and the Great Depression that broad segments of the body politic were calling into question the basic framework of free markets. Eugene Debs, for example, had run for president in 1920 and received 920,000 votes, on the Socialist party ticket.[4]

Free institutions, economic and otherwise, were in retreat around the globe. The Soviet Union, under the tyrannical Stalin, was growing in strength and global influence. Germany's Weimar Republic had essentially collapsed and would ultimately be replaced by the National Socialist, or Nazi, government. More than a few Americans wondered whether capitalist institutions could withstand such competition and whether they could adequately provide materially for their citizenry in a modern technological economy.

It was part and parcel of the political genius of FDR that he at all times outwardly displayed an exuberant confidence in the durability of U.S. institutions, even as many others were wracked with doubt. But at the same time he indulged the side of the American psyche that had lost confidence in the ability of the existing institutions of markets, families, and churches to be adequate shields between individual citizens and destitution. The federal government, in FDR's view, could and should accept that role, to a degree that it had not before. And there were few places where FDR thought it more highly necessary than in protecting senior citizens from poverty.

Roosevelt knew that he could potentially come into conflict with the values of a nation that had practically been founded on the premise of opposition to intrusive government power. He knew that "welfare" held unsavory connotations for many Americans, and so he frequently touted his programs as providing "relief" for those afflicted by an economic emergency. But however temporary the term "relief" sounded, what Roosevelt had in mind in the case of social insurance for the elderly was a permanent set of institutions that would be able to withstand any swing of the political pendulum away from FDR's own views.

The system that FDR and his advisors proposed was a neat solution of several simultaneous problems. The federal government would manage the old-age pension program itself, on the premise that states could not adequately do so in a society where individuals often moved from one state to another, especially to retire. Individual Americans would be assessed for contributions to these pensions, which would be used to pay benefits for those already in retirement. There was some disagreement at first about how much of a reserve fund to build up. Roosevelt himself favored building up a larger reserve fund (perhaps he would have approved of the 1983 Social Security Amendments), but others felt that this would leave the government in control of too much investment; the enacting legislation was ultimately amended to function on a pay-as-you-go basis.

The move away from advance funding had long-range political significance that did not escape FDR. Moving to pay-as-you-go meant that liabilities would henceforth be met on a contingency basis—and there was no guarantee that future generations would always be willing to contemporarily produce the revenues that the system might ultimately require. This left the program with one significant element of political vulnerability. Despite losing on this issue, this aspect of FDR's political vision has been borne out. There is some recognition of this principle in the prescriptions of President Clinton and others today, who wish to lock in an excess of future funding commitments to the program to shield it from alteration by fiscal conservatives in future decades.

FDR's timeless—and double-edged—political contribution was the creation of the Social Security card and account number. This decision has constrained policymakers for decades since, as was Roosevelt's willful intention. Individual Americans do not currently have an individual Social Security account, nor are their contributions to the system tabulated and invested separately in order to provide them with an eventual benefit. The benefits they receive are strictly a function of formulas that, while based on their wage history, do not in the end need to relate in any tangible way to contributions made. The establishment of the card and the account number were willfully created so as to foster the illusion of such a connection and a perception of an earned benefit.

One of the ironic aspects of the current Social Security debate is that many reform proposals now would involve the incorporation of some features which are, in substantive reality, what the current system only pretends to be—one in which individual contributions are, at least to an extent, tabulated and invested and in which benefits truly are owned by individuals in their own names.

Even as this is written, examples abound of the state of misunderstanding and of the press's inability to get it right. On November 7, 1998, there aired a teaser for a television news broadcast by Channel 7 in Washington, D.C. Viewers were shown a graphic entitled "Social Insecurity" and asked to imagine the horrors that would come from having one's Social Security number stolen, as apparently happened to the subject of that evening's exposé. The reporter solemnly asked viewers to imagine how they would feel if they had worked hard to pay their Social Security taxes, only to find that those contributions were not put in their own account, but put in the account of another person! *Que horrible!*

This news broadcast was telling viewers that they had Social Security "accounts" already—precisely the element of reform that many were being pilloried for trying to create. It is difficult to develop support for such a feature when the press is telling the public that they already have it.

The great irony is that the horror described by the newscast is not visited solely on the unfortunate soul whose Social Security number has been stolen; it's visited on *everyone* by the current system. Each of us labors to pay payroll taxes, and then those taxes are used to pay benefits to someone else. There's no "account" there, and our payroll taxes aren't saved in any meaningful way. We are simply promised that someday, someone else will be taxed to pay benefits to us. For Channel 7 to imply to viewers that under normal conditions their Social Security contributions are put in a savings account shows how successful FDR and his successors were at advancing a potent fiction.

A tremendous amount of the current Social Security demagoguery industry is fed by this perception that individuals' contributions have "earned" certain benefits which government is "thieving" if it attempts to change formulas or otherwise "take them away." Individuals often say that all they want to do is to get their own money back out again, and they can't understand why government should get in the way of that. Direct-mail groups to seniors feed this perception, telling beneficiaries that "you paid for these benefits" even when in reality the individual's benefits may have exceeded the compounded value of anything they put in and are paid only by taxing current workers.

FDR did all of this on purpose. He knew that "welfare" benefits for the elderly could ultimately be cut or even eliminated. Suppose that he had simply set up a system of temporary relief for senior citizens, paying exactly the same benefits during his presidency as Social Security in fact did. Nothing would have prevented a subsequent administration from scaling back that program once the economy recovered. No one, in all likelihood, would have consulted the amount of taxes that they had paid during FDR's presidency and demanded to be paid back, even though in a strict sense under FDR's system they hadn't "paid for their own benefits" in any more meaningful way.

This point was not lost on early bureaucrats, who approached FDR to complain about the needless expense of keeping track of Social Security numbers, issuing Social Security cards, and responding to requests for information about benefits to be received. Since benefits would be paid out of future taxes anyway, why bother with all of this infrastructure simply to create the illusion of a firm tie between contributions and benefits?

To FDR, the answer was simple. It was to make certain that the system was perpetual and that individual Americans would forever feel that they had a right to whatever the system was supposed to pay them. With such political support, the program could never die. As FDR put it, "That account is not useless. That account is not to determine how much should be paid out and to control what should be paid out. That account is there so those sons of bitches up on the Hill can't ever abandon this system when I'm gone."[5]

FDR knew what he cared about and what he didn't. He was not in the least concerned about whether individual contributions matched benefits or not. FDR knew what he wanted, and he got it—a system constructed to perpetually provide its own political support.

This is, in the end, why Social Security is financed via a separate collection, the FICA tax, and not through general revenues. Were it mixed in with other general revenues, no one would be induced to believe that they should keep track of a lifetime of contributions and then demand back a certain amount of benefits at the end of the game. Again, to quote FDR, "With those taxes in there, no damn politician can ever scrap my Social Security program."[6]

It was, in many ways, a political rout of conservatism, to the extent that conservatism might advocate the scaling back of government paternalism. I have spoken many times in front of panels of conservative thinkers who would, in the instance of any other federal program, advocate its scaling back, regardless of what investments each taxpayer had made in it. FDR's creation of such symbolism has sent conservatives scrambling to assure themselves and one another that everyone has to get his or her share out of the Social Security system in a fair way, evaluating rates of return, trying to outbid the left in terms of benefits promised. Can you imagine this being done by self-styled conservatives with respect to any other government program?

This represents a wholesale intellectual surrender by conservatives and libertarians to FDR, foregoing their usual wishes to scale back government expenditures and accepting the premise that the government-run system must forever parcel out a bigger and better level of benefits. The willingness of so many conservatives to engage in this bidding war, with precious little recognition of how FDR's structure has hoodwinked them into abandoning their normal concerns about spending and tax burdens, represents one of the greatest political masterstrokes of all time.

This should, however, be a cautionary tale. FDR's vision extended to the behavior of future Congresses—it did not extend to a society in which the average American lived beyond the age of 80. Nor did it extend to how future Congresses would *expand* upon his program and inadvertently threaten it in that way.

After FDR, the program took on a life of its own, as determinative in its own way as the determination of an individual's eventual physical attributes are by his DNA. The program could be nothing but popular at first. Before it had fully matured, beneficiaries received something good after having paid in little or nothing at all—why shouldn't it be popular with them? Payroll tax rates remained low for decades, creating windfall benefits for the first generations of beneficiaries. A society that respected its elderly was pleased that more of them were receiving additional safeguards from poverty. The system's "winners" were quite visible, and any "losers" that it might create were either too young to know it, or had not even been born.

And so the program grew. One surefire method of gaining political support was to promise to enhance the unalloyed blessing of Social Security. In 1972, cost-of-living adjustments (COLAs) were added as a permanent feature of Social Security benefits (becoming effective in July 1975). Later in the same decade, double-digit inflation, wreaking its havoc upon the COLAs, threatened the program with immediate insolvency. One must be somewhat cautious in describing the effects of the COLA legislation. On the one hand, it prevented senior citizens from being horrendously and disproportionately injured by the hyperinflation of the late 1970s. On the other, it assured that the program's financial problems would accelerate and, in some ways, become permanent aspects of Social Security.

One moral of the COLA story is how the press and public selectively interpret the "contract" pertinent to Social Security. There is no sense in which automatic COLAs can be said to be an original feature of the Social Security "contract," having been added almost two generations after the program began. When one discusses changes that must be made to assure the future solvency of the program, one is frequently hit with the argument that the "contract" cannot be altered with respect to the promises made to beneficiaries, even if those beneficiaries aren't retiring until two generations from now.

As a point of fact, the Social Security "contract" has been rewritten time and again, usually to the benefit of current retirees and to the detriment of future ones. For some reason, no one interpreted the addition of COLAs, vast though the implications were, as a violation of the "contract" with current taxpayers and thus with future retirees. As a political matter, the contract has been enforceable primarily in one direction, higher spending only.

This is not to say that we should eliminate COLAs. COLAs are an even more indispensable feature of the program now that so many retirees live for decades after they begin to collect, during which time inflation would erode a fixed benefit and send many into poverty. The COLA tale is here provided merely to show how the program has evolved and expanded through time and how even spending features that were not part of the original "contract" at all are now defended tooth and nail as though they were.

This pattern of program development is not at all unique to the United States. The World Bank has conducted studies the world over of the "life cycles" of public pension programs and has found that they tend to go through predictable phases.

The first stage is distinguished by such features as very high ratios of workers to retirees and low total costs relative to the size of the economy (less than 1 percent of GDP). During this time, beneficiaries are those who have paid very little, if anything, into the system, and thus pension benefits are paid out with a generous relationship to contributions.

In the second stage, people who have paid into the system for a few decades begin to collect benefits. Their rates of return aren't as high as is the case for the first few retirees, but the absolute size of the wealth transfer in their direction is higher (because they are getting full benefits, though they have only contributed for part of their lives). The program remains popular because people are generally still getting a good deal from it. Because everyone seems to be a winner, few object when the program is expanded, as it often is during this stage.

In the third stage, the pyramid scheme collapses. It becomes apparent that the existing setup cannot be maintained without significant new infusions of tax revenue. Spending on the program begins to squeeze out other national priorities, causing cutbacks in programs aimed at youth, such as education. Now young people begin to perceive that they will not receive a good deal from the system, and talk of change becomes politically more acceptable, ultimately leading to a shift towards a partially funded system that no longer depends on an unrealistic perpetual expansion of the population pyramid.[7]

A glance at payroll tax rates in the United States shows how we are passing through these stages. Early on, both the contribution base and the tax rate were extremely low (in 1940, 2 percent of the first $3,000 of wages, and in 1950, 3 percent of the first $3,000 in wages).[8] By the 1960s, retirees were entitled to substantial benefits, despite having spent much of their life paying in at a very low tax rate. This necessitated higher tax rates upon current workers (in 1960, 6 percent of the first $4,800 in wages, and in 1970, 8.40 percent of the first $7,800). By the 1990s, the tax burden (12.40 percent of the first $51,300 of wages in 1990) was such that current workers could not expect to recoup a lifetime of contributions in the manner of current and past beneficiaries.

It is clear that at some point in the last few years, the United States entered the third stage of development identified by the World Bank and that political as well as policy factors will require the incorporation of some advance funding. When I entered public service in 1989, the lion's share of the political weight was still lavished on defending the status quo, and fundamental change was only discussed by individuals who were comfortable outside of the political mainstream. But in the last several years, this political legacy has given way to a new dynamic in which the vast critical mass in the political center recognizes the need for fundamental change, and only some political "outliers" on the left sincerely believe that the system can continue to exist as it has in the past.

Though the vast predominance of opinion has made this leap, structural change will not necessarily be possible within the next few years, when it would still be significantly more advantageous. Much political muscle is still flexed by the most reactionary of forces, in organized labor and among some of the more ideologically constrained senior advocacy groups. But regardless, we have come a long way in the last decade in our ability to come to grips with the legacy that was bequeathed to us, and the share of the population in denial will inevitably continue to shrink.

NOTES

1. Congressional Quarterly (CQ), *Congressional Quarterly Almanac* (Washington, D.C., 1985), p. 450.

2. *Congressional Record*, June 26, 1985, p. 17398.

3. CQ, *Almanac* 1985, p. 456.

4. Joseph Nathan Kane, *Facts about the Presidents* (Ace Books, 1976), p. 331.

5. Richard Neustadt, and Ernest May, *Thinking in Time* (New York: Free Press, 1986), p. 102.

6. Arthur Schlesinger, Jr., *The Coming of the New Deal* (Boston: Houghton Mifflin, 1958), pp. 308–309.

7. World Bank Policy Research Report, *Averting the Old-Age Crisis: Policies to Protect the Old and Promote Growth* (New York: Oxford University Press, 1994), pp. 315–317.

8. Peter Ferrara, and Michael Tanner, *A New Deal for Social Security* (Washington, D.C.: Cato Institute, 1988), p. 45.

4

The Kerrey-Danforth Commission

Senator Bob Kerrey of Nebraska seems to relish a challenge. The bigger the obstacle, the more likely it seems that Kerrey is inclined to take it on. He demonstrated his physical courage in combat during the Vietnam war, losing part of his foot as a result. He ran an uphill race for president in 1992 against the well-financed anointed front-runner Bill Clinton. He accepted the job as the chairman of the Democratic Senatorial Campaign Committee at a time when the campaign money and the votes were tending in the Republican direction.

Most of all, however, Kerrey seems to relish a moral or intellectual challenge, fighting on the battlefield of ideas, challenging ossified attitudes. It was Kerrey, more than any other, who pointed out to fellow Democrats how runaway spending growth in the very entitlement programs that they had long defended would ultimately threaten the objectives that the party held dear.

His work has been vital. In the same way that only Nixon could go to China, only a Democrat could tell the truth about Social Security, Medicare, and other entitlements, in a way that the public and press would hear.

Jack Danforth of Missouri was also an unusual man among senators. Possessed of the deep resonant voice of the preacher that he was, Danforth was a moderate, though not a compromising, Republican. Though considered to be a compassionate and upright man, he would not back away from a challenge if he thought he was right, whether or not this put him at odds with the majority of the nation's press or at odds on occasion with his own party. During much of Danforth's career, the Senate was a tolerant environment for independent-minded senators, but by the end, it was clear that the party demanded greater loyalty and that senators like Danforth would be well advised to get on the team.

Very much against his will and inclination, Danforth was brought further into the public's eye during the time of the Clarence Thomas confirmation hearings. Thomas had worked for Danforth, who believed implicitly in his character, his honesty, and in his innocence of the allegations being leveled against him. Much of America's choices about whom to believe in the Anita Hill–Clarence Thomas divide had everything to do with the partisan affiliations of the observers. Danforth, the least partisan of men, stood by his friend and thus received much of the partisan wrath that surrounded the case. Though Thomas survived to win confirmation, Danforth emerged from the ordeal a fatigued and disappointed man.

The President's Bipartisan Commission on Entitlement and Tax Reform that Senators Kerrey and Danforth were given was reluctantly assembled. The president had agreed to create it only as a concession during negotiations pertinent to his 1993 budget. Republican Leader Robert Dole made his appointments only after satisfying himself that the commission would not be overly tilted towards the president's loyalists. Many of the participants on the panel itself felt an engrained skepticism about what it could accomplish—including, from the left, Richard Trumka of the United Mine Workers and, from the conservative side, Senator Malcolm Wallop. Enthusiasm for the work was limited only to a few members of the panel—Kerrey, Danforth, Al Simpson, Pete Peterson, and Congressman Alex McMillan (R-NC), to name a few.

The staff of the Entitlement Commission were assembled and led by two individuals whom I would come to know very well—Fred Goldberg and Mark Weinberger. They put together an excellent team of young staffers, many of whom graduated from their work with the commission to take important staff positions on Capitol Hill.

Relations between the staff of the Entitlement Commission were not always smooth. Early on in the process, there was a sentiment among Republican staff that Republicans needed to coordinate their message in a concerted way, because they were in the minority and had no desire to be overrun by a prevailing political agenda with which they might disagree. As my boss and I were among the early enthusiasts for the work and as I had developed good relationships with Weinberger, with Pete Peterson's staff, and others, we were occasionally in the awkward position of balancing our commitment to a bipartisan effort with our loyalty to our fellow Republicans.

In the end, there proved to be no conflict, because the commission was able only to unite behind a series of factual findings, not behind recommendations. Consideration of the latter proved so divisive that the parties, had they tried, could not have formed organized voting blocs for one approach or the other. In the end, it was simply a question of which commission members would take the initiative to develop proposals on their own and whether they could attract a handful of colleagues to endorse them. In this, the chairmen proved no more successful than any of the other commission members. The final report of recommendations contained the work of scattered individuals and an occasional bloc of two or three.

Still, the findings justified the commission's existence. They reveal the value of public education. Nothing in the Entitlement Commission's interim report to the president of August 1994 was really news to policymakers. Everyone who worked on budget and fiscal issues and who bore responsibility for studying entitlement programs had known well everything that was in it. There was something of a sense, as we were putting the document together, that we were simply going over a too-oft-told story for the zillionth time. Did we really need yet another pamphlet, yet another memo, yet another series of charts showing what was happening with entitlement programs?

It turned out that we did. This commission, starved of active presidential support, given little or no respect by the nation's press, issued a pamphlet that quickly became something of a Bible on Capitol Hill, a set of findings that began to be cited not only during debates within the beltway but also around the country, whenever problems with Social Security and other entitlement programs were discussed.

One chart in particular is an emblem of the commission's work. Just as Leonardo had his Mona Lisa, overshadowing everything else he painted, and just as Melville was forever known for Moby Dick, no matter what else he wrote, most of the members of the Entitlement Commission will never, in their collective lives, produce anything more durable than the "Current Trends Are Not Sustainable" chart, which appears on page 7 of the Entitlement Commission report (see Figure 4.1).

It's a good chart, and it certainly makes a good point. When it was first unveiled, however, I had no idea just how well it made that point. The number of senators from both sides of the aisle who displayed this chart on the Senate floor within a year after the commission's report must be at least one dozen. My boss, Senator Judd Gregg, still displays this chart today, albeit with updated numbers to reflect current budget projections.

Part of the chart's popularity was rooted in the way that it forcefully communicates a very important message, that—well, that "Current Trends Are Not Sustainable." As others have noted, when something is unsustainable, it tends to stop. Change will come and must inevitably come. The only question is whether we can accommodate ourselves to those changes and make them work for the type of society and the type of government that we wish to have, or whether we will allow ourselves to be overrun by them, with no planning, no attempt to distribute burdens and responsibilities

Figure 4.1
Current Trends Are Not Sustainable

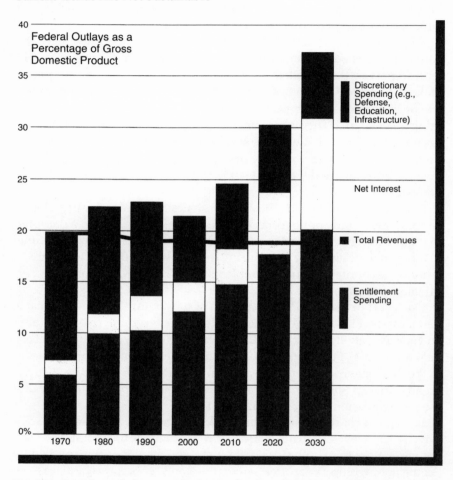

Note: This chart shows the long-term budget implications of current spending and tax policies. In projecting entitlement spending, Medicare and Social Security outlays follow the Medicare and Social Security Trustees' "best estimates." Medicaid outlays are assumed to reflect demographic changes and the increases in health care costs that underlie the Medicare projections. All other spending and revenues are assumed to follow Congressional Budget Office projections through 1999 and to grow in proportion to the overall economy thereafter.

Source: Bipartisan Commission on Entitlement and Tax Reform, *Interim Report to the President* (Washington, D.C.: GPO, 1994).

fairly, and no assurance that our nation's economic viability can be maintained.

What the chart showed in very stark detail was that entitlement spending—mostly Social Security, Medicare, and Medicaid—would by itself, left unrestructured, swallow up all federal spending by the year 2012. (That date has since been postponed significantly by recent success in balancing the unified federal budget.) If this occurred, it would leave not one penny for national defense, education, highways, or any other priority that the nation wished to pursue, unless it chose to finance them with new debt.

Many of the commission members started out seeing these as budgetary problems more than philosophical or structural ones. We knew that the sum total of entitlement spending was on an unsustainable course, but the commission had not begun to probe the inner workings of these programs in a comprehensive way that would place each on a sounder policy footing. We were still focused on symptoms, rather than causes. The commission's mission was limited—to sound an alarm and to show that we had to change our course. The right course to take was not something that a strictly budgetary view of the problem could illuminate.

To the extent that we budget hawks suffered from some myopia on these problems at that time, we were not the only ones. Commission members from the opposite political faith also made statements in their final views that can clearly be seen as at least problematic today. Richard Trumka: "There is clearly no crisis in Social Security, either in the short or long term." Former Congressman Tom Downey (D-NY): "There is clearly no crisis in Social Security either short or long run."[1] I do not know whether the authors of these statements (which were frequently uttered almost in exact duplication by several commission members) would retract them now, but clearly they do not square with the facts of the program as outlined in the annual trustees' reports. If a program requires more than $7 trillion in general tax revenues just to get it through from 2014 to 2034 and then becomes insolvent anyway, some contortions of language are required not to acknowledge a looming crisis.

Lest it be perceived that fiscal realism on the commission was limited to one side of the aisle, let us note also the contributions made by Robert Greenstein. Greenstein was appointed by the president, largely on the basis of Greenstein's work with the Center on Budget and Policy Priorities, an organization he founded to monitor and to defend the proportion of federal spending going to those in greatest economic need. Though Greenstein and my own boss often pursued different policies, we admired his intellectual integrity and his willingness to face facts that were inconvenient to his own position, when most in Washington simply ignore those facts that seem to contradict their own views.

Though the commission didn't move fully down the road toward a set of solutions that would turn Social Security and Medicare into viable, internally consistent programs, the thinking of the chairs and of the commission members did in fact progress as the commission hearings went forward.

It was the chairmen and their staff who first made the conceptual leap to realize that the problems within Social Security could not be viewed as budget problems alone. The Kerrey-Danforth proposal to include personal accounts within the Social Security system stemmed from their recognition that the program could not adequately provide for retirement income benefits were it balanced solely by benefit cuts or tax increases. The chairs advocated a personal account contribution carved out from 1.5 percentage points of the existing payroll tax, in combination with various changes in eligibility ages, calculation of CPI, bend point indexing, and other aspects of Social Security's benefit structure, to bring the program into balance.

Though the Kerrey-Danforth recommendations on Social Security were not yet as sophisticated as what was to follow—proposals that would ultimately also examine such factors as the work incentives and distributional aspects in the traditional Old-Age, Survivors, and Disability Insurance (OASDI) system—they were nonetheless a turning point. In our Simpson-McMillan-Goss alternative to the chairmen's (Congressman Poter Goss, R-FL) mark, we also incorporated a voluntary version of the chairmen's individual Social Security account component.

In the waning days of the commission, it became clear that no consensus would be reached. The Kerrey-Danforth recommendations were presented to the commission with a fairly short timespan in which to support, oppose, or amend. Had there been a serious prospect at that point of a majority opinion, we would undoubtedly have worked with Kerrey and Danforth to negotiate an agreement based on their proposal. Since there was no chance of that, Senator Simpson decided that he would be taking nothing away from the chairmen by offering his own. "If I'm going to go down in flames," he said in his vivid way, "I'm going to go down having proposed something."

In retrospect, our Simpson-McMillan-Goss alternative was not half bad. Though incompletely analyzed, there are a couple of elements of it that stand up well when viewed from a distance. One was that we included personal accounts in our Social Security recommendations and resisted the apparent budgetary pressure to fix Social Security through benefit restraints alone. Second, we rejected means-testing in Social Security and in entitlements across the board, except in the specific case of the Medicare Part B premium, a distinct policy case because it was not a contributory program in the sense of Medicare Part A or Social Security. Third, we did not seek to bring the medical health insurance programs under control simply through restraints upon benefits, and we recognized that structural reform of the health care purchasing systems would be necessary, incorporating a proposal by Congressman Alex McMillan to bring increased consumer choice into Medicare. (Meanwhile, Senator Gregg's counsel Stan Sokul was working with Senator Gregg to develop more sophisticated Medicare Choice provisions that would ultimately be included in the budget reconciliation bill of 1997.)

In the end, what did the Entitlement Commission really accomplish?

1. It sounded an alarm and gave bipartisan credibility to a message that the U.S. public needed to hear, namely, that "current trends are not sustainable."
2. It moved key decisionmakers from viewing entitlement programs mainly from a budgetary perspective toward realizing that fundamental structural changes would be required to make them function adequately for beneficiaries and taxpayers alike.

The commission's work recast the debate about entitlements, especially Social Security, challenging lawmakers to review the basic philosophical premises of these programs and to understand that their basic purposes could not be met if Congress took a reflexive budget-cutting approach to them. Accordingly, at this point it seems appropriate to review those long-standing purposes of Social Security and how it attempts to meet them.

NOTE

1. Entitlement and Tax Reform Commission, Final Report to the President, 1994.

5

Social Security: Its Purposes and How It Works

What exactly is the purpose of Social Security? Perhaps the most common answer is: to allow Americans to retire with dignity. Dignity has many facets. It requires self-respect and also that an individual can feel respected by others. It is difficult, if not impossible, to retain such a feeling when in a position of economic or physical dependence. No one likes to feel like a supplicant.

Impoverishment of either children or the elderly rightly strikes us as disgraceful. Children cannot be expected to fend for themselves. It is the obligation, if not indeed the preeminent purpose, of families that they provide children with the emotional, tutorial, and material support that they require until they achieve self-sufficiency. When a child is in poverty, it is rightly perceived to be our collective fault, not the child's.

Poverty among the elderly strikes us similarly. We do not believe that an individual's obligation to work and to earn should be perpetual. As nature has decreed that our physical capacities decline as we age, however this decline is retarded by science, so do human societies now tend to believe that some respite is due in the twilight of life, during which it is understood that the material and emotional needs of the elderly will not be contingent upon continued labor. When the elderly are in poverty, we do not believe that this is because they are shiftless or worthless, but because the proper arrangements have not been made to provide for a period of retirement.

That Social Security attempts to provide the elderly with the dignity of retirement income security is almost axiomatic. The means that it uses to do so are what is frequently debated.

Of all of the businesses that government is rightly involved in, the dignity business is probably not among the first that comes to the average citizen's mind. Indignity, yes—*that's* something that the man on the street may associate with government. But Americans are so unaccustomed to associating dignity with government operations that they sometimes fail to recognize it even when they do. During the debate over the 1995 budget, many seniors contacted Congress to say, "Keep the government out of my Medicare!"—it apparently being inconceivable that a popular program, one that seniors most assuredly believe provides them with a greater opportunity to lead a dignified life, actually comes courtesy of government.

More seriously, people *do* associate the Social Security program with a dignified retirement. An inevitable corollary of this association is that government must be doing something to add to that dignity—something that adds to the likelihood of a decent retirement instead of subtracting from it.

An elusive and precious thing, dignity. It cannot be equated naively with the income itself. We do not acquire dignity by accepting charity. On the contrary, perceptions of our own dignity may require us to reject it. A position of dependency, whether on family, friends, or the government, does not confer dignity. That people wish to associate the concept of dignity with Social Security implies as a matter of course, that they wish it to be a benefit perceived as honestly earned through a lifetime of work. Social insurance, yes; protection against poverty, yes. But the connection between one's productivity in one's working years and the benefits granted in retirement must never be wholly severed, if the program is to remain consistent with the goal of providing a dignified, as well as a secure, retirement.

Just how does the government provide this retirement income? Does it do it by investing the contributions of wage-earners wisely, more wisely than they could have, to produce a level of retirement income for them that they could not have for themselves? Is it possible that the operation of Social Security by the government adds to net national income in some way? Or is government merely giving to some with one hand and taking from some with the other?

The reader need not know much about economics to know that the government is not a generator of wealth. What it provides to some as retirement income, it must extract from others.

The Social Security system is a "social insurance" system in a real sense. It is not, nor has it ever been, a savings program. Today's payroll taxes go to support today's retirees. Tomorrow's Social Security income—at least under current law—will be provided by taxing tomorrow's workers.

The term "social contract" is often applied to Social Security, as a means of reinforcing the principle that it is not a program under which individuals save for themselves. It is a program that binds Americans together in a sort of reciprocal contractual relationship. We who pay payroll taxes today, pay to support today's retirees. We hope that tomorrow others will pay sufficient taxes to support us. In that sense, we feel that we have a somewhat contractual arrangement—we are required to give something today, and in return we will receive something tomorrow.

However, it takes two to make a contract. No one has asked tomorrow's workers about this arrangement. There is a touch of unseemly arrogance in the assertion that today's Americans have an enforceable "contract" that gives us a right to their earnings. We could, if we chose, pass a law tomorrow raising Social Security benefits, starting in the year 2015, to $1 million a day. This strikes us as ridiculous, because it is obvious that the money that we put into the system does not justify such awards and because it is immoral to expect tomorrow's workers to carry that level of tax burden.

This is a critical point. Rhetoric about a social "contract" does not obviate the need to ensure that everyone is treated fairly under the current system, nor does it obviate the need to ensure that it can adequately function. Saying that there is a "contract" does not relieve us of the obligation of reviewing it to make sure that everyone is treated fairly, including those who aren't here now to sign on to it.

So when we discuss the purposes of Social Security, we must pay careful heed to how the federal government attempts to achieve the purpose of a dignified retirement for Americans through the Social Security program. It does not do this through a savings program. It does this through a program of income redistribution—from one generation to previous ones and from some income classes to others.

It is often noted, correctly, that Social Security represents a poor investment deal for young workers, in the sense that many of them will not receive back the value of the contributions that they have been forced to pay in—in other words, that they have been forced, essentially, to lose money through the system. It is said by some traditional defenders of the current structure that this really doesn't and shouldn't matter, because the program is not a savings or a pension program, but "social insurance" pure and simple.

This is true to a point, but there are certain factors that this overlooks. First of all, it is manifestly inconsistent with the way that Social Security is presented to the U.S. public. It is routinely represented that Social Security is not a "welfare" program, but that benefits received will bear a reasonable relationship to contributions made. In fact, this connection is precisely what FDR attempted to establish when he created the Social Security numbers that were discussed earlier.

Social Security's political support depends explicitly upon this perception. Welfare is much less popular politically than are "earned benefits." Social Security's benefit formulas are progressive and redistributive, but they are not withheld (with the exception of the earnings limit and benefit taxation) as a function of non–Social Security income. The designers of Social Security knew explicitly that, in order to be supported, the public must be-

43

lieve that all Americans, rich and poor alike, were getting something out of the Social Security system that they had earned.

Second, and more subtly, whether one "wins" or "loses" under Social Security is more deterministic than whether one, say, happens to experience a health crisis that justifies the payments made for health insurance. In health insurance, a pool of insured put their money in together, and some of them benefit more than others from that choice. In Social Security, the rules are set up so that whole classes of beneficiaries are advantaged or disadvantaged by design. Early retiree cohorts received enormous windfalls, benefits received after little to no contributions at all, and thus it is small wonder that the program was popular with them. Subsequent classes of workers, having paid extremely modest FICA tax rates, also received a tremendous return on their investment in the system. With each generation of then-retirees supported by an ample generation of workers, it was easy for the pay-as-you-go system to thrive and for generations of seniors to feel that the program had worked well for them.

As long as the working population continues to grow in a pyramidal shape, workers can continue to provide such gains to retirees without experiencing a sharp increase in tax burdens. However, if the ratio of retirees to workers grows, these benefit levels can only be sustained by higher tax rates, which in turn reduce the chance that the generations that paid those higher tax rates will get a good deal.

We will soon enter a period in which retirees will not have received a good deal for their Social Security investment and when a good number of them would have done much better had they been able to invest that money for themselves. One might make the argument that Social Security has increased the certainty of that income and that this is ample compensation for the lost opportunity to earn more. However, as the generations go by and rates of return drop, the likelihood increases that each would have received more money investing on its own; thus also the likelihood increases that the Social Security program has forced them into a net loss. This situation will be detailed in chapter 12, and is dramatized in tables 12.2 and 12.3.

Left unchanged, the Social Security system will head to a place in which workers, rather than receiving the security of retirement income insurance, will for the most part be receiving only the assurance that they will lose money through the Social Security system. Not knowing how well they might have fared by investing their money themselves—for some, no doubt, would have invested even more poorly than through Social Security, making the social insurance a good buy for them—they will all know only that, net, their entire birth class has lost money through the Social Security system. Most people will not believe that they could not beat a 1 percent rate of return.

44

This experience will lead to an entirely different dynamic than the one that existed in Social Security's early years, when beneficiaries received a windfall. The term "social insurance" may sound pleasant to some policymakers in Washington, but that will be small comfort to those who could have purchased such insurance on their own, through different means and at lower cost. In time, this will mean almost everyone under current law.

In the final analysis, a thriving Social Security system must continue to serve a dual function—both as social insurance and as a reasonable return for the individual's investment. It must provide protection against poverty, but must not so completely divorce contributions and benefits that it takes on the appearance of public welfare. In order to achieve this, it cannot afford to assess tax rates that cannot be presented to the public as ultimately relating to the benefits that they will receive. If it did so, the prevailing logic behind Social Security would collapse, and it would simply become one more tax that wage-earners pay in order to put bread on the table of others, with no hope of reaping a similar net benefit for themselves.

This is not the concern of an isolated few. It is shared by students of the system across the political spectrum. The Social Security Advisory Council put it this way in 1996: "Social Security should provide benefits to each generation of workers that bear a reasonable relationship to total taxes paid, plus interest."[1]

HOW THE SYSTEM WORKS

Social Security is designed so that an individual's wage history is used to compute his or her eventual benefit level. With some simplifications, it works as follows.

The Social Security Administration (SSA) keeps track of every year of "covered earnings" (years in which the individual is employed and paying payroll taxes) and then "wage indexes" each one forward to produce its current value. "Wage indexing" is a way of comparing your wages to the average national level in the particular year that you worked, so that the wages you earned in different years are corrected for inflation and for national income trends. If you earned $10 an hour in 1970 and $12 an hour this year, "wage indexing" would correctly perceive that your wages would in effect have gone down, not up, relative to the rest of the country, and thus 1970 would be considered as a higher-wage year for you.

Wages in an individual's highest 35 years of covered earnings are thus indexed, averaged, and converted to a monthly basis, to produce a figure called the AIME, or "averaged indexed monthly earnings." That number, an attempt to capture one's typical monthly earnings level, is then turned into a Social Security benefit by the following formula (as of 1999):

90 percent times the first $505, plus

32 percent times the next earnings on up to $3043, plus

15 percent of anything above that.

The income levels at which 90 percent turns into 32 percent, and 32 percent turns into 15 percent, are called "bend points." The different percentages are designed to create a progressive distribution of retirement income. One "earns back" one's contributions much more quickly with the first few dollars of earnings than with dollars earned and contributed after that. At all times, there is a relationship between contributions and benefits, so this is not "welfare" in that sense, but the formula is designed to redistribute down the income chain.

At the moment, the normal retirement age is 65. This is scheduled to gradually increase under current law, starting in the year 2000, going up two months each year through 2005, plateauing for twelve years, and then resuming again from 2017 to 2022, so that it will be 67 from that point on. There is a lot of confusion out there amid journalists and the public at large about this. This is already the law. The current projections of the Social Security Trustees *already* take this normal retirement age increase into account. The fiscal situation will *not* improve when this begins to happen. We have already credited ourselves for the savings to the system that it will produce.

Our office occasionally receives calls from disgruntled citizens who suggest that the system's difficulties can be resolved simply by allowing the retirement age to drift upward to 67, as it is currently scheduled to do. Senator Gregg's opponent in the 1998 election made this claim at one point. Unfortunately, there is no new savings, beyond that already calculated, to be received from this upcoming event.

Social Security beneficiaries need not wait until normal retirement age. They may retire early, as early as 62. Under current law, they will still be able to retire at 62 even when the normal retirement age reaches 67. If an individual retires right now at age 62, he or she receives a benefit that is 80 percent of the benefit that would be received had they waited until 65. This is called an actuarial adjustment, and it is intended to work matters out so that an individual's lifetime of benefits would be equal, if they lived an average lifetime, whether they retired at age 62 or at age 65.

There is also something called the delayed retirement credit, which increases benefits for individuals who work beyond normal retirement age. This is scheduled to increase in coming years, so that it reaches 8 percent per year in the year 2007. In other words, for every year an individual waits until after normal retirement age to begin collecting benefits, benefit levels go up by 8 percent.

There are significant policy problems with these arrangements. Consider an individual who is 62. We have attempted to construct the system so that this person will get an equivalent amount of benefits if he or she starts collecting now as compared with waiting until 65. Knowing that—and knowing that the individual, should he or she continue to work, will keep pouring payroll taxes into the system—why would the individual continue to work and to pay payroll taxes if in the end that work produces no net increase in benefits? Those taxes are simply lost. As work incentives go, the policy operates in the wrong direction.

This is not a theoretical assessment; it is reflected in the data that reveal when people are retiring. A number of factors determine when an individual retires, but consider the following information: (1) a mature Social Security system has made early retirement more affordable, (2) individuals will do better, net, if they retire early and start collecting benefits than if they keep working and paying payroll taxes, (3) only an individual's top earnings years are counted toward benefits, reducing incentives for part-time work by individuals at the end of their careers, and (4) individuals are actively discouraged from working by an earnings test applied to their Social Security benefits once they start receiving them.

On balance, people are living longer and leading healthier lives and can be productive and healthy for many more years than was true a generation ago. And yet the incentives for early retirement are so powerful, the data reveal that individuals are retiring earlier rather than later. The average age at which individuals began to receive Social Security benefits in 1940 was 68.8.[2] This was reduced to 66.8 in 1960 and further down to 63.7 in 1990.

Now, don't get me wrong. I think early retirement is as attractive an idea as anyone else does. It's one reason why I don't deem myself able to afford a house with land around it or a car larger than my little compact. But if we want to induce people to retire earlier and earlier, then we're going to pass to posterity a bill of the magnitude outlined in the first chapter.

Take another look at the preceding figures. The average person retiring at age 69 in 1940 was born in 1871. I've never known anyone born that long ago. The oldest individual I remember was my great-grandmother Pearl, my mother's mother's mother. She would correspond to 1950's class of retirees, being roughly 69 years old then, having been born around 1881. I learned a lot from listening to great-grandmother Pearl talk about her childhood, but I don't recall her saying anything that suggested that life was, on the whole, cushier for everyone then to the extent that people stayed healthier for five years longer than they do today.

The age of eligibility is a powerfully emotional issue. Often people enter the question by asking, "Why should people be forced to retire at a later age than they want?" A more accurate way to put the question is, "Should we force others to pay for us to spend longer and longer periods of our lives in retirement?" Many people like the idea of retiring at age 65 more than they do at age 68. Many of us like the idea of retiring at age 55 better still. Unfortunately, that desire itself does not make this option affordable. One can't answer the question as to how to set the age of eligibility and how to set the actuarial adjustments until one carefully reviews the effects on all sides of the law and then makes a balanced appraisal of what is fairest for everyone.

Many considerations should go into how we set the age of eligibility for full benefits, which is not the subject of this chapter. Study of both the causes and the effects within the current structure leads powerfully to the conclusion that our Social Security system induces people to retire early, precisely at a moment in history when we need to figure out how to prevent the plummeting projections of the ratio of workers to retirees from coming to pass.

Of course, Social Security does much more than to provide retirement income to the primary insured individuals that we have been dealing with so far. The disability insurance program, a major component of Social Security, is under more severe financial strain than the larger and more-publicized retirement income portion of the program. Spouses, widows, and some dependent children also receive benefits. Social Security includes the concept of a "dual entitlement," which specifies that one may be entitled to benefits based on one's own earnings history or as the spouse of a covered worker. One collects, effectively, the larger of the two amounts, determined by the two ways of computing the benefit. Nonworking spouses can be entitled to an amount equal to half of the benefit level paid to the primary insured worker (widows, 100 percent; children, 75 percent). These formulas are somewhat arbitrary and lead to some inequities in the current system, including regressive transfers of wealth that will be discussed in an upcoming chapter.

NOTES

1. Report of the 1994–1996 Advisory Council on Social Security, p. 17.
2. Green Book, 1996, p. 20.

6

The Trustees' Reports and What They Say: Beyond Actuarial Solvency

Each year, the financial status of the Federal Old-Age, Survivors, and Disability Insurance (OASDI) Trust Funds—otherwise known as Social Security—is reported by the Social Security and Medicare Trustees. These include the sitting Secretary of the Treasury, the Secretary of Labor, the Secretary of Health and Human Services, the Social Security Commissioner, and two publicly appointed trustees, typically one Democrat and one Republican.

The trustees have no crystal ball. Predicting the future is no easier for them than it is for anyone else. But for the most part, the trustees' report, though it may be challenged on intellectual or analytical grounds, is traditionally viewed by all sides in the Social Security debate as an objective appraisal of the program's future course. Analysts may take issue with an assumption here or a projection there, but political figures from left to right credibly cite the trustees' report to buttress their own assertions about Social Security.

In recent years, the reports of the trustees have included projections that the program is, under current law, slated to become insolvent in little more than a generation. As of this writing, 2034 is the projected insolvency date most frequently cited in news reports. The net actuarial deficit over 75 years is, we are told, a mere 2.07 percent of the national payroll tax base.[1]

The reader may be forgiven for asking at this point: This is a crisis? What is the big deal?

The big deal is that these numbers do not begin to tell the story of Social Security's fiscal problems. Though useful, the trustees' report is a bland factual document that can be selectively cited to make whatever point one wishes to. It is only when the fine points regarding the future evolution of the program are dissected that a clear, and profoundly disturbing, picture emerges.

Seldom has public understanding of the nuts and bolts of a complex government program contained such significant stakes for the future of the United States. As the national debate regarding Social Security unfolds, it will be the easiest thing in the world for individuals to present contextless figures to the public that are, to borrow a phrase, "legally accurate," but nonetheless misleading in the extreme. The more that interested citizens and policymakers are willing to delve into these substantive matters, the better equipped we will be to protect posterity from the consequences of grave mistakes that we might otherwise make.

The normal course in a Social Security discussion is, unfortunately, to begin with one's sweeping conclusions and then to fill in the details that support them. Here we will do just the opposite. We will walk through the current-law course of Social Security as projected by the trustees, proceed from that to arrive at the most frequently cited summary characteristics, and only then analyze what it all means and whether we should take these projections seriously.

In 1999, Americans are projected to pay $453 billion in payroll taxes to the Social Security (OASDI) system, a burden equally shared between employers and employees. Taxation of a portion of the benefits paid to senior citizens will bring in less than $11 billion, for a total non-interest income to Social Security of approximately $464 billion.

In recent years, as most of us know, the Social Security system has collected more revenue than is needed to fund current benefits. Under decades-old Social Security law, this surplus is invested in securities of the U.S. Treasury. What this means is that it is invested in the federal government itself, which uses the investment to finance its current operations. When people speak of the Social Security Trust Fund, they are referring to the accumulation of the Treasury securities that it holds, assets "belonging" to the Social Security program—which, someday, the federal government will have to redeem or, in other words, pay back.

This method of investing the surplus causes ceaseless controversy. Senior citizen organizations write in to Congress by the truckload, charging that Congress is "raiding" or "spending" the surplus, which in turn sparks legislative proposal after legislative proposal to move Social Security "off-budget." As a consequence, Social Security has been moved "off-budget" in ten quadrillion different ways in the past few decades. In 1999, for example, a projected unified budget surplus brought renewed calls that we must "save the surplus for Social Security," with various forms of "lockbox" legislation, whose aim was to ensure that Congress stopped "spending" the Social Security surplus.

In reality, there is only one factor that ensures that the Social Security surplus is "spent." It is the requirement that surplus Social Security taxes be invested in Treasury securities. As long as that continues to happen, those Treasury securities will finance the federal government, and Social Security will hold debt that, someday, the federal government will have to repay.

For now, however, the point is that the accumulated Social Security Trust Fund, at the start of 1999, consists of roughly $762 billion dollars. This Fund earns interest—also charged to the federal government—equal to $54 billion in 1999.

All told, therefore, the total income of the OASDI program in 1999 was roughly $518 billion ($464 billion in tax revenue, plus $54 billion in interest).

In 1999, benefit payments were projected to be $387 billion. Adding in administrative expenses and a few odds and ends such as railroad retirement benefit interchanges, the total cost of the system in 1999 was projected to be $394 billion.

This $394 billion contains a variety of different benefits, which fulfill different functions of the Social Security system. Retirement income is but one of these. Disability benefits are another—$54 billion of the total. Also included are spouse benefits, widow(er) benefits, benefits for dependent children, and even survivor benefits for certain parents. These other benefits are considerable elements of Social Security. Fewer than two-thirds of the beneficiaries are retired workers. The disabled, the spouses of retirees, and widows and widowers by themselves make up more than one-quarter of beneficiaries. The benefits for all of these depend greatly upon the basic formulas that determine the benefit levels for the primary insured population.

With $518 billion in income and $394 billion in outlays, Social Security would have a total surplus of $124 billion in 1999. This $124 billion surplus means that the Trust Fund's net assets would grow in 1999 from $762 billion to $887 billion. (These figures are rounded, so they may not appear to add up exactly.) That's $887 billion that, someday, the federal government will have to pay back. It is $887 billion of future claims by Social Security upon the general tax revenue of the United States.

The 1999 surplus is projected to come in the form of $70 billion from surplus taxes and $54 billion in interest earned on the Trust Fund. The $54 billion in interest currently exists as nothing more than an accounting entry. That amount isn't currently needed to pay beneficiaries, so the government doesn't have to write a check for that amount—yet. It simply notes the amount of Treasury bills that the Social Security system is holding and says, "OK, now we will have to pay you another $54 billion some time down the road, as your interest payment for not cashing in the Trust Fund at the present time"—and adds that figure to Social Security's total assets.

Sound harmless enough? Wait.

Reforming Social Security

In 2010, the Social Security cash surplus—the excess of tax revenue over spending—will dip below $50 billion and be heading downward. This will force the federal government to tighten its belt, as there will no longer be an infusion of that much in new T-bill purchases. No more will the federal government be able to count on that extra $50 billion each year to finance federal spending and thereby reduce other federal borrowing. However, since some surpluses still persist, the Trust Fund will continue to grow, and thus the federal government will continue to credit Social Security with higher levels of interest earned every year.

In 2014—not in 2034—Social Security will, according to the trustees, begin to suffer a shortage of annual revenue relative to annual outlays. These outlays will have more than doubled from their current levels—to $929 billion dollars. Annual revenues will only be $917 billion. Thus, additional money must be found to make timely payments to beneficiaries. Not only will every penny of FICA tax revenue be needed to pay current benefits, but the federal government will need to budget for an additional $12 billion in order to get the checks out. It will need to trim other spending, raise taxes, or borrow the money.

It may be the case that only the last two options exist in practice. The Entitlement Commission found that by the early 2010s, all federal revenue would be needed just to fund spending on entitlement programs alone, most especially Social Security and Medicare. Though this projection has since been postponed, it's still the case that, within a few decades, there wouldn't even *be* any other spending—on defense, education, highways, you name it—unless the government began running deficits again. Of course, it is doubtful in practice that we would, by this point, have no other spending to cut. The nation must be defended, after all. But it may not be a realistic option by as early as 2020 to do anything other than to raise taxes or to borrow.

Unfortunately, that $12 billion is just a starting point, the veritable tip of the iceberg. The gap in benefit payments that the federal government must thenceforth plug will begin to grow exponentially: $35 billion in 2015, $61 billion in 2016, and on up to $200 billion by the year 2020.

All the while, a peculiar fiscal situation exists. Social Security's annual revenues are insufficient to meet current benefit payments, requiring the federal government to make cash payments of interest owed. But as these interest payments, through 2020, are less than the amount of total interest that the Social Security Trust Fund is earning each year, it will still grow larger despite the annual deficits. The Trust Fund, under current law, would grow to a peak of $4.46 trillion in 2021.

From the point of view of the taxpayer, nothing significant happens in 2022. All that happens is that the amount by which taxes would have to be raised, above and beyond current payroll tax collections, would continue to climb—in 2022, to $282 billion. But from Social Security's perspective, a corner has been turned. The Trust Fund would only earn $278 billion in interest that year. Thus, the Trust Fund must start drawing down principal in order to make current benefit payments.

In 2022, benefits stand to cost $1.60 trillion. Of this, $1.32 trillion would come from payroll taxes. Another $56 billion would come from taxation of benefits. The federal government also needs to pay off $278 billion in interest that year to Social Security alone. Another $4 billion in payments of principal is needed. It is clear that the payroll taxes collected in 2022 do not begin to measure the total cost of the Social Security system to the nation's economy.

The reader can no doubt anticipate that annual payments of principal will thenceforth accelerate, as interest payments have already done to this point. In the year 2033, the gap between revenues and outlays stands at a cool $814 billion, money that must be raised above and beyond payroll taxes already being collected, through general taxation.

Then, in 2034, the program would become insolvent anyway. Revenues would be insufficient to fund outlay obligations, and there would be no money remaining in the Social Security Trust Fund. Unless the law were changed—for example, either to raise taxes directly or to grant Social Security borrowing authority—beneficiaries would not receive the income that they had been promised.

This is not to suggest that we will allow this dire scenario to play out, because we, as a nation, would not possibly permit this. It is to make the point, however, that when it is said that we have until 2034 to confront this problem, this assumes that all of the suggested actions can be plausibly taken without adverse economic, political, and social consequences. The insolvency date of 2034 assumes that, somehow, the federal government has managed to raise more than $7 trillion in additional tax revenue, above and beyond an already onerous payroll tax.

Moreover, it is to show that the figure of a "2.07 percent actuarial deficit" is in a sense misleading. This figure is a net figure, summing Social Security revenues and outlays over a 75-year valuation period. However, because of the particular shape of the U.S. demographic curve—due to the aging of our population—Social Security outlays will grow much faster than can the economy that is required to support them, in a way that a 2.07 percent figure does not begin to describe.

We currently have payroll taxes at the point where they are above the line needed to pay current benefits, but under current law they will only stay above that line until 2014. We will collect more revenue than we need in the short term and have far too little in the long term. The "2.07 percent actuarial deficit" measure arises from subtracting the size of the near-term surpluses from the long-term deficits. This accounting maneuver does not obviate the fact that those long-term deficits are still there, and the federal government, at that time, will need to fill in those financing gaps in order to pay benefits. In the year 2070, for example, the net financing gap is not 2.07

percent of the national payroll tax base, but 6.29 percent. The federal government would need to hike FICA taxes by over 50 percent if it wished to meet benefit payments that year on a pay-as-you-go basis.

The 2.07 percent figure is particularly misleading in the case of a system such as Social Security, a pay-as-you-go system in which surplus taxes are, by law, invested in the federal government. This is not savings in a meaningful sense. It is an acceptance by the federal government of the obligation to assess the necessary amount of taxes at some future date to repay those debts. Hypothetically, for example, it does us little good to run a 1 percent surplus this year, face a 3 percent deficit next year, use that 1 percent surplus to finance current government spending, and thus claim that our net actuarial deficit over the two years is 2 percent. In reality, we still have to come up with a 3 percent tax increase the next year, having spent the 1 percent on ourselves.

To anticipate an objection: Isn't it possible, in some way, to bank those near-term surpluses, so that they can indeed offset the long-term cost of the Social Security system? Surely we must get something out of collecting extra money this year. Can't we put that "in the bank" this year and then use the earnings from that saving in order to defray future costs?

In a sense, this is exactly what many Social Security personal account advocates are trying to do—to see to it that Social Security taxes are invested in real assets that can be used to finance the retirement income of the twenty-first century. But under current law, the answer is no. The money is not invested in the production of real goods and services that then generate a return down the road. It is invested in the federal government, which says, "thank you," and then promises to pay the money back in the future—a promise that it meets through its power to tax, not through any ability to generate real economic growth.

But surely, you might say, if the money is invested in the federal government, the government's overall fiscal health is improved by that amount. If the federal government gets $50 billion in subsidies from Social Security, isn't that $50 billion less in borrowing that the federal government has to do otherwise? Isn't there a net increase of $50 billion in national savings?

This is the only sense in which near-term surpluses can count in any way against future Social Security deficits. Let's put it in specific terms. In the year 2020, when the financing gap between revenues and outlays in Social Security is $200 billion, the federal government will be in better position to raise that extra $200 billion if it had collected the extra $50 billion this year than if it had not. If its other borrowing today were $50 billion more, non–Social Security debt and interest on that debt would be higher in 2020 than if it received the extra money from Social Security. In fact, were it institutionally capable of completely balancing the non–Social Security books and running annual unified surpluses each year equal to the annual surpluses of Social Security, then indeed it might be possible in theory for the federal government to become a net creditor, holding $4.46 trillion in assets in the year 2021, which it could then make available to finance retirement benefits from the years 2021–2034.

But of course, no such thing has happened in American history. When the federal government gets an extra $50 billion in Social Security, that is merely $50 billion less in additional borrowing that it might otherwise do. It is institutionally incapable of accumulating a nest egg of $4.46 trillion, or any other figure, that can be used to advance-fund future spending obligations. Even in 1998, the first year of unified budget surpluses in more than a generation, Congress was unable to resist the temptation, and prodding by the president, to reduce those surpluses through additional supplemental appropriations. And this was before the non–Social Security budget was yet balanced. In 1999, projections of an on-budget (non–Social Security) surplus finally appeared and immediately dissipated. Congress and the president immediately set to blaming one another for the supplemental appropriations spending that threatened to require, once again, that Social Security surpluses be tapped to provide overall budget balance.

One moral is very simple. If we want to have $4.46 trillion in assets—or any other figure—sitting around in the year 2021 to cover a yawning gap between current revenues and outlays of Social Security, we had better create a place for those assets to accumulate without government's being able to spend them. The current system does not provide one, no matter how many times Congress declares that the surplus is "off-budget." Investing it in Treasury securities guarantees that the money is gone and can reappear only when government levies taxes at some day in the future.

Another moral, just as undeniable, seems to glance off the skull of the nation's press. Mesmerized by the small figure, "2.07 percent of national taxable payroll," so many journalists and political observers fail to note that a solution could be devised that purported to eliminate Social Security's actuarial deficit, but would in practice solve nothing. In order to claim that the system has been "fixed," we have to be able to demonstrate how future benefits are to be funded. To build a "Trust Fund" of $4 or $5 or $6 trillion is not an answer—it simply raises the question of where posterity will come up with $6 trillion. In other words, it simply punts.

Were we to enact a package of legislative reforms that, on paper, attained actuarial solvency but was predicated entirely upon future citizens ponying up $7 trillion in two decades, on top of the payroll taxes they are already scheduled to pay, we would be guilty of a massive fraud. No solution to Social Security's financing problems is a true solution if it leaves such enormous financing gaps in place.

BEYOND ACTUARIAL SOLVENCY

Total outlays of the Social Security program, under current law, can be expressed in nominal dollars or as a percentage of the national taxable payroll tax base. Each worker in 1999 contributed OASDI taxes on the first $72,600 of taxable wages, and it is this taxation that serves as the predominant source of revenue for the program.

The Social Security actuaries tend to use nominal dollars in their long-term projections, and these lead to some fairly eye-popping figures. Given that the number of elderly in this country will increase drastically, that they will be collecting benefits for a longer number of years, that inflation will continue to rise, as will economic growth and wage growth—it's no wonder that the nominal figures in the out-years become so large as to be difficult to view with perspective.

The real question is whether all these costs are growing at a rate that is faster than the economy's ability to keep up. Each year the cap on taxable wages is indexed upward for national average wage growth. What are SSA's estimates of the total size of Social Security outlays as a fraction of this taxable payroll (Table 6.1)? Beyond 2035, the cost figure continues to go up, with no end in sight. At the end of the valuation period, in 2070, costs are 19.63 percent of national taxable payroll.[2]

What this means is that we have a fundamental structural problem that will outlast the baby boom. As long as lifespans continue to lengthen, the costs of the program will grow, not only relative to inflation but also faster than economic growth can sustain.

A program cannot be sustainable if it perpetually grows faster than the economy that must support it. These figures tell us not only that we must restore Social Security to actuarial solvency, but also that we must do so in a

Table 6.1
Projected Social Security Outlay Costs, Revenues, and Cash Flow Balances*

Year	Cost Rate	Income Rate	Balance Requiring Additional General Revenue Outlays
2005	11.18	12.70	(1.52)
2010	11.91	12.75	(0.84)
2015	13.25	12.82	0.45
2020	15.03	12.91	2.12
2025	16.62	13.01	3.61
2030	17.71	13.09	4.62
2035	18.19	13.15	5.05

*As a percentage of taxable payroll

way that keeps total outlays from permanently outpacing economic growth.

Let us return to nominal dollars as a means of illustrating the specific financing problems that must be solved within Social Security. As we have seen, it will not be sufficient to restore actuarial solvency to the program if that solvency is achieved through implausible means, such as the requirement that future taxpayers redeem trillions in Trust Fund assets. Chapter 12 will cover this subject in greater detail, and the cash flow operations of the system are projected in Table 12.1.

A couple of things are clear from those projections. One is that we are missing a critical opportunity by not saving the surplus taxes that are coming in the years prior to 2014. Were those saved and used to finance future benefits, instead of invested in treasury bills, they could offset some of the gaps in subsequent years.

Second, it is clear that actuarial solvency is only part of a larger puzzle. The gaps between revenues and outlays in years such as 2025 and 2030 are so large that they cannot realistically be filled in only by taking action at the moment that the gaps occur. If this program is to operate soundly and to continue to pay promised benefits in a timely manner, then the first two columns of Table 12.1 must be kept in rough proximity to one another in perpetuity, regardless of whether or not we have ruled that the program is "actuarially sound." If in any one year we lack the means to send out the benefit checks, actuarial soundness will be a small comfort to beneficiaries.

Thus far, we see that the program must not only be made actuarially sound but also must be placed on a course that the economy can sustain and show a reasonable balance between outlays and revenues in every year. But what about the most important considerations of all—the impact upon beneficiaries? Clearly we could solve these problems simply by recklessly cutting benefits, but that would be inconsistent with our goals for the program, that it provide fairness and income security.

In a subsequent section we will examine the treatment of beneficiaries under Social Security by the measures of money's worth, replacement rates, and rates of return. Suffice to say here that we must look beyond actuarial solvency alone. We must fix the system in a manner that gives every generation and every beneficiary a fair deal.

NOTES

1. Social Security and Medicare Trustees, *Annual Report*, 1999.
2. Ibid.

7

Dissecting the Trustees' Assumptions

The assumptions of the Social Security actuaries frequently come under attack, from both right and left. Not coincidentally, each side wants the actuaries to estimate a little more optimistically, for obvious reasons. The left wishes that the financing problem could be made to vanish with just a little bit of creativity in the assumptions, and the right wishes that the actuaries would be willing to estimate a higher rate of return from personal accounts invested in the private sector. The incentives are clear: the more optimistic our long-term economic projections, the fewer tough choices we have to make, and the better deal that we can promise under our favored Social Security reforms.

From the standpoint of history, however, no such creative optimism is justified. When the 1983 Social Security amendments were passed, the Social Security Trustees estimated that they would be sufficient to guarantee 75-year actuarial solvency for the program. Now their estimate is that the Trust Fund will be exhausted in 2034. Though careful analysts might point out that the redemption of such a large Trust Fund was never a realistic scenario, the fact remains that changes in the trustees' estimates have moved the date of insolvency up by decades relative to the estimate when the last Social Security rescue was adopted.

The Social Security actuaries make Intermediate, Low-Cost, and High-Cost estimates. The Low-Cost estimate is essentially what will occur if everything goes "right" from the standpoint of Social Security solvency, and the High-Cost, if everything goes "wrong." (These evaluations are in quotation marks, because it is a dubious "right" if individuals die earlier, as they do under the Low-Cost estimates.)

Historically, reality has tended to arrive at somewhere between the Intermediate and the High-Cost estimates. There is not much basis, as some have suggested, for the belief that things will turn out as the trustees project in their Low-Cost estimates. But let us look at what those estimates are, nonetheless.

Under the Low-Cost scenario, Social Security does not go bankrupt during the 75-year valuation period. The financing crunch begins somewhere around the year 2018, when outlays first exceed revenues. It becomes its most severe in the years 2030–2035, when annual costs and revenues are out of balance by approximately 2 percent of the national payroll tax base, producing financing gaps on the order of roughly $300 billion per year, to be raised from general taxes. But assuming that the federal government can raise this without dire incident, the Trust Fund will have enough assets to call in these claims without itself running dry.

Before we rejoice too much over this scenario, let us keep in mind a critical aspect of the Low-Cost scenario. Social Security, even under the "Low-Cost" Estimate, would never again be in the black on an annual cash-flow basis after 2014. Permanently—let that be understood—the program's annual tax revenues would be less than outlay obligations, meaning that additional taxes would be required in order to fund benefits. The program would have the statutory authority to make these claims on general revenue, but it would permanently suffer an excess of outlays over revenues.

Now, what are the assumptions that underlie this Low-Cost picture? They are:

- Real wage growth 0.5 percent higher each year than in the Intermediate estimates.

- Unemployment rate 1.0 percent lower (4.5 percent perpetually).

- Interest rates 0.3 percent lower.

- Fertility rates equal to 0.3 children more for every mother.

- Life expectancy at birth 3.0 years lower.

- Annual immigration 250,000 higher.

Not *some* of these factors, but *all* of them, operating simultaneously.

Each year the trustees publish a report on the sensitivity of their analyses to changes in the actuarial estimates. Perhaps the most oft-studied of these are the Intermediate assumptions with regard to life expectancy. Currently, the average male, at birth, is expected to live for 73.6 years, while the average female is expected to live 79.5. years. At age 65, these expectancies are 15.8 and 19.2 years, respectively.

Dissecting the Trustees' Assumptions

This is a significant change from 1940. Then the average male only lived to 61.4, and the female 65.7. The average male, at birth, had a life expectancy that was *less* even than the early eligibility age. Those who did make it to 65 were expected to live for another 11.9 and 13.4 years, for males and females respectively.

If any one issue is the crux of the entire Social Security financing problem, this is it. It is not that benefits are too high, or taxes too low, in any absolute sense. It's not that the rich are receiving too many benefits, or that we spent all of our Social Security money on the Marshall Plan, or that waste and fraud are depleting the funds. All of these real and imagined effects pale in comparison to the fact that people are living longer. Even after the baby boomers pass through their retirement years, the system still won't return to a flat cost rate, simply because people are living longer than before.

What do the actuaries project for the growth of the elderly population? In their Intermediate assumptions, they expect life expectancy at birth for men to rise by three years from 2000 to 2030, from 73.8 to 76.8. At the same time, for women, it would increase from 79.6 to 81.7. Life expectancy at age 65 would increase, over those 30 years, from 15.8 to 17.1, and 19.2 to 20.2, for men and women respectively.

The trustees also make Low-Cost and High-Cost assumptions. The High-Cost assumptions are particularly important here. Under the High-Cost assumptions, the trustees assume that by 2030 life expectancies at birth for men and women will be 78.5 and 83.5, and at age 65, 18.4 and 21.7.

What does this by itself do to the actuarial estimates? If these higher life expectancies are accurate, it would throw the estimates off considerably, worsening the net actuarial imbalance from 2.07 percent in the red to 2.75 percent—an increase of 33 percent in the net actuarial deficit.

This is especially significant because many scholars believe that the Social Security actuaries severely underestimate the number of "old-old" who will be alive by the middle of the twenty-first century.[1] The high-cost estimates of the Social Security actuaries are that there will be 17.8 million Americans above the age of 85 by the year 2050, significantly higher than their intermediate estimate of 14.6 million, but still lower than the intermediate estimate used by the Census Bureau (18.2 million). Such a figure could push the long-range estimate of the actuarial deficit to higher than 3 percent.

Here we have a situation in which two government departments are using vastly different projections of a most critical piece of data for the future of Social Security. The timing of the cost implications inherent in these figures is as important as their total magnitude. Return for a moment to the fact that the 75-year actuarial deficit is a net figure, subtracting near-term surpluses from out-year deficits. The real financing gaps that must be filled in are those out-year deficits. If the Census Bureau's intermediate projections turn out to be right, then not only would the 75-year deficit be worse than 3 percent, but the annual deficit in the years around 2070 could be well beyond 7 percent of national payroll, requiring effective tax increases of more than 60 percent of the current OASI tax levels.

Just to add to an already serious picture, we should note that the Census Bureau's estimates of individuals over the age of 85 in the year 2050 also include low, intermediate, and high-cost estimates—9.6 million, 18.2 million, and 31.1 million respectively. The latter figure would worsen the cost picture much more severely than the figures previously cited.

In summary, the Social Security actuaries' estimates are quite sensitive to the assumptions that are used for mortality rates and life expectancy—and their intermediate estimates of costs are significantly lower than what would result from the assumptions that our own Census Bureau would use. This fact in and of itself reveals that there is little substantive reason to simply sit back and hope that the problem will vanish on its own.

Perhaps the most frequently discussed factor with respect to the trustees' report is their set of assumptions regarding future economic growth. One congressman recently wrote that the 2.07 percent actuarial deficit, despite being the trustees' Intermediate estimate, is a "worst case scenario"—largely because the trustees have made "conservative" assumptions regarding economic growth, which we as a nation should exceed easily, and thus reduce the long-term actuarial deficit of the program.[2] At the December White House summit on Social Security, NOW President Patricia Ireland also suggested that the trustees' assumptions about economic growth might be creating needless worry about the program's fiscal future.

The trustees assume real GDP growth over the next ten years of approximately 2.0 percent per year, slightly lower than the 2.4 percent of the last ten years, the difference "mostly due to slower projected growth in labor force and employment."[3] This is key. They are not assuming that worker productivity growth will slow down so much as noting that the fraction of the population that is working will drop. Because of this, in the long run, they assume that real growth slows gradually, staying roughly constant at about 1.3 percent from 2050 onward.

In their optimistic projections, they assume that the steady growth of the last decade will accelerate slightly, to 2.5 percent over the next year, and remain fairly close to that, leveling out at 2.2 percent, even though the ratio of workers to retirees has dropped significantly. Alternatively, the pessimistic scenario shows what would happen if a recession hit the country in 2000, economic growth rebounded to 3.0 percent in the year 2004, then dropped quickly as the baby boomers begin to retire, down to 0.9 percent in 2020, and then moved further downward with population aging, with barely positive 0.3 percent real growth by the end of the valuation window in 2070.

Dissecting the Trustees' Assumptions

No economist can tell you what the economy will do over the next couple of decades. Certainly it will grow faster if we save more and work longer than if we save less and all quit working earlier, but the precise course of events is anyone's guess. We can, however, look at what happens with different rates of increase in wage growth that would result from faster or slower economic growth. (Wage growth increases are correlated with, but not exactly the same as, economic growth, but it is the wage growth sensitivity analysis that is contained in the actuaries' report.)

Basically, improvements in projected wage growth are not able to help the system as much as deterioration resulting from longer life expectancy could harm it. In the optimistic economic growth assumptions of the trustees, the long-term actuarial outlook improves from 2.07 percent to 1.55 percent (the pessimistic ones deteriorate from 2.07 percent to 2.57 percent). In other words, even if the trustees are wrong, and real wage growth in the next ten years exceeds that of the last ten years and stays there, we still have a major financing problem.

What's perhaps more significant—though one rarely hears about this from the proponents of the "cross your fingers and hope we grow our way out of it" school—is that the extra help that we would get from economic growth does not really achieve that much when the program is in desperate need of cash. Consider the information about the optimistic projections shown in Table 7.1. Through 25 years, it's "so far, so good." We have a larger actuarial balance in the short term, when we're already in surplus (if we count interest). We get extra cash when we really don't need it, resulting in a

Table 7.1
Projected 25-Year and 50-Year Income and Cost Rates under Alternative Assumptions*

	Intermediate Projection	Optimistic Projection
25-year income rate	13.81	13.75
25-year cost rate	13.04	12.65
25-year balance	+0.77	+1.10
50-year income rate	13.54	13.46
50-year cost rate	14.80	14.24
50-year balance	-1.26	-0.78

*As a percentage of taxable payroll

63

larger Trust Fund that future taxpayers have to pay off. Now look at the picture over the first 50 years, considered together.

Think for a moment about what is happening here. Increased economic growth is producing higher wage growth, which in turn increases the size of the payroll tax base relative to the program's costs. That's why the income *rates* go down slightly under the optimistic projection. We're taking in a slightly smaller fraction of the nation's payroll simply because there's more payroll around even though we are collecting more money.

But greater revenues also lead to higher initial benefit levels. We collect more in taxes from workers, and we have to pay them *more benefits* later on. It's not a wash, of course: Economic growth does make the problem easier to manage; when those workers are collecting more in benefits later on, more wages are being earned at the same time to support them. But the net drop in real costs is not as great, proportionally, as it was at first.

Higher average economic growth rates would bring costs down pretty sharply at the beginning—from 13.04 percent down to 12.65 percent, a 0.39 percent drop—at a time when we can afford the program already and don't need to raise taxes to fund it. The surplus then goes to create a bigger Trust Fund, and then the working population later faces a larger liability and takes longer to pay it off. As for whether their burdens are reduced while doing so because the economy has grown further—yes, they are, but not much. Net costs over the first 50 years have dropped from 14.80 percent to 14.24 percent, a 0.56 percent drop, but as we have seen, a good portion of that has occurred in the first 25 years.

Let's make the math very simple and approximate to make the point clear, even if inexact. Higher economic growth has improved the situation from the years 1999–2023, when the comparative need for improvement is less. But in the years 2023–2048—the critical years—not much has been accomplished. One can estimate that under current law, the program would have an income rate of 13.27 percent and a cost rate of 16.56 percent in those years, or an imbalance of 3.29 percent. Under our optimistic economic growth assumptions, those numbers would change to 13.17 percent and 15.83 percent respectively—an average imbalance of 2.66 percent of taxable payroll every year.

That isn't much of an improvement. The high-growth scenario simply doesn't result in that much help during the program's years of untenability. On paper, it might appear to. It will take much longer to pay off the Trust Fund, for example, and thus the program will be considered to be "solvent" for longer—but in reality, the financing gaps that the country will face—the gaps that determine whether or not beneficiaries can be paid—would not change by so much as 20 percent. The qualitative picture is unchanged by improved economic growth projections.

The skeptical reader may need a little bit more than this to go on. Let's try it another way. The late 1990s have been a tremendous period for the economy. Economic growth has been up, wages have been up, and inflation has been down: exactly the conditions that one would expect would lead to an improvement in the outlook for Social Security. More wages to support payroll taxes, less inflation to drive CPI-indexed benefit payments, and low unemployment to keep the revenues up as well.

In 1998, the trustees also issued a report that implied an improvement in the long-term outlook for Social Security, postponing the date of insolvency of the OASDI Trust Funds from 2029 to 2032:

The economy performed better than expected over the past year. Real GDP grew more than 1 percent faster than was expected, as did the average real wage level. The factors contributing to this favorable growth, higher than expected productivity growth, the temporary cessation of the historical decline in average hours worked per employee, and an increase in wages as a portion of GDP, are assumed to persist through much of the short-range period in this report.[4]

How much did this really do for us? Table 7.2 shows the changes between the 1997 and the 1998 projections. Increased economic growth made the outyear financing gaps *larger*, not smaller. The insolvency date was postponed from 2029 to 2032, not because things were to be better in 2030 than previously thought, but simply because it would take longer to pay off the Trust Fund. The extra payroll taxes projected as a result of improved growth estimates in the years 2025, 2030, and so on, did not move upward as fast as benefit obligations increased. The best that one could say was that, with a larger economy, the financing gap itself, which needs to be made up

Table 7.2
Annual Balances, OASDI Program (in billions)

	1997 Estimates	1998 Estimates
2000	+$32.5	+$54.5
2005	+$31.6	+$51.9
2010	+$13.0	+$31.6
2015	-$64.6	-$49.1
2020	-$217.6	-$213.6
2025	-$425.3	-$433.3
2030	-$661.9	-$684.2
2035	-$890.6	-$924.5

Source: 1997 and 1998 Social trustees' estimates.

through general tax collections, might be slightly smaller relative to the size of the economy—though by the year 2035, even this was untrue.

In other words, the increased economic growth from 1997 to 1998 gave us a more optimistic projection date for insolvency, but not much in the way of real improvement. That is what happens with a pay-as-you-go system in which benefit levels are tied to wage growth. You can't grow your way out of the real problem, even though you might, if all things go well, grow your way into a smaller estimate of the net actuarial deficit.

Shall we put it bluntly? The argument that the trustees' conservative economic growth estimates should console us is simply fallacious, premised on the audience's ignorance of the factors behind the naive measure of actuarial solvency. We shouldn't hide from reality according to an argument that doesn't have much relevance to the issue at hand.

Of the remaining factors that affect the trustees' projections, the most significant is the projected fertility rate. Some commentators have offered the titillating recommendation that we simply start breeding faster as a way of meeting the Social Security financing problem. However enticing this "solution" may be, it would only perpetuate the basic structural problem with the current Social Security program, in which we hope that the workforce will grow to the extent necessary to produce benefits tomorrow that relate well to today's contributions.

Now that the population "pyramid," in Judd Gregg's words, is becoming a "box or a rectangle," the financing system is experiencing strains. We can keep trying to expand the base of the pyramid as long as we can, but at some point it simply isn't going to work, and it makes much more sense from a policy standpoint to build some advance funding into the system, a closer relationship between one's own contributions and one's eventual benefits, than to simply hope that in another time and place more babies will be born.

That being said, fertility rates, within the valuation window, can impact the actuarial analysis. The actuaries' projections assume that they will stay at or near the levels of that last 20 years or so (a little lower than 1987–1997 rates, but higher than rates in 1975–1987). If the twenty-first century is marked by higher fertility rates, more in keeping with what was seen just around 1972, approximately 0.33 percentage points would be shaved off the net actuarial deficit. A major baby boom would help out still more. But a continued decline in fertility rates, down to 1.6 in the high-cost estimates, would increase the net actuarial deficit to 2.42 percent. As our fertility rates have stayed relatively stable, within one-quarter of a child, for the last twenty years or so, it is difficult to believe that changes in fertility will ultimately have a decisive impact upon actuarial solvency.

Two other assumptions should be mentioned, even though they do not affect the totals as much. Immigration projections are also evaluated, but unless there is a major change in the nation's immigration policy, this is unlikely to affect the long-range picture by more than a small part of a percentage point.

Also, it may come as a surprise that the trustees' projections do not vary that much with their projections for the Consumer Price Index (CPI), for measurements of inflation. The reason is that the key factor that affects actuarial balance is not CPI per se, but real wage growth—in other words, the relationship between the growth of payroll taxes and the growth of benefits after they begin to be received (as a consequence of being indexed to CPI). The trustees' estimates of future inflation do not fundamentally change the relationship between wages and inflation, nominal wage growth being expected simply to rise and fall as CPI does. A change in how CPI is figured, however, could in fact change the trustees' estimates significantly, if it alters this relationship between wage growth and CPI measurement, increasing the projected difference between the two. But as CPI and wages rise and fall together, though this impacts the estimates somewhat, there is not a huge effect.

NOTES

1. Martin Holmer, "EBRI Social Security Reform Analysis Project Progress Report: Phases 1 and 2, Assessing Social Security Reform Alternatives," *EBRI*, 1997, pp. 43–56.
2. Congressman Jerrold Nadler, *Roll Call* magazine.
3. Social Security and Medicare Trustees, Report, 1999, p. 54.
4. Social Security and Medicare Trustees, Report, 1998, p. 130.

8

A Cottage Industry of Demagogues

Washington employs a cottage industry of organizations and individuals whose job it is, essentially, to complain. These organizations are not in the business of making and selling products, nor are they even in the business of governing. They are in the business of convincing citizens to give them money on the premise that government is doing something wrong. After most of the money is distributed to the organization's employees, a little bit is spent now and then to remind those in government of their failures.

There is nothing intrinsically evil about such employment. Lord knows, government does plenty that should be complained about. Many believe passionately in their causes. But individuals of lesser convictions, but of surpassing ambition, can employ the same appeals as those who bear a legitimate grievance. Given that Americans have a tradition, a healthy one, of mistrusting government, it takes no great amount of ingenuity to separate citizens from their money with the pitch that government is going to abuse them. Thus, a thriving market exists for the individual who wishes neither to be productive himself nor to be accountable to the electorate at large and yet desires a healthy income.

Every day, thousands upon thousands of envelopes are delivered to the homes of U.S. senior citizens. These envelopes reflect the findings of direct marketers everywhere, that whether the cause is charitable, commercial, religious, or political, seniors are more likely to be persuaded into parting with their money than is the average citizen. Some may have reached a stage of life where disposable income is greater. Often, however, this is not the case, and the willingness to contribute has much more to do with the credulity of the donor than with any spare income.

Seniors are not the only citizens targeted by political pressure groups, but they are the most convenient target in part because they themselves inspire sympathy. Some organizations shake down seniors for direct contributions, some generate revenue by selling them commercial products tax-free (exploiting a loophole in the tax code for such organizations), and some, believe it or not, get their revenue principally from the United States Treasury.

The National Council of Senior Citizens is a case study in everything that is wrong with our political process. This organization has received the overwhelming majority of its income directly from the U.S. taxpayer, in the form of federal grants. The organization, at the same time, lobbies essentially for the hastening bankruptcy of every senior entitlement, through increased spending.

And guess what? You have been paying for them, whether you agree with them or not. You may believe that Social Security should be expanded or that it should be abolished. No matter; your tax dollars are the essential source of support for this organization, which then goes out and showers the senior population of the United States with nonsense.

Perhaps the single most effective way to frighten a senior citizen half to death is to emblazon on a mailing a warning that Congress is preparing to "cut" Social Security benefits, an attention-getting threat considering that for the vast majority of seniors, Social Security is their largest source of income. Perhaps the single most effective way to incite rage is to suggest to seniors that their rightful level of Social Security benefits is being denied to them.

To take one case in point: the "notch baby" issue. The "notch" issue is, for lack of a better word, blather that is used simply to raise money for senior-scaring organizations such as the National Committee to Preserve Social Security and Medicare, and the increasingly shrill The Retired Enlisted Association (TREA). First, let's review what happened, and then see what is said about it.

In 1972, Congress enacted legislation to add COLAs to Social Security, indexed the benefits of current retirees, and also accidentally markedly raised the benefits of future retirees. In effect, Congress screwed up. They created a sort of "dual indexing" that would create compounded increases in benefits. Whenever an automatic benefit increase for current retirees came into effect, this changed the formula that was used to calculate the benefits of future retirees. In effect, the benefits of future retirees were being indexed twice. Once in the calculation of their own wage histories, and once again in the benefit formula.

Had this been allowed to continue, the results would have been perverse. The system would have been driven into insolvency within a few years; even had it not been made insolvent, beneficiaries would soon have received benefits actually higher than what they had been earning when working. So Congress in 1977 had to fix the formulas so that the "replacement rates"—the relationship between retiree benefits and previous working wages—would return to contemplated levels. The fix was phased in so that it would not affect any then-current retirees (those born in 1916 and before). Individuals born after that point would still receive higher benefit levels than had been intended, but not as grossly so as if the error had been perpetuated. As a consequence, the "notch" was allegedly created—the birth years from 1917 to 1921—during which the error was phased out.

In reality, there is no "notch." There is a group of retirees born before 1916 who received an unintended windfall. If you compare the individuals born between 1917 and 1921—those for whom the error was not phased out—to that group, of course the benefits of subsequent cohorts will be lower than for those who received too much. However, these supposed "notch babies" receive a much better rate of return on their Social Security contributions than those who follow them (Table 8.1).

In fact, most of the "notch babies" are enjoying replacement rates from their benefit levels that are significantly higher than those received by other birth years because of where they fit into the phase-out of the erroneous formula. The average individual born in 1918, for example,[1] is receiving a higher replacement rate than any subsequent birth year. Second place would go to 1919. Even in the worst-case "notch" years, replacement rates are still higher than will be the case for workers born in 1960 and beyond. A number of opportunistic fundraising groups, however, such as the National Committee to Preserve Social Security and Medicare, decided to beat the drum on the notch issue for all that it was worth.

Table 8.1
Number of Years to Recover Retirement Portion of OASI Taxes, Plus Interest

Birth Year	Payback Time
1915	1.4 years
1920	2.8 years
1925	4.0 years
1935	7.3 years
1950	9.5 years

Source: "Social Security Notch Debate," CRS Issue Brief IB92129, p. 9.

Reforming Social Security

In 1994, a bipartisan Commission on the Social Security "notch" issue completed a final study of the subject and concluded that "no remedial legislation is in order." And yet the subject still gets brought up from time to time, whenever an organization feels the need to do a little extra fundraising. Nipping along at the heels of the National Committee to Preserve Social Security and Medicare is a group that has more recently wormed its way to the forefront of notch demagoguery, The Retired Enlisted Association, engaging in the splendid practice of suggesting to seniors that if they send membership dues to TREA, they may receive an immediate lump-sum windfall from the U.S. Treasury.

On TREA's website,[2] listed as its third highest priority resolution, is one that begins as follows: "WHEREAS, the "notch" occurred in 1977 when Congress reduced the Social Security benefit levels for all eligible persons born after January 1, 1917, and before January 1, 1927."

This isn't a good start. First of all, the benefit corrections included transitional benefit rules for those born between 1917 and 1921. There is no inherent reason to single out people born from 1917 through 1927. The 5-year phase-in was over by birth year 1922, and though one could argue that individuals born in 1927 were receiving lower benefits than they would had the error been perpetuated, the same could be said of any subsequent birth year. So the years here are at worst wrong and at best arbitrary. Further, it's fairly misleading to say that Congress "reduced the Social Security benefit levels," as those individuals had not yet retired and had not yet been collecting benefits, and there was thus nothing to reduce. They did change the method that would be used to index—that is, increase—benefit levels.

Further, the site states: "WHEREAS, notch babies then have been receiving an average of 20 percent less in Social Security payments than people born before 1917."

Possibly, but this is because people born before 1917 were getting an unplanned windfall, and Congress didn't feel able to take it away, however undeserved, because most of these people had already retired. One could argue—and apparently TREA is arguing—that because people born before 1917 got comparatively higher benefits, the error should be perpetuated for everyone, regardless of equity concerns and regardless of what it does to tax levels and to Social Security solvency.

Moreover, these figures hardly tell the whole story. As the Congressional Research Service puts it,[3] "many individuals born in the above-referenced years were not adversely affected—in fact a significant but undetermined number of them received a higher benefit than they would have under the old rules."

No matter. TREA wants a $5,000 lump sum payment for each of them anyway, or at least they claim they do. CRS estimates that the cost would be roughly $60 billion, more than wiping out last year's annual cash surplus in Social Security.

A Cottage Industry of Demagogues

As former Social Security actuary Robert Myers put it, the proper way to deal with the error might have been to limit the "undue windfalls" of people born before 1917. But he figured that it was too late for that, and the best that could be noted was that "legislative action to give more bonanzas, all at the expense of younger workers, is not needed."[4] His statement recognized that the only true victims of the "notch" issue were the taxpayers, who were left holding the tab for the extra benefits given to those who retired in the mid-1970s.

Plenty of groups on the left side of the aisle recognize that the notch issue is a phony. The American Association of Retired Persons (AARP) stuck its neck out responsibly and refused to agitate for additional notch benefits. You would think that the issue would be dead and gone, having been stripped of all credibility by analysts on both sides of the ideological spectrum, but as long as there are organizations out there in need of an issue to hammer on in mass mailings to seniors, the notch issue will continue to serve that purpose. That there are still legislators who will introduce bills authorizing payments to individuals who are not entitled to them is a shameful bit of pandering that still, regrettably, occurs every now and then.

Of course, none of these tactics would be possible were it not for the particular way that Social Security is structured. Because benefits are set through a political process each year, not by the level of savings that each individual has accrued and over which he has property rights, the charge can perpetually be made that individuals are being ripped off and that they need someone to lobby on their behalf. This is the true agenda of these organizations: to convince seniors that they will be helpless against a vicious Congress, unless the National Council of Senior Citizens or whichever group is there to fight for them. If seniors were guaranteed ownership, not forfeitable to political processes, of their own savings, these groups would lose their major reason for existence: to frighten seniors out of their money.

The National Council of Senior Citizens is, along with the AFL–CIO, one of the many voices that purport to speak for laborers on questions of national policy. The posture of organized labor on such questions has long been puzzling, inasmuch as they have drifted into positions that seem to run counter to the interests of their own membership.

Organized labor has been an indispensable part of the political coalitions overseas that fostered reform of sagging public pension programs. In such countries as Australia and Great Britain, labor took on the task of delivering a system of wealth creation and savings to their members, understanding it as a positive benefit that negotiators would be credited with facilitating. Here in the United States, however, organized labor has positioned itself inflexibly against any personal ownership of accruing Social Security benefits and on the side of government control.

In an effort to dissect the behavior of labor on these questions, let us review the main categories of options for restoring solvency to the Social Security system and juxtapose with them the logical, and then actual, positions of labor.

TAX INCREASES

One option, of course, is to do nothing to arrest or to fund the growing liabilities of the Social Security system and simply to raise taxes as is necessary to meet the demands. As we have seen from previous discussion, this would amount to enormous and unprecedented increases in tax burdens. The conflict with the interest of wage earners is manifest.

While labor has not explicitly endorsed using tax increases as a means of resolving the financing problems, they are peculiarly open minded on the subject. Moreover, they seem to be working to produce this result by default, in agitating against the only reforms that could avert the increases. Labor has not advocated a tax increase, but is fond of pointing out that the problem "could" be solved with a tax increase (Gerry Shea of the AFL–CIO opined at the 1994–1996 Advisory Council on Social Security meetings that this might not be so bad).

Moreover, labor continues to defend the practice of financing future Social Security obligations through the buildup of a Trust Fund, which in practice means assessing a tax burden on future generations to redeem it. While it is true that this displaces some of the burden away from the payroll tax and into the more progressive income tax, labor is curiously tolerant of the tax increases that are more a threat to wage-earners than to any other segment of society.

BENEFIT CUTS

The second route is simply to cut benefit levels. Again, confining solutions to this course is manifestly against the interests of laborers. The possibility does exist that low-income individuals can be shielded from the worst effects of this tactic, because benefit changes can always be made in a highly progressive manner. But in general, acting solely to cut benefits, without increases in national savings that otherwise generate retirement income, would undermine the retirement income security of the U.S. worker. On this matter, labor takes the position that one might expect—firmly against benefit cuts. They oppose, however, even progressive benefit changes that would target them chiefly to higher-wage individuals, reasoning that such changes would ultimately affect the low-income worker as well. As a strategic position, this is dubious, for the mathematical realities are that within a given level of spending, the benefits of low-income individuals are threatened to the extent that those of higher-income individuals are protected.

Moreover, labor resists the creation of accounts through which individuals might be able to earn back the benefits lost in the course of balancing the existing system, an arguably self-contradicting position. While one may quibble with the specific choices that labor makes on these questions, there is no mystery to their position here, as there is elsewhere. They oppose cuts in projected levels of government-provided benefits, pure and simple.

SHUFFLING INVESTMENT AROUND

After we see that both tax increases and benefit cuts are against the interests of U.S. workers, the necessity of exploring other options becomes clear. Is there a way to minimize the impact of changes in both taxes and benefits? Such changes are so problematic, in terms of both policy and politics, that the temptation to avoid them if at all possible is almost irresistible. Unfortunately, too many policy students, searching for "magic bullets" to avoid the first two categories of choices, hit upon solutions that seem to promise a by-pass but in reality do not.

The most prominent of these is the proposal put forth by Robert Ball, Henry Aaron, and Robert Reischauer, among others, to paper over the need for changes on the revenue and benefit sides, by having the government invest the Social Security Trust Fund in a different way, in the equities market. (Various incarnations of this proposal would make some minor changes in revenue levels and outlay levels, raising the cap on taxable wages and changing the calculation of CPI. However, for the most part, such proposals seek to duck these choices and simply redirect as much of the Trust Fund as is deemed necessary to bypass such decisions.)

That this proposal has set off various alarm bells is not surprising, and we will return to the policy problems with this suggestion in a later chapter. What is particularly striking in this particular discussion, however, is the way that such a proposal would affect the interests of organized labor. Of the three routes to reform thus far considered, it would be by far the most direct assault on the income of organized laborers. The National Council of Senior Citizens seems to recognize this, and some labor unions have expressed opposition to the idea, whereas others such as the AFL–CIO, have remained largely silent.

To understand the effect of such a change in investment requires a moment of reflection. Recall that the essence of the Ball approach is to avoid, to the extent possible, changes in the revenue and outlay levels associated with the Social Security program. Rather than to do what others have proposed, which is to change revenue and outlay levels to bring the Social Security program into balance, the whole point of the Ball approach is to appear to provide a free lunch. No increase in tax rates, no significant decrease in benefits—just move some investment around from here to there, and the problem is solved.

Were it not immediately apparent that if the government closed a multitrillion-dollar funding gap, someone would have to pay for it, a number of analysts have stated quite clearly why such an approach achieves nothing, in net terms. Alan Greenspan put it this way when testifying before Senator Judd Gregg at a hearing of the Social Security Task Force of the Senate Budget Committee:

As I have argued elsewhere, unless national saving increases, shifting Social Security trust funds to private securities, while likely increasing income in the Social Security system, will, to a first approximation, reduce non–Social Security retirement income to an offsetting degree. Without an increase in the savings flow, private pension and insurance funds, among other holders of private securities, presumably would be induced to sell higher-yielding stocks and private bonds to the Social Security retirement funds in exchange for lower-yielding U.S. treasuries. This could translate into higher premiums for life insurance and lower returns on other defined contribution retirement plans. This would not be an improvement to our overall retirement system.[5]

Translated for the layman, this means: If we do nothing to increase net national savings, then one entity's gain in investment income comes at the expense of another's. If government gets a higher rate of return for Social Security, then other forms of retirement saving—through insurance, through private pensions—will earn less money.

This is not unrecognized by the proponents of this approach. Robert Reischauer, for example, has straightforwardly admitted that such an approach does not produce a net increase in national savings. Rather, he couches the argument differently—that by running a surplus in the past and being required to invest it only in government securities, Social Security has been in effect subsidizing savings returns for the rest of the country. By providing a cushion against the amount of borrowing that the federal government would otherwise have to do, the environment for private retirement savings has been indirectly strengthened. To be fair, he argues, we should give Social Security a portion of that return. It doesn't solve anything in net terms, but there's a *fairness* argument advanced by the idea.

The problem is that "not solving anything" is anything but a trivial detail. The phrase "rearranging the deck chairs on the Titanic" is overused, but it seems appropriate to simply rearrange the forms of national retirement savings that are inadequate to the tune of trillions of dollars.

No one has more of an incentive to look skeptically at this than the labor unions. If such a change in investments is made in an effort to duck the other changes required in the Social Security system, then additional Social Security income will come through the indirect tax increase of taking investment returns away from private retirement savings—none more obviously than the pension plans provided to laborers. Reinvesting the Social Security Trust Fund in the stock market takes money directly out of the pockets of employees with other retirement (pension) investments and puts it into the coffers of the federal government. It is a targeted revenue grab from the very people the union leadership is responsible for protecting. If this is where the AFL–CIO winds up, it would be an astounding rejection of the direct remuneratory interests of their members.

INCLUSION OF PERSONAL ACCOUNTS

Including personal accounts in the Social Security system is the only option that has a chance of working in the interests of wage-earners. Still, a personal account approach is not without perils similar to those previously mentioned. For example, were we to do nothing to balance the outlays and revenues of the Social Security system, but simply placed Social Security money placed in personal accounts; then we would have exactly the same situation as predicted earlier. Net investment income in the Social Security system would increase, and net investment income outside of it would fall. There would be no dynamic effects on the economy, no overall improvements in national retirement income projections. However, it is far more likely that other changes would be made that would result in a net improvement for tomorrow's workers.

First, personal accounts can be a facilitator of additional saving, beyond that already provided to the Social Security system, whether through additional mandated contributions or purely voluntary ones.

Second, the federal government, losing the additional revenue coming in from the Social Security system to cover its own borrowing, would likely enact some offsetting changes in its own spending levels; to the extent that such offsets were enacted, the money placed in personal accounts would in fact add to national savings.

Third, the accounting procedures for Social Security permit government investment to be counted as occurring within the Social Security Trust Fund, whereas most personal account proposals count the investment in personal account proposals as outside it. As a consequence, most responsible personal account proposals also would eliminate the imbalances, the dissaving, within the traditional Social Security system and thereby add to net national savings income, whereas government investment advocates deliberately bypass the choices necessary to make this happen.

This is not a trivial exercise—it would indeed be possible to develop a personal account proposal or any other kind of proposal that would work against the interests of U.S. wage-earners, perhaps even relative to an untenable current-law scenario. *The fact remains that the incorporation of personal accounts the laborer's only hope.* The three alternatives—tax increases, benefit cuts, and shuffling of government investment—are direct attacks on the retirement income of wage-earners. It is something of a disturbing paradox, however, that the one option that promises at least some hope for their members is the one that organized labor in the United States, alone among the world's labor movements, seems resolutely to oppose.

Why would they do this? The answer is simple—and daunting.

The leaders of organized labor enjoy a particular form of power and influence in their role as seeming protectors of retirees' income and benefits. It is the annual negotiation between the taxpayer and the beneficiary, into which the labor leaders can insert themselves, that justifies their existence. Remove the dependence by the beneficiary on the taxpayer, and thus vanishes the intermediary.

If the individual beneficiary owned his or her own benefits and if they were not subject to the annual voting process on Capitol Hill, how then could one frighten the retiree? What role would there be for the agent acting as the safeguard against government imposing cuts in retirement income?

None whatsoever—And labor knows this. Consequently, the notion that individual wage-earners would be liberated from the whims of government, and thus from the efficacy of labor leadership, strikes fear in their hearts. They need wage-earners to be perpetually dependent—on government and therefore on those who derive their employment from it.

Those who believe that personal accounts pose a threat to labor are right, but it is not the individual worker they threaten, but the lobbyist walking the halls of Capitol Hill and the fund-raiser mailing inflammatory missives to seniors across the United States. Their existence is tenuous when individuals control their own economic destiny, free from threats by government, and they will spend millions to defend that lucrative sinecure.

The reader should remember this whenever labor solemnly intones that seniors would be put out to pasture by any attempt to provide them with ownership and control over a portion of their retirement benefits. The beneficiary does not lose by possessing such benefits, but the labor leader does.

While the motives of such organizations are patently disingenuous, that is not the main issue of this work. What is of concern here is the misinformation circulated about Social Security and plans to reform it.

A typical example is the NCSC analysis of Senator Moynihan's Social Security reform proposal. Moynihan's proposal makes several substantially different policy choices than did the NCRP plan. It could be fairly criticized on the grounds that the benefit changes were not sufficiently limited to higher-income retirees. However, it is an example of a serious plan that, because it faced up to some difficult choices, is subjected to the sort of misleading analysis in which these organizations specialize.

The following is taken from the NCSC's website: "The backbone of the Moynihan plan—the policy choice that drives all others—is the idea that everyone can get rich, over time, by simply putting 2 percent of annual payroll into the stock market."[6] This is, for lack of a fancier word, a lie. The inclusion of personal accounts was anything but the "backbone" of the Moynihan proposal. They were included on a voluntary basis only, and

78

their inclusion did not affect the other components of the plan. To suggest that this was the "policy choice that drives all others" is a distortion of Senator Moynihan's approach. Senator Moynihan drafted a plan that would achieve solvency for the traditional Social Security system, as scored by the Social Security actuaries, with or without personal accounts. The inclusion of personal accounts did not affect those policy choices by so much as one penny.

The accusation is made by the NCSC for a specific purpose—so that they can continue to allege, wrongly, that the choices Senator Moynihan made in facing up to the financing deficits in the current-law Social Security system were in some way the product of personal accounts. By making this allegation, the NCSC can therefore imply that such choices would not be necessary if one did not create a personal account plan. This is untrue. The problems that exist with financing the current system require substantial changes if they are to be averted, and they are not the creation of Senator Moynihan or of any other advocate of personal accounts.

Another choice phrase appears later on the website: "The Moynihan plan would cut Social Security payroll taxes today by one percent for both employer and employee, and then raise them again after 2030, when today's politicians have, conveniently, retired."

To understand why this is disingenuous, one must note that today's payroll taxes are higher than they need to be in order to pay current benefits and that the surplus taxes are not being saved in any meaningful way to finance tomorrow's benefits. To put a halt to the collection of surplus taxes that are not being used for the appropriate purpose is hardly the stuff of venality.

As for the tax increases that Senator Moynihan would postpone until today's politicians are retired, let us note that even the highest tax rate proposed by Senator Moynihan—13.4 percent—is significantly lower than the effective tax rate required under current law within a generation. In fact, the NCSC, which is so fond of saying that the current system can be fixed with "only" a minor 2.07 percent net payroll tax increase, would see effective tax rates rise from 14.5 percent today (with the tax increase) to more than 18 percent by 2035 (the net cost that the NCSC's approach would require, the sum of payroll taxes collected and general taxes required to redeem the Social Security Trust Fund) and—moving upward to 19.79 percent at the end of the actuaries' valuation window, rising perpetually after that.

The allegedly diabolical Pat Moynihan would actually aim to *lower* the net tax burden substantially in the twenty-first century relative to the NCSC's favored approach. It cannot be otherwise, because Moynihan would do what is necessary to lower the long-term costs of the system. But one wouldn't know this from reading the NCSC analysis. That analysis appears to imply that Social Security, under Pat Moynihan's vision, would pay fewer benefits, but from a much higher tax level, than the NCSC's approach. Something is very wrong with that picture. If Moynihan is raising taxes so severely and the benefits are not higher, what in the world is he doing with the extra money?

The answer can only be understood in reference to the NCSC agenda. There is no significant "extra" money under Senator Moynihan's plan. Revenues and outlays balance somewhat neatly throughout the valuation period, albeit rising throughout. The reason that the NCSC can imply that it stands for paying higher benefits and for not collecting as much in taxes as Senator Moynihan is that it is content to leave the previously described financing gaps in the system to be tomorrow's problem. It's the NCSC that is lobbying for the highest tax rates, not Senator Moynihan. The only difference is that Moynihan tells us what tax rates he proposes, and the NCSC doesn't.

This is not an endorsement of Senator Moynihan's Social Security proposal. He made different choices in his legislation than were made in the NCRP plan, but his plan represents an honestly developed solution to the Social Security problem and certainly a higher level of commitment to the health of the program than displayed by anyone who has ever written for the NCSC.

Thus the challenge of reforming Social Security requires not only the intellectual courage to face up to its financing difficulties, but also the moral and political courage to overcome the substantial political muscle of those entities who base their livelihood on frightening senior citizens. Today's public servants will need to confront not only an enormous and complex problem but also the baying voices who clamor to perpetuate it.

NOTES

1. Congressional Research Service (CRS), "Social Security Notch Debate," CRS Issue Brief IB92129, table on p. 8.

2. http://www.trea.org/resolutions.html.

3. Congressional Reference Service, "Social Security Notch Issue: A Summary," p. 4.

4. CRS Issue Brief IB92129, p. 8.

5. Alan Greenspan, Testimony before the Senate Budget Committee Task Force on Social Security, November 20, 1997.

6. http://www.ncscinc.org/issues/ssmoyn.htm.

9

Into the Lion's Den with the AARP

No discussion of the interest groups influencing Social Security policy could possibly be complete without a description of the most powerful lobbying group of all, the American Association of Retired Persons (AARP). It warrants a separate chapter, for various reasons. On the one hand, it is unfair to the AARP to include it in the previous chapter, under the title "A Cottage Industry of Demagogues." On the other hand, it is unfair to imply that any of the groups covered in that chapter wield more than a small fraction of the AARP's influence.

It so happens that the election of 1994 (more on this next chapter) indirectly threw me into a clinch with the AARP. Shortly after Senator Simpson was named to chair the Senate Finance Committee's Subcommittee on Social Security, I was with him at a speech, when he introduced me to a crowd and said, "And this young man is about to lead an investigation into the AARP!"—drawing a round of laughter and applause from the audience.

I would have passed it off as one of the senator's many jests, but it was not the first time that he had made such remarks. During a hearing of the Entitlement Commission, he had gone full bore after the representatives of the AARP, suggesting that its business entanglements contradicted its public posture as a disinterested voice for the elderly.

In subsequent consultations with the senator, it became clear that he was seriously interested in probing the public policy implications of the AARP phenomenon and its interaction with federal law. He did want to have hearings if possible.

Reforming Social Security

Before I begin to briefly describe this work, let me make two points—a disclaimer and a summary of Senator Simpson's concerns, of why he felt some review (he shied away from the word "investigation") was necessary.

First, the disclaimer: Whatever improper things were done within the AARP—and there have been some—it should not be implied that the current group of people who run the organization are in it for profiteering or to engage in a corrupt enterprise. The current leadership appears genuinely motivated by a desire to represent the interests of senior citizens, and any improper actions were likely conducted by the founders of the organization. The persisting problems tend to be institutional, growing out of the policy contradictions that have allowed AARP to reach its present size and status.

Now, the concern. The AARP is easily the most powerful lobbying organization in Washington, D.C., beside which such organizations as the National Rifle Association and the Christian Coalition seem puny and ineffectual. Al Simpson was perhaps the first to refer to the AARP as the "800-pound gorilla" of U.S. politics. Driving its power was its claim to represent an enormous and monolithic voting bloc of 30 million members—not just any members, but politically the most courted voters of all, senior citizens. No other group of voters combines such numbers and power at the voting booth with such a hold on reflexive public sympathies.

For years, the AARP has used its power and influence to press tirelessly for ever greater expansion of government spending. When the National Taxpayers Union Foundation conducted a study of the AARP's legislative agenda, it found that the organization was actively working to increase federal spending by more than $1 trillion over the decade following the study. The AARP's legislative activity saw to it that, as the costs of mounting entitlement spending continued to swell, almost all of those costs would be passed onto taxpayers, rarely any to beneficiaries.

Were the AARP simply another member political organization, even if it were selfishly promoting the interests of only its members at the expense of other Americans, past and future, the public policy issue raised by its clout would be limited, though still substantial. But it is not just any organization. It was and is a vast commercial empire—moreover, a vast tax-free commercial empire. Less than half of its revenues came from members' dues. The vast majority came from a combination of royalties and other premiums on the sales of products, in combination with the interest accruing from a massive investment portfolio—$38 million in interest alone in 1992.[1] The AARP brings members in for only a nominal fee—$8 a head—which membership entitles the individual to receive periodic mailings that contain advertisements only for products endorsed by—and thus producing a royalty payment for—the AARP itself.

Thus, the AARP is not simply a member organization representing the interests of its members. It was a thriving, massive business, which has fig-

ured out that if its customers pay dues and make it a "member organization," its business can get away without paying taxes on its income.

The original brains behind this whole operation was a fellow named
Leonard Davis, a man whose license to sell insurance was revoked by the
state of New York because of his "untrustworthiness to act as an insurance
agent."[2] Davis diagnosed that there could be massive profit in selling
health insurance to senior citizens, especially if he didn't have to pay taxes
on the income. He teamed up with Ethel Percy Andrus to work out an arrangement by which a fledgling group called the American Association of
Retired Persons would be established and would charge only a nominal fee
for membership. Davis established an insurance company named Colonial
Penn, and with some strategic interlocking management arrangements, he
guaranteed that the AARP board always gave his insurance company the
AARP contract, which meant the exclusive right to advertise through
AARP publications. AARP would endorse the Colonial Penn products.
Members would buy their insurance from Colonial Penn. For this endorsement, a certain percentage of the premiums would be paid back to AARP as
tax-free income. Everyone would make money—AARP, Colonial Penn,
and not least of all, Davis himself.

Thus was born a major business empire, through the loopholes in the tax
and regulatory laws. Though Davis and Colonial Penn were ultimately
broken away from AARP as the consequence of a messy lawsuit in the early
1980s, the essential framework still remained intact. AARP operated
through a number of business affiliates—handling health insurance, life insurance, financial services, pharmaceuticals, and a host of other products.
The AARP would give an exclusive endorsement to one carrier of each of
these services, and the businesses would each pay the AARP a royalty in
exchange for this endorsement. Steered to these businesses by the AARP
literature—all mailed at subsidized not-for-profit mail rates—seniors
would preferentially buy these products. The more they bought, the more
tax-free royalties came back to AARP.

Essentially, the AARP figured out how to run a massive business without being taxed like one. This raises a whole host of issues with regard to the
"level playing field" for business competition and whether we can expect
other businesses to organize themselves and pay taxes appropriately, when
they are forced to compete against business empires such as the AARP that
have managed to avoid the normal taxation.

Moreover, this tax-free income meant an enormous revenue base that
could be used to support the political views of its leadership, most of whom
were advocates of greater federal spending. The fact that it had a large and
diverse group of members, with a diverse range of political views, need not
necessarily matter, because most of the money used to finance the operations of the AARP didn't come from its dues. Members joined up to get the

discounts, bought the products, and were cited as implicitly giving their stamp of approval to everything that the AARP was lobbying for.

The plums didn't stop there, though. Because the AARP had managed to create the illusion of being a disinterested advocate for seniors' interests, it was tapped to run a number of federal programs and received millions of federal grants each year to do so, another great deal for the AARP. Although the AARP makes a strong case that it provides good service for the grant money received, there is still a fundamental conflict of interest at work. The grant money enables the AARP to pose as a great benefactor of senior citizens, providing services to them that are in reality being funded by general taxpayers through the federal government. It's splendid publicity, which fuels AARP's benign image.

There was a serious public policy question here. Is it appropriate for the federal government to be subsidizing the activities of the most powerful political force in the nation? Imagine for a second that the federal government decided to fork over millions to the National Rifle Association or the Christian Coalition so that these groups could give benefits to their members. The citizenry would scream bloody murder at being required to indirectly subsidize the activities of overtly political organizations that they might disagree with on many issues. Here was the most powerful political organization in Washington, receiving federal grant money and simultaneously lobbying furiously for expansions of federal spending that would accelerate patterns already projected to bankrupt the nation, claiming all the while that its members supported this agenda.

Senator Simpson didn't expect to change much of the legal environment in which the AARP operated. He did, however, hope to learn—and to expose—some of what the organization was actually up to. Extremely striking was that the deluge of mail that we received after beginning the work— 92 percent by our count—was favorable to the investigation, hostile to the AARP. One thing one learns in Washington is that it's always easier to be against something than for something. Thus, we should not have been surprised that so many people who contacted us would have been complaining about the AARP instead of praising it. You just can't keep 30 million members happy. When you do well, people will forget it, or won't say anything. When you tick them off, they'll let you know—and let others know.

There were still surprises. We had assumed that people distrusted the federal government much more than they distrusted the AARP and that given the choice of two entities to complain about, they'd complain about Senator Simpson's work. And yet the vast majority of mail that we got cheered us on. Political cartoons were drawn up in which the senator was pictured as a Don Quixote–like figure, tilting not at windmills but at an oversized monster. One political cartoon showed a giant in the shape of a grandmother, swooping down on the U.S. Capitol and picking up a tiny (and terrified) Al Simpson, squeezing him in her giant fist, and shouting, "Alan Simpson, you naughty naughty boy! Picking on a poor defenseless little old lady like me!"

Curiously, AARP did not actively defend itself. *Nightline* hosted the senator, while AARP declined a similar invitation. No doubt annoyed by the AARP's refusal to discuss its operations, *Nightline* showed a lengthy introduction in which the whole range of AARP financial interests was displayed and its conflicts of interest laid out. Then Al Simpson was given the stage to himself to describe his concerns. The senator enjoyed himself hugely, with no rebuttal time.

The AARP controversy had a decidedly positive effect on the Senator's reputation as a stand-up performer. "Thirty million members, united by a common love of airline discounts," he would call AARP. He perfected an impersonation of the Gen-X voter, wearing a baseball cap backward, approaching him and pleading, "Who speaks for me?" "Why don't you speak for yourselves?" was his rehearsed reply. "You have the vote, and only 18 percent of you use it." When he showed up late for speeches and meetings, he would crack, "Sorry about the delay. The AARP mined my driveway."

At the staff level, it was a little more tedious. The vast majority of the AARP's operations were behind a wall of secrecy that really could not be penetrated. The small fraction of the overall income that came back to the AARP in royalties was disclosed on federal form 990, but the vast majority of the proceeds stayed within the coffers of various affiliated for-profit businesses under no obligation to tell us anything.

To take a case in point: We knew the amount of royalties being paid to the AARP from Retired Persons Services, its pharmacy. We also knew that several members of the AARP's board also sat on the pharmacy's board of directors. They weren't paid for their AARP duties, and the money sent back to AARP from the pharmacy was comparatively limited (at least compared to the rest of AARP's money). But how much was being made within the pharmacy and by whom was anybody's guess.

We knew that a settlement had been reached by the AARP and the Internal Revenue Service, for $135 million in lieu of back taxes. This was a tantalizing finding, as $135 million in lieu of taxes suggests a large amount of income being shielded from taxation. We had no way of knowing just how much the AARP should have been paying and what arguments they were using to protect income from taxation, but clearly vast amounts of revenue were floating around. The AARP evinced no desire to tell us the precise terms of the dispute.

One thing that AARP had been doing was to send out advertisements for its insurance products using nonprofit mailing rates. These health insurance benefits were provided by Prudential, a taxpaying for-profit corporation that is not supposed to have the benefit of nonprofit rates. The AARP engaged in a series of mailings starting in January 1992—as it had several times before—that were documented by the Postal Service as using the lower nonprofit rate. The Postal Service contacted the AARP and reminded it that mailings at such rates were illegal.

What happened then was a remarkable example of the extent to which the AARP, at that point, essentially viewed itself as above the law. Not only did it continue the mailings—through August of 1992—but it replied with a draft agreement that the Postal Service would "not bring any enforcement action"—further stipulating that the Postal Service would lobby Congress to change the law to make AARP's actions legal again! ("The parties shall use their best cooperative efforts to secure an amendment, set forth in Appendix A to this agreement, to Section 3626 of Title 39, United States Code, to replace the test of qualified insurance mailings . . . with statutory language eliminating the qualification of such insurance mailings for n.p.o. special third class bulk rates as of January 1, 1993."[3])

Space and subject limitations prevent us here from reviewing even a fraction of the litany of such findings that emerged. Suffice it to say here that Senator Simpson's hearings sharpened the picture and disclosed that this was not a simple matter of balancing the interests of seniors against those of other taxpayers. Clearly, enormous business enterprises had waded into the mix; they were willing to use their scope and influence to advance their interests, in a way that could not always be reconciled with the AARP's public posture of disinterested advocacy. Senator Simpson did much to strip the veneer of objectivity from the AARP.

Not that the members didn't already know. Discontent within the organization was so high that people were voluntarily feeding us information that we would never think to ask for. Senator Simpson, during a hearing on June 20, 1995, was questioning AARP chair Horace Deets about why the AARP had taken particular legislative positions that its membership often seemed to oppose. Examples included catastrophic health care insurance, the president's health care proposals, and the balanced budget amendment. Deets implied that the AARP surveyed its members and chose its legislative positions according to where they stood.

Said Deets:

I am concerned with the implication that we do not represent our members' wishes. Certainly we disagreed with Senator McCain over catastrophic. You yourself disagreed with him. We have reason to believe that easily over 60 percent of our members supported that, because they would not have paid a single cent more. That was a progressively funded program. That legislation has gone away, but the issue of health care has not gone away.[4]

Deets did not specify how the AARP had surveyed its membership to get marching orders on its positions. But at that very moment, someone within AARP downloaded an internal AARP survey and sent it to us in the anteroom behind the hearing chamber. It showed that in fact the AARP's decisions on these matters were driving members out of the AARP ranks and that departing members were citing AARP's spending-increasing, deficit-expanding stances on these issues as the major reasons for their discontent. Senator Simpson gleefully confronted Deets with the information that he had just been passed:

Let me just share with you, modern technology being what it is, something that I have just received that shows you how Washington works. It is a memorandum of May 15, 1995, to the membership department directors, the membership division section managers, from Keith Hardy, re: HCR impact study. That is health care reform. And it goes directly in opposition to what you are just telling us.

This is apparently a confidential document. It shows that 35 percent of those ending their AARP membership did so mainly because of AARP's position on health care. Another 15 percent said it was a very important reason. So 50 percent of [those ending their] . . . membership have said this. Sixty percent of your members did not even know AARP had taken a position on this issue. This is a fascinating document. It flies exactly in the face of what you have just told me.[5]

In another instance, the AARP shared with us one of its polls on the balanced budget amendment, supposedly justifying why the AARP had lobbied against it. In actuality, the polling data showed that a higher proportion of seniors, relative to the general population, favored the balanced budget amendment. ("Seven out of 10 Americans 50 and older favor a balanced budget amendment."[6]) In some of the more detailed questions, seniors also said that they did not believe that a balanced budget amendment would result in cuts in Social Security and Medicare. ("Older Americans dominate the group who think that a BBA would not affect them—they simply feel 'immune' and think that programs like Social Security and Medicare will not be touched."[7])

The AARP legislative shop took this polling information and turned it into an endorsement of exactly the opposite position. Its reasoning went something like this: The AARP leadership believed that the balanced budget amendment would lead to cuts in Social Security and Medicare (even though much of the debate on the balanced budget amendment dealt with how to formally guarantee that it would lead to no cuts in Social Security, indicating a wide bipartisan commitment to shielding Social Security from any such effects). Thus, since the AARP leadership believed that the BBA would make such cuts inevitable, they convinced themselves that their members would oppose the BBA if only they knew enough to know that it would lead to cuts that they didn't like. (Most of those polled did say that they wouldn't support cuts in Social Security and Medicare to enforce the BBA.) Thus, even though the members said that they favored the BBA, the AARP leadership lobbied the other way, essentially assuming that their membership didn't know any better and would change their minds if they did.

This is not to suggest that responsible parties should take a position on public policy based solely on polling data. But in the case of an organization like the AARP, it is worthwhile to know that positions taken by lobbyists in Washington may bear absolutely no relationship to the viewpoints and interests of their membership.

What is the moral of all of this? Just that in the areas of Social Security and other budget and entitlement issues, things are not always as they first appear. There are various reasons why the programs for seniors are constructed as they are, and not all of them are based on what is best for seniors. The loudest voices in the public policy debate are in many instances deriving their clout and their power, not from their degree of connection to the will of the electorate, even the senior electorate, but from the skill with which they have exploited the loopholes in the laws relating to unrelated business income taxation (UBIT) of nonprofit organizations, the lobbying regulations, and access to federal money.

The AARP is very much in transition, and internally it has started to recognize that it is not to its long-term benefit to continue to promote a statist agenda in opposition to the views of the baby-boom generation, their future members and customers. The AARP has enough staying power and institutional strength to look beyond the next direct-mail scare piece, unlike some other seniors' organizations. It doesn't survive from month to month by provoking hysterics, and it can take a longer view.

A number of factors have gone into this apparent change in direction within the AARP: President Clinton's deftness in recruiting it to be an honest broker of the 1998 Social Security discussion, it own internal looks at the changing characteristics of its future membership, and others. But one of the factors was the spotlight shined on it by Alan K. Simpson of Wyoming. When the lights were turned on the AARP operations, many Americans—and many AARP members—did not like what they saw. If any changes at all were induced by this exposure, they will benefit those whom the AARP leaders ultimately wish to help.

NOTES

1. AARP, Form 990, 1992.
2. State of New York Insurance Department, Stipulation by Richard E. Stewart, Superintendent of Insurance, August 13, 1969.
3. Letter from Jack Lahr to Donald Dillman, U.S. Postal Service, February 26, 1992.
4. Hearing of the Senate Finance Committee Subcommittee on Social Security and Family Policy, June 20, 1995 (transcript).
5. Ibid.
6. Wirthlin Group, "A National Survey Measuring Sentiment Towards the Balanced Budget Amendment," January 1995.
7. Ibid.

10

The Congressional Debate Evolves: 1994–1997

The year 1994 was a watershed in national politics, featuring the conquest by the Republican Party of both the House and the Senate—the House majority being its first in 40 years. Writing at a distance of five years, it is difficult to convey the momentous feeling of that event.

In 1998, Americans elected Republican majorities to both chambers of Congress for the third consecutive time. The public has already become so acclimated to Republican stewardship of Congress that most press attention focused on why Republicans had not *increased* their majorities.

But since I was young—and indeed for a decade before I was born—the House had been in Democratic hands. Republicans might break through and capture the presidency as often as not, and they could even gain an occasional majority in the Senate, given the equal representation there given to more rural, more Republican states. But the political alignment that ensured Democratic dominance of the House seemed etched in stone. The Democrats had long maintained superior party organizations at the congressional district level, and they had mastered the principle that, in Tip O'Neill's words, "All politics is local." While Republicans might be entrusted with the president's responsibilities for matters of war and peace, for foreign policy, and to rein in the excesses of congressional spenders, voters felt that only Democrats knew how to bring home the bacon from the House of Representatives.

Forty years of Democratic dominance had created a work environment in the House that was unknown on the Senate side. In the Senate, majority and minority exchanged hands from time to time, and moreover, the minority was explicitly protected in various ways. A minority can filibuster a bill, and even one senator may object to a unanimous consent agreement that is necessary to expedite Senate action. The rules and traditions of the Senate are designed to retain the prerogatives of each individual senator and to involve the minority in routine decisionmaking.

Not so in the House. The House is an institution that still can mystify the Senate. The rules for floor action are established anew for each bill by the House Rules Committee, which is stacked heavily in favor of the majority party, even if that party's overall House majority is slim. These rules, of course, can be set up to limit debate, to limit the consideration of amendments, to determine how those amendments are considered, or to make whatever other decision the majority finds advantageous.

Not only is the legislative deck stacked on the House side, but so is everything else, including for example the amount of staff provided to the majority and the minority. Republicans labored for 40 years in an environment where the rules of debate were established to still their voices, and the resources were eagerly provided by a Democratic majority to themselves. Voters for decades made the quite rational calculation that it did not pay to elect a member of a perpetual minority party, given the nature of House operations. The Democrats seemed to have determined how to make congressional control a self-perpetuating phenomenon.

Until, that is, 1994. One after another of the first results that trickled in were tending Republican. Not, it seemed, merely a majority of them, but every race that had been considered at all competitive was going into the Republican column. It was something like the feeling one would get if one were flipping a coin and it kept coming up heads—5, 10, 15 times in a row. With each flip one thinks, "This can't possibly come up heads again"—and then, somehow, it does. Screen after screen rolled by, with each result tilting the Republican way.

I don't want to be misunderstood here as attaching too much glory to a partisan gain. Few people are more vexing than those who, tribally, associate their own political party with all that is right and good, and the opposing one with everything pernicious and evil. This tale is not aimed at convincing the reader that the creation of a Republican majority was a splendid thing simply because this happened to be the party of the senator for whom I worked. Rather, it is to convey a sense of how much the political world seemed to turn upside-down in 1994, how significant was the overturning of a long-entrenched order, and how the election results catapulted many new people into the operating majority of Congress, when there was previously little reason to assume that such an outcome was possible.

Republicans in the House tried to make up for 40 years of wandering in the political wilderness with a flurry of action, passing item after item from the "Contract with America." They slashed personnel budgets, and they dismantled the staff empires that had been built up over the decades. This new majority did not simply want to seize the reins that had restricted them throughout the decades; they wished instead to eliminate much of this machinery of control so that it could never be used again. In effect, the serfs stormed the gentry's mansions and, instead of taking them over, burned many of them down. It was something to watch.

In the Senate, Democrat Bob Kerrey won reelection easily, one of many instances of a public official directly taking on Social Security, Medicare, and other politically sensitive issues and prospering at the ballot box. Thus we see that, while these issues can indeed be fatal politically to those who attempt to run from them and who cast their votes without adequate public explanations, those who take them on full-bore are not, generally, penalized for their courage. My current boss, Judd Gregg, offered his Social Security plan in the middle of an election year and was returned to the Senate with the highest percentage of any senator in New Hampshire history. Democratic Congressman Charles Stenholm, a coauthor of the Social Security plan, was supposed to have a tough race in 1998, but actually he improved upon his 1996 margin of victory. This should be a lesson to all of those who think that the 1985–1986 electoral experience still represents the politics of Social Security.

Kerrey's Entitlement Commission cochairman, Jack Danforth, retired. In the wake of Danforth's retirement, Senator Kerrey approached my then boss, Al Simpson, about creating legislation based on the recommendations of the Entitlement Commission. There began a fruitful collaboration.

The resulting Kerrey-Simpson legislation was groundbreaking. It would have achieved actuarial solvency for the Social Security system and also created a system of individual personal accounts, funded with two percentage points of the existing payroll tax.

We were still learning when we put the legislation together, and a couple of choices were made that we would not repeat today. One element of our proposal was to invest a portion of the Social Security Trust Fund in the equities market. Since we developed that original legislation, we have had many chances and reasons to think better of the proposal. But we intended then to craft something that would advance the debate, and we did.

We divided the legislation into several bills, which were numbered as Senate bills 818 through 824. We also crafted a comprehensive package of proposals, S. 825, which united the main features of the others and which would ensure solvency for the Social Security system. The reason that we put out the bills in several pieces, according to Senator Simpson, was that "when they take down some of the proposals, we'd still have a few left." Democratic Senator Chuck Robb was the only other senator to cosponsor S. 825.

The Kerrey-Simpson bills did not come near to legislative enactment in the Congress of 1995–1996. They did, however, set a standard for Social Security reform proposals that is still a fairly good one. Had we effected even portions of this legislation when it was introduced, the country would be in far better shape than it is now to deal with the long-term challenges facing Social Security.

The years following Kerrey-Simpson were ones of intense creativity and activity both on and around Capitol Hill on Social Security. Senator Simpson held a number of hearings on Social Security in his subcommittee, which were scrupulously avoided by the other senators on the subcommittee. We were grateful for one exception, Senator John Breaux, the ranking member, who diligently attended whatever hearings he could. For the most part, however, in Senator Simpson's words, the hearings were "like a bowling alley at 2 A.M." He would joke that staff were positioned in the hallways outside the hearing room, intercepting their bosses and whispering, "Don't go in there! He's talking about Social Security!"

Over on the House side, other proposals were cropping up. Congressman John Porter (R-IL) had previously developed a proposal to establish a funded component within Social Security. Toward the end of the congressional session, Congressman Nick Smith (R-MI) introduced a proposal of his own, including personal accounts, that was also judged as attaining solvency by the Social Security actuaries.

Perhaps the single most newsworthy development in the area of Social Security reform proposals, however, was the work of the Social Security Advisory council. This council, which reported to the Social Security Commissioner and the Secretary of Health and Human Services, worked from 1994 to 1996 to develop recommendations to shore up the Social Security program. Its report, the details of which will be covered in chapter 11, would give new energy to the Social Security reform debate.

But though the Advisory Council's report undoubtedly received the most publicity among developments on the Social Security front, action was picking up elsewhere around town and would continue to accelerate throughout the 1995–1996 period.

Organizations surrounding Capitol Hill had already written much about Social Security, and their work began to pick up in pace and intensity. The Cato Institute, the Brookings Institute, the Heritage Foundation, the Progressive Policy Institute, and the Urban Institute were among the many that began to publish and speak about the Social Security issue with increasing frequency. Another commission, the Committee for Economic Development, also produced a well-publicized proposal, similar to the Gramlich (Advisory Council) proposal in including "add-on" personal accounts.

Few things stuck in Senator Simpson's craw more than the fact that Congress listened regularly to the phone banks generated by the AARP and other seniors' organizations, but rarely to the concerns of the young about the way that their fiscal future was being sold down the river. Third Millennium's (an advocacy group representing the interests of young Americans) entry into the advocacy picture was beginning to change that.

On the one hand, Senator Simpson blamed the young for not being more involved, not voting more, not walking the halls of Congress. He was impressed by the way that AARP would come in the door and say, "We represent 30 million members, and they vote!" That's an effective way to get the attention of a senator.

But on the other hand, it was not right simply to blame the young for not having more of a political voice. Is Congress only supposed to listen to the concerns of those who vote? Are we not to concern ourselves with the environment that we create for children, even though they aren't permitted to vote at all? Surely political activity should be something more than a raw contest of numbers and power, in which whoever muscles more individuals to the voting booths turns the resources taken coercively by government in their own direction. Were that the case, there would be nothing wrong with simply running massive debts, spending extra money on ourselves, and leaving posterity to foot the bill.

Third Millennium became an increasingly vocal force for fundamental structural reforms of Social Security and other entitlements. With no specific recommendations of their own, they were a resolutely bipartisan organization—going so far as to require that they maintain a 50/50 balance between Republicans and Democrats. All they asked was that Congress bear in mind that the decisions it made—even on programs designed for the elderly alone—would affect the young, tomorrow's elderly, as much as today's.

Something was definitely changing in the political environment. Economist Larry Kotlikoff's methods of "generational accounting"—assessing the tax burden on future generations as a consequence of current practices—became part of federal budget debates.

The changes, however, involved more than awareness of the budgetary implications of entitlement spending, but a gradual shift away from a narrow budget outlook to broader questions of the structure of the entitlement programs themselves.

During the deliberations of the Entitlement Commission, I had the good fortune to meet Senator Judd Gregg and his chief counsel Stan Sokul. I found myself agreeing with Stan as often as with any staff associated with the commission, and I was impressed by the seriousness with which he and the senator approached their work.

It was Senator Gregg, with Stan Sokul handling the staff work, who first offered the Medicare Choice legislation in the Senate, advancing principles that would greatly influence the way that Congress approached health insurance policy. Senator Gregg had made the conceptual leap that the Medicare program could not be perpetually stabilized simply by enacting various cost-saving formula changes. Rather, the entire dynamic of

Medicare health benefit delivery had to be changed. The essence of Choice Care was that competitive market forces must be brought into the Medicare health benefit delivery system, or else it would continue to be subject to hyperinflation. As long as there was little cost accountability to consumers, spiraling costs would forever be distributed between taxpayers and beneficiaries (and providers as well), with nothing being solved.

Senator Gregg's insights about Medicare—partially and imperfectly implemented in the 1997 budget reconciliation bill[1]—were analogous to those that were gaining force with respect to Social Security. Gradually, Congress was beginning to understand it was not enough to add some revenue here and to cut some benefits there. The operations of the program itself had to be fundamentally transformed. Senator Kerrey's own language evolved significantly during this time. During the Entitlement Commission's deliberations, he had spoken chiefly of generational equity, moral responsibility to posterity, and willingness to bear burdens equitably. In the next Congress, he began to discuss more forthrightly the shortcomings of the system itself, talking about the need to turn it into a true savings system and employing the language of "wealth creation."

Moreover, this period also saw a leap into the fray by certain individuals associated formerly with the political left. Sam Beard, a former assistant to Robert Kennedy, formed Economic Security 2000, a grassroots organization aimed at building support for personal accounts within Social Security. Again, here the message was one of economic empowerment, or wealth creation, not balancing the federal books. Beard was a veteran of economic assistance efforts in U.S. cities, and he was troubled by the consigning of large segments of the U.S. citizenry to a system that offered no opportunity for the compilation of real assets. He began to pitch Social Security reform as a means of enabling low-income Americans, as well as those with higher incomes, to create real savings and ultimately real wealth in a way that the current system prevented.

By the end of the 1995–1996 Congress, Social Security reform had grown into an issue that had absorbed the attentions of an increasing number of players—from Senators Simpson and Kerrey, to Congressman Nick Smith, to advocacy groups such as Third Millennium and Economic Security 2000, to think tanks such as the Brookings Institute and the Cato Institute. Interest swelled to a critical mass. Only a small number of representatives and senators had stuck their necks out publicly, the rest confining their activities to whispering approvingly in the ears of the few who had done so. But an increasing number now stood ready to take a bolder position on the subject.

When Senator Simpson announced his retirement, Senator Gregg invited me to join his staff. The senator clearly wanted to become more involved in the Social Security issue and immediately directed my drafting of a bill, S. 321, to save the existing Social Security surplus in personal accounts. We put together a bipartisan working group of senators and Senate staff to explore Social Security issues. We also arranged matters so that Senator Gregg would cochair, along with Senator John Breaux, Congressman Kolbe, and Congressman Stenholm, a commission convened by the Center for Strategic and International Studies, to make recommendations to deal with the coming pressures on retirement income in the twenty-first century.

Senator Gregg had essentially designed S. 321 as a way of jump-starting the discussion on Social Security in the Senate. It would simply have saved one percentage point of the payroll tax in personal accounts and made some additional adjustments to the age of eligibility and to the calculation of the Consumer Price Index. It did not aim at actuarial solvency, nor did it represent the full extent of what Senator Gregg believed necessary to do. But he thought it was important to put something out there that focused senators' attention on certain specific issues. The main issue was the fact that we were not saving the Social Security surpluses, but instead were using those surpluses to finance current government consumption.

Conversations with Brad Belt of CSIS revealed we had a major policy objective in common with the organization's upcoming project. I mentioned to him that Senator Gregg was greatly interested in advancing the debate on retirement income policy, that he saw this as the principal policy challenge facing this Congress and this president. Brad and CSIS agreed, and they were in the midst of assembling a commission that would be cochaired by public and private sector individuals, would involve both Senate and House members, and would bring together a coalition of experts on retirement income policy.

The National Commission on Retirement Policy (NCRP) was modeled on the CSIS Strengthening of America Commission, an enormously successful project chaired by Senators Sam Nunn and Pete Domenici, working with leading opinionmakers in the public and private sectors, to issue a report detailing the upcoming policy challenges to the United States' long-term economic strength. CSIS hoped that the NCRP product would enjoy a comparable status when completed.

The NCRP began work in early 1997, studying the vast spectrum of issues pertaining to population aging and retirement income policy. How its work concluded will be reviewed in later chapters. First, let us review the specific recommendations made by the Social Security Advisory Council of 1994–1996.

NOTE

1. The imperfection resided principally in limiting consumer empowerment to a choice between services, with no opportunity to shop for lower costs, the principal tool of the consumer. Senator Gregg worried aloud that scaling back the proposal in this way would reduce its chances of having a positive effect.

11

A Divided Advisory Council Unites Behind Advance Funding

The report of the 1994–1996 Advisory Council on Social Security accomplished nothing less than a fundamental transformation of public debate surrounding the program. It was one thing for iconoclastic senators like Bob Kerrey and Al Simpson to call for an overhaul of Social Security, but it was quite another for the nation's acknowledged experts to issue a report that made the same point.

Most press accounts focused on the split of the Social Security Advisory Council into three camps, unable to agree among themselves as to how to solve Social Security's financing problems. The split was real, symptomatic of the tremendous difficulty of finding a tolerable medium between different philosophical approaches. It is precisely the difficulties that the Advisory Council and many other distinguished groups faced in pursuing agreement that makes the NCRP's reaching unity such a special achievement. But deep though the divide on the Council was, its members were able to find common ground on a number of points.

The press likes disagreement more than agreement, controversy more than concord. The common principles endorsed by the Advisory Council took a back seat in press accounts to the issues in contention. One central principle endorsed by the Advisory Council was that Social Security must move to an advance-funded system. They couldn't agree on how to do it—some favoring personal accounts, and some government investment in equities—but they agreed upon the need.

They further agreed to oppose moving to general revenue financing of Social Security, opining that Social Security's benefits should continue to be based on an individual's contributory taxes. Severing this connection would undermine the program's political basis. Unremarked upon at the time, this recommendation was significant for being the one most disregarded by the Clinton administration.

Moreover, the Advisory Council specified that Social Security must maintain a reasonable relationship between contributions made and benefits received. This may sound like an obvious finding, but it is not. It is very much at the heart of what FDR set up in a unique way within the Social Security system. He didn't want something indistinguishable from other forms of means-tested welfare programs.

Robert Samuelson, the columnist who has over the years written powerfully about the shortcomings of Social Security, has opined that such emphasis on "payback" is illusory and is doomed ultimately to failure—that we as a nation will ultimately be unable to finance a system that provides much more than welfare for those most in need. But the Advisory Council endorsed a structure for the system such that perceived relationships between benefits and contributions had some grounding in reality.

The council also agreed that action needed to be taken—and fast. The earlier the action taken to restructure Social Security, the more gradual the planned changes could be, and the less expensive would be the ultimate cost of balancing the system.

The council also agreed that 75-year actuarial solvency was something of a misleading and inadequate standard. Under the current structure of the system, a solution could be legislated tomorrow that purported to attain actuarial solvency but then, one year later, be deemed insolvent again. The first year, a year of surplus, would vanish from the projection, and year 76, a year of deficits, would be added, throwing the program out of balance all over again. The council agreed that the system should show perpetual balance. We should not project deficits and declining Trust Fund assets at the end of the valuation period if we claim to solve the system's problems. (This was another of the council's findings disregarded by the president and by some congressmen.)

The council also made a stand against conventional "means-testing." They put it quite succinctly and well: "The fact that benefits are paid without regard to a beneficiary's income and assets is the crucial principle that allows—and encourages—people to add savings to their Social Security benefits and makes it feasible for employers and employees to establish supplementary pension plans."[1] The council wasn't declaring opposition to increased progressivity for the system, but it did oppose penalizing individuals for the saving that they did outside of the Social Security system. After all, given that private savings are also inadequate nationally, it makes little policy sense to reduce one source of retirement income automatically as another builds up.

A Divided Advisory Council Unites

These were but a few of the principles that found wide agreement within the Advisory Council. But there were also fundamental gaps between policy views that could not be bridged. The council split into three factions, each endorsing a different plan. No plan attracted a majority of supporters.

One approach became associated in the minds of the public and press principally with two figures—Syl Schieber and Carolyn Weaver. Each would make, through their work with the Advisory Council and afterwards, a major contribution to the Social Security reform discussion. Both were willing to make a straightforward assessment of the costs as well as the benefits of a personal account approach. It is easy to make a case for personal accounts if one simply ignores issues pertaining to the transition from an unfunded to a funded system. Schieber and Weaver's proposals directly addressed the costs of such transitions and put forward the case that the shift in policy was still worth it. The Schieber-Weaver plan was important not only because of the contents of their advocated position but also because of the analysis that accompanied it.

The chairman of the Advisory Council, Ned Gramlich, is now with the Federal Reserve. He took something of a middle-of-the-road approach, but was unable to attract more than one supporter on the council for his plan. Still, the fact that this plan attracted the smallest number of votes on the council did not mean that it had the least staying power.

The Robert Ball group within the Advisory Council also endorsed the principle of advance funding, but they opposed personal accounts in favor of aggregate investment of the Social Security Trust Fund. They referred to their plan as the "maintain benefits" plan, which is a fair title, given that every effort was made to leave the basic benefit formulas of Social Security untouched to the maximum practicable extent. For various reasons that will be further explored, the Ball approach lacked practical or political viability. It is significant that, though the Ball approach adhered most closely to the traditional structure of Social Security—even with the new investment advocated for the Social Security Trust Fund—a majority of the Advisory Council would not support it.

For a Social Security Advisory Council, appointed by HHS Secretary Donna Shalala, to produce a majority finding that personal accounts must be a part of a Social Security reform solution was a strong statement before Washington and the body politic at large. This council was not by any stretch the creature of an ideological construction. These were the leading experts on Social Security, and if biased in any specific direction, they certainly would have been expected to hew to traditional solutions, were these tenable. Yet a majority of the council was saying that such solutions would not work and that personal accounts needed to be included.

Division, however, is what captures the attention of the nation's journalists, and thus tremendous print space was devoted to playing the various members of the Advisory Council off against each other, glossing over the surprising new consensus. This was, it was portrayed, yet another commission that had failed to reach agreement as to how to fix Social Security. If this council, an unelected one, with members free to go on with their life's work regardless of political repercussions, was unable to forge a consensus, what hope was there of Congress doing so?

Significant hope, actually. Academics and other thinkers are not accustomed to having to compromise their views. But members of Congress don't enjoy any such luxury. Decisions have to made; majorities reached. They don't get to vote "maybe," nor do 100 senators get the luxury of seeing their separate plans acted upon.

The great temptation that Washington seems forever to indulge—to farm out the most controversial issues to politically independent commissions—is a less than efficient path to consensus and no substitute for the give and take of political negotiation, which must be done in any event. After a commission has spoken, its findings must still be subject to the test of what the balance of political power will allow. So the fact that the council had failed to reach agreement did not in any way preclude the likelihood of Congress's being able to do so.

Moreover, the specific elements of the Advisory Council plans themselves clearly bore the signature of plans that had not been devised by legislators. None of the plans, useful though they were, could be passed by Congress into law in the form presented. Let us, therefore, wrap up this discussion of the Advisory Council's work by briefly describing the three plans and the political problems that they contain.

THE SCHIEBER-WEAVER PROPOSAL

The centerpiece of the Schieber-Weaver proposal, the PSA (Personal Savings Accounts) plan, was to use five percentage points of the current payroll tax to establish personally owned accounts. When the system was fully phased in, the traditional Social Security benefit would be a flat one, a basic protection against poverty, with the remainder of benefits coming from the personal accounts. The new benefit structure would be phased in over 30 years, with individuals over 55 continuing under the old system and individuals under 25 being wholly within the new one. For those in between, a transitional formula would be used, reflecting their age and thus the amount of time that they spent participating in the new personal account system.

Needless to say, placing five percentage points of the payroll tax into personal accounts would create a transition issue, because a good portion of that money is needed today to pay benefits to current retirees. Schieber-Weaver would fill in that gap with a combination of additional taxes (roughly 1.52 percent of payroll), and new debt. The system would require new debt in the short term, when it has an excess of outlay obligations (personal account investments, plus traditional OASDI payments) over revenues; in the out-years, when revenues exceed outlay obligations, the system would pay that debt off from surpluses.

Schieber-Weaver demonstrated that things will work out better under this system than current law. Workers at all income levels, especially those born from 1965 or so on, would ultimately receive higher benefit levels than under a traditional solution, even when fairly conservative rates of return are assumed and the costs of administering the accounts are subtracted out. They opted for larger accounts in part because it would maximize the rate of return for individual beneficiaries relative to administrative costs and because the larger amount of advance funding would ultimately mean higher benefit levels.

Moreover, they did not gloss over the real problems of transition. For example, a tax increase equal to 1.52 percent of payroll would be assessed, although in the near term there would still be a significant gap between revenues and outlays. In the year 2005, for example, a significant amount of new borrowing would have to be done—another 1.50 percent of taxable payroll. Even with the tax increase and the new debt issuance, there would still be a gap in the system between benefit payments and available revenues. So the federal government would buy down the existing OASDI Trust Fund a little bit—never more than $100 billion per year, and generally confined to payments of interest owed to the Trust Fund, but a real payment nonetheless.

By the later years of the plan—2050, for example—the 1.52 percent tax increase would enable the system to enjoy sufficient surpluses that the extra borrowing can be paid off without bringing the system to insolvency. Schieber and Weaver budgeted for all debt issuance and payoff within their proposal.

What Schieber and Weaver achieved was to show how the transition to a significantly funded personal account system could be accomplished, what it would mean to overall benefit levels even if one assumed only conservative return rates, and even if one assumed fairly hefty administrative costs (subtracting a full percentage point off of rates of return). For their efforts, they met with the political attacks that beset anyone who makes an honest accounting of all costs associated with financing benefits.

There were significant political as well as policy obstacles to enacting a Schieber-Weaver type of plan. First, there is not at this time a consensus among the U.S. electorate that they wish to move to a system in which a large chunk of Social Security benefits come ultimately from personal accounts, leaving the defined benefit portion of the program as a flat benefit. Such a proposal makes two philosophical leaps, perhaps even politically contradictory ones, at the same time—first, that Americans are willing to have a fairly large component of the Social Security system funded for the first time as a defined contribution system, and second, that the defined benefit component of the program should shed its relationship with an individual's wage history and thus with contributions made. While the program as a whole under Schieber-Weaver may retain a total mix of redistribution similar to current law, detractors would not portray it that way. They would portray the remaining flat benefit as something more akin to a welfare system, unfamiliar to their expectations of the Social Security system.

It is terribly hard to tell what Americans really want even now, let alone what they will want in the future from the Social Security system. Syl Schieber points out that the current relationship between an individual's contributions and benefits is becoming so tenuous that the public may not miss it in moving to a flat-base benefit. The attacks against Schieber-Weaver, however, do suggest that significant controversy would attend such a proposal. If the public is not, as a whole, certain that this is where they want to go, this may constrain the sacrifices that they are willing to make to get there.

In the case of the Schieber-Weaver plan, the sacrifices seem larger in the 1996 report than they do now. The extra 1.52 percent contribution required to fund Schieber-Weaver could be afforded in the near term from non–Social Security surpluses, as could some additional borrowing by the Social Security system from general revenues.

But even so, moving from a system that is unfunded to one with this degree of funding will take a good amount of transition time. The transition in Schieber-Weaver is over roughly in the year 2030, producing a net improvement in the federal budget balance of $9 billion in that year, and increasing thereafter.

Why is it negative through the 2020s? Because the changes to the Social Security system don't begin to save it money, net, until the year 2016. At that point, things have only evened out because the Social Security system has been permitted to do additional borrowing. The debt service costs of the new borrowing initially outweigh the savings on the outlay side, a situation that will not reverse until the year 2030. And then it may not have evened out nearly enough to have moved us from an untenable place to a tenable one.

This is an explanation of the barriers to transition to something as large as a 5 percent plan, not a criticism of the outstanding Schieber-Weaver work. There are a lot of plans out there with phony numbers, and this isn't one of them. But the nation may not be willing to do what is necessary to get to 5 percent accounts. This accounting in and of itself is a valuable service. Privatizers often imply that anyone who does not press for accounts of larger than 5 percent is guilty of a tremendous moral failing. But we know from the work of Schieber and Weaver that even getting to 5 percent requires tremendous exertions and transition costs, which we may find difficult to terminate before costs have reached their currently projected high levels in 2030.

The Schieber-Weaver work was groundbreaking. They showed that their plan will increase benefit levels and that government finances will simultaneously be much better off in the long run, with no gimmicks, no funny assumptions, and no tricks—even relative to the dubious assumption that money not used for this plan would otherwise be saved by the federal government. Whether the nation is willing to be similarly bold is another matter entirely.

THE GRAMLICH PROPOSAL

The Gramlich proposal, being the "centrist" proposal of the group, is the one most often compared with other "centrist" proposals developed by members of Congress. It would create a 1.6 percent personal account, managed in a way similar to the federal employees' Thrift Savings Plan, that would be funded through additional mandatory contributions. Steps would be taken—such as changing ages of eligibility, benefit formulas, and others—to balance the finances of the traditional OASDI system. The personal accounts would be created on top of this structure so that beneficiaries could recoup the benefits that would have been lost through traditional cost savings measures alone.

Implicit in the Gramlich proposal is the finding that the current contribution rates for the Social Security system are inadequate to fund the benefits that society would deem the minimum necessary. Thus, the additional 1.6 percent contribution is required. Otherwise, Gramlich finds, the benefit levels that would result from constraining the growth of benefits in the traditional system to the point where balance is achieved would be too low. Since supplemental revenues are required, Gramlich wants them used to create advance funding—specifically meaning invested on behalf of individuals in assets other than treasury securities—and that also improving the rate of return that individuals would receive from Social Security.

The Gramlich proposal is similar to, but not quite like, other plans offered by legislators. It has more in common with the Moynihan plan than with the others. Like Gramlich, Moynihan would restrain cost growth in the traditional system to reach balance and would also create supplementary personal accounts. But there are also critical differences. Moynihan's personal accounts would be voluntary, not mandatory. Moreover, the cash flow under Moynihan is very different, reducing revenue in the short term and increasing as is necessary over the long term. Thus, Moynihan's voluntary personal accounts can be funded with the tax reduction if the individual chooses, though in the long run the tax reduction is not really there, as tax rates have increased. Gramlich doesn't change the FICA tax rates and mandates the additional 1.6 percent contribution.

Reforming Social Security

The Kerrey-Simpson and Gregg-Breaux-Kolbe-Stenholm bills would also have included accounts of comparable size, 2 percent. Unlike the Gramlich proposal, they would "carve out" the personal account contributions from within the current payroll tax, noting that an additional mandatory contribution is tantamount to a tax increase. Consequently, their restraints on the liability growth in the traditional system are greater than under Gramlich. Moreover, because the personal account contributions are collected on top of currently projected revenues under the Gramlich proposal, the revenue flow ultimately looks very different under Gramlich than is the case under the NCRP proposal. (More on that later.)

Though it does not appear to be so at first glance, there are also some similarities between the Gramlich proposal and the Gramm-Domenici plan offered in 1998. Gramm-Domenici uses a different philosophy on some matters—phasing down the liabilities of the traditional system as a function of the buildup in personal accounts, for one thing, and having larger personal accounts (3 percent), for another. However, in terms of the cash flow that each plan would provide, Gramlich and Gramm-Domenici, in the short term, resemble each other more than they do Kerrey-Simpson, NCRP, and Moynihan-Kerrey. Both Gramm-Domenici and Gramlich would keep the current projected levels of revenues flowing into the Trust Fund—Gramlich because the mandatory contributions to personal accounts are collected in addition to FICA contributions, and Gramm/Domenici because general revenues are used to reimburse the Trust Fund for the revenues moved into personal accounts. Whereas Gramlich would assess the additional contributions to the Social Security system directly, through a 1.6 percent mandatory additional contribution, Gramm-Domenici would do this through the general tax base (to a greater extent, 3 percent, but only for a limited period).

Because Gramlich would balance the traditional OASDI system through benefit growth restraints only, the basic shape of the solvency curve would not be altered qualitatively, but would simply be shifted in a positive direction. Larger surpluses would build up in the short term and persist for the first two decades of the twenty-first century. From that point on the cash flow balances would turn negative, but not so negative that the Trust Fund would need to be drawn down and depleted. Rather, the federal government would need to make a cash payment of part of the interest owed to the Trust Fund, for something close to perpetuity, but would never reach a crash point when payments of principal would ultimately deplete the Trust Fund.

The Gramlich proposal would not promise the rates of return for beneficiaries that Schieber-Weaver would, but like it, would effectively require a payroll tax increase of 1.6 percent in the long run. This is more than problematic in view of the other fiscal pressures that will face the government, in terms of Medicare expenditures and in terms of promoting other retirement saving outside the Social Security system. The political credibility that one would attach to the Gramlich proposal would exist in proportion to how likely one believes it is that the nation will want to turn to permanent tax increases to solve the Social Security financing problem. (It should be noted in fairness to the Gramlich and Schieber-Weaver plans that the payroll tax increases they envision are actually smaller than the general tax revenues required to fund the Clinton, Archer, or Gramm proposals, but that the Advisory Council plans were simply more explicit in identifying the proposal's costs.)

THE BALL PROPOSAL

The third proposal, put forth by Robert Ball and others, is remarkable for the concession that this traditionalist group has made to the necessity of advance funding of Social Security. One of the great ironies of the Social Security program is that this program, born during Depression-era fears of poverty in the wake of a stock market collapse, now finds itself seeking a bailout from precisely that same stock market; moreover, its most traditional defenders are proposing the most direct mixing of the market and the fortunes of Social Security. It is now the left, not the right, that wants to force Social Security recipients into the stock market.

In a future chapter we will review the various political and practical obstacles to the implementation of such a plan. Suffice to say here that the Ball approach is the least politically salable of the three Advisory Council plans, even less so than the bold and creative Schieber-Weaver plan, because it contains elements that will never be accepted by the U.S. body politic, most notably direct ownership by the Social Security system of significant portions of the equities market. It also achieves the least in terms of resolving the financing problems.

Essentially, the Ball approach is to try to avoid the difficult decisions to balance the revenues and outlays of the Social Security system and to obtain a higher rate of return for the Social Security system, at the expense of rates of return in private retirement savings. (Recall Alan Greenspan's testimony.) Thus, there is an apparent "free lunch" in the Ball plan, in that the costs of it to the private savings market do not appear on the ledgers describing the plan.

Even with that caveat, the plan does not seem to significantly improve the long-term cash flow outlook. For example, it would leave in place more than two-thirds of the existing gap between the system's revenues and outlays in such a difficult year as 2030. Instead of filling in that gap, however, with general tax increases to redeem more than $600 billion in treasury bills, only a smaller amount of such payments would need to be made, similar to the level in the Gramlich plan, and the lion's share of the difference would come from the government's unloading hundreds of billions of dollars in stock. From 2020 onward, the Ball plan would not promise a system in which revenues and outlays were balanced, but one in which government would finance the system by selling more than $100 billion in stock annually starting in that first year and rising dramatically afterward.

The Ball group itself had considerable doubt about the wisdom of investing the trust fund in the equities market and phrased its recommendations to fall somewhat short of outright recommendation of such a step. As a consequence, it was left with a proposal that effectively fell short of the solvency mark—even with another little-discussed element of the proposal, to increase taxes by 1.6 percent of national payroll after 50 years. In its unwillingness to make the decisions necessary to bring the OASDI system into balance straightforwardly, the Ball group resorted to proposals that were on the one hand politically unfeasible and on the other, not truly successful in bringing the system into balance.

The Congressional Research Service's most recent study of the Ball approach found that, under the Intermediate and Low-Return assumptions applied by the Advisory Council to the personal account proposals, the Ball plan did not even balance in an actuarial sense.[2] Only if the high return assumptions were employed would the plan even work actuarially. For the traditionalist wing of the Social Security community to be banking the entire solvency of the system on aggressive rate-of-return assumptions for the stock market is one of the more intriguing conversions of modern times.

Each of the three groups on the Advisory Council did its work diligently and well and presented a set of important proposals to the public. Even the Ball group's recommendations carried the forceful message that the system cannot work without some form of advance funding and of investment reform. The Advisory Council completed the journey begun by the Entitlement Commission and was the final nail in the coffin for any plausible suggestions that the system could be repaired by traditional means alone.

NOTES

1. Report of the 1994–1996 Advisory Council on Social Security, vol. 1, p. 18.

2. Congressional Research Service, *Social Security Reform: Projected Contributions and Benefits Under Three Proposals*. Report for the U.S. Congress. December 3, 1998.

12

Where Will Future Benefits Come From? A Sound and Fair System

If the government guarantees the payment of a benefit, someone somewhere will have to pay for it.

Most individuals would probably not have difficulty accepting this statement as an unavoidable reality. It is not that wretchedly difficult a concept to comprehend. Government has no magic powers to produce benefits out of thin air. It can redistribute existing wealth, surely, and some among us may also believe that it can facilitate conditions that better enable productive citizens to generate it. But it can't create something from nothing.

As the Social Security debate evolves, it is surprising how seductive is the idea that there is a magic bullet lurking somewhere that will sever the link between the benefits that the federal government will guarantee and the burden that is placed on taxpayers of the twenty-first century. Every manner of clever means is employed to create alternate Social Security reform proposals, in which beneficiaries "can't lose," the federal government guarantees them a generous defined benefit, and yet the result is not an untenable burden on the economy of the future.

It doesn't work that way. You would think this would be obvious, but such is the power of self-deception that plan after plan has come out that purports to work such magic and to avoid the necessity of making "tough choices." This magic is done both with solutions in which all benefits are funded from a Social Security Trust Fund and with solutions that create personal accounts but guarantee the investor a certain minimum result. No matter how these guarantees are disguised, analysis reveals that the benefits come from the taxpayer's pocket.

Gene Steuerle of the Urban Institute has noted that a singular failure of Communist systems was that they set about first making grand plans regarding the quantity and the form of the services and benefits that the government would allocate. As to the production of the resources that government would tap, this would be controlled by the government's ability to target capital investment, to will those resources into existence by fiat.

The hubris of centrally planned economies was manifested in their claims that they could simply decide to grow at a certain pace and in a certain way and that thus it was not folly in the least to decide years ahead of time how government was going to distribute the fruits of that productivity. We see similar hubris today in the words of many who say that we can simply decide in advance to pay trillions in currently unfunded benefits, if we just make the decision as well to have the economy grow quickly along the way.

We are in a situation without exact precedent. Seldom have we as a nation been forced to allocate a huge share of our resources in accordance with the whims and wishes of individuals who controlled the government a century before. Fortunately, the founding fathers of the United States thought it immoral to bind posterity in such a way and dedicated themselves to ensuring that each generation paid its own bills, leaving subsequent ones free to chart their own course. Even FDR, in setting up the Social Security program over a half century ago, did not presume to bind us today to the amount we are currently projected to spend on it.

We need to tread carefully. Instead of falling all over one another in a race to boast that our plans will guarantee higher levels of benefits than our opponents, we should be dissecting these plans to determine what exactly those commitments mean to future generations of taxpayers.

This, of course, is the negative side—how we can go wrong if we don't change our ways. But we are still in a position that enables us to achieve positive reforms, if we take advantage of a fleeting opportunity.

The first element required of any practicable plan is that it must work. There must be no mysterious "asterisks" in the plan, no enormous gaps that posterity is required to fill. It is no achievement whatsoever to outline a program for spending resources without generating the means to provide for them.

The total cost to taxpayers of a Social Security program can be the sum of several factors in a given year, including:

1. Revenue from payroll taxation
2. Revenue from benefit taxation
3. Interest payments to the Trust Fund, required in cash from the federal government to underwrite checks to beneficiaries

4. Payments of principal to the Trust Fund, required in cash from the federal government to underwrite checks to beneficiaries

5. The cost of new debt established by the federal government to finance Social Security benefits

These elements all require the collection and allocation of tax dollars.

Table 12.1 is a snapshot of a few years in the future of the Social Security program. On the left are the amounts that the program must pay. In the second, fourth, and fifth columns are the components of the financing: the tax revenues that are projected for the Social Security system each year, followed by the amounts that the Trust Fund will need to "call in," in interest and principal, to fill in any negative balances and to meet benefit payments. (The zeroes in the interest and principal columns in the earlier years do not mean that the Trust Fund is not building interest and principal during those years, but rather that none of those interest and principal payments are yet needed to finance benefits.)

It is the column on the left that accurately represents the cost of the program to posterity. According to the trustees, this cost will approach 18 percent of the national payroll-tax base in the year 2030—almost one-fifth of the total of taxable wages to support one program.

Suppose that we enacted a solution that left these enormous outlay obligations in place but simply changed the method of financing, perhaps raising payroll taxes, or making other changes that swelled the size of the OASDI Trust Fund in the near term. We could create a scenario in which we decreed the system to be actuarially solvent, but left enormous gaps between the first two columns in the years 2025, 2030, and 2035. We would still foist on posterity an enormous unanswered question, where will the money come from to produce the revenue shown in the last two columns?

Table 12.1

Components of Projected Financing of Future Social Security Outlays (in trillions)

Year	Outlays	OASDI Revenues	Balance	Interest Payments	Principal
2000	$0.409	$0.479	+$0.070	$0	$0
2005	$0.524	$0.595	+$0.071	$0	$0
2010	$0.710	$0.759	+$0.049	$0	$0
2015	$0.995	$0.960	-$0.035	$0.035	$0
2020	$1.40	$1.21	-$0.200	$0.200	$0
2025	$1.92	$1.50	-$0.420	$0.264	$0.157
2030	$2.54	$1.88	-$0.666	$0.165	$0.501
2035	$3.25	$2.34	-$0.910	(not available)	(not available)

Reforming Social Security

Almost daily, columns are written by journalists that miss this point. In November 1998, Peter Coy of *Business Week* wrote a hopelessly misinformed column that suggested that Social Security could be "fixed" with just a few tweaks in assumptions, benefit levels, and tax rates (and also stating that the perceived need to advance-fund was based purely on the "politicization" of the debate). Such claims rest on the author's and the reader's not realizing that there is a lot more to this problem than simply getting a net "zero" in the actuarial balance over 75 years.

This problem, despite its complexity, can be solved. It requires, however, that we move a portion of the liabilities of the program off the federal ledger. If they remain on the ledger of Social Security as defined benefit payments, there is no avoiding the increases in tax liabilities, no matter how they are disguised in the cloak of interest and principal payments.

There is room in this situation for a variety of approaches, which may vary widely according to the political philosophy of the observer. You could, and Senator Moynihan would, simply eliminate the excess of payroll taxes today and raise payroll taxes as necessary to finance future benefits without leaving the payments of hundreds of billions of interest and principal as an enormous "asterisk" for posterity to deal with. Moynihan restrains the growth on the benefit side to a more realistic level and then comes up with a gradually increasing stream of payroll tax revenues that roughly matches the pace of outlay growth. Senator Moynihan is willing to quantify the tax increases that he believes are necessary, rather than simply pretending that they don't exist if they are provided through general revenues. Not everyone does this.

The other method, the approach taken by the NCRP, is to hold the growth of liabilities on the federal ledger to a sustainable level, which must be defined as one that does not ultimately grow faster than the economy's ability to keep pace. No program can be said to be perpetually stable if it commands an ever-increasing share of the nation's resources. Permanent growth of the benefits within any program cannot exceed the economy's ability to provide that growth.

Because of the peculiar shape of our own demographic curve and the fact that the baby boomers did not have as many children as did their parents, there will of necessity be at least a temporary period during which the Social Security program will grow faster than the economy. There is no way to avoid this unless baby boomers receive a disproportionate level of cuts in promised benefits. However, the temporary increase in costs must not be permanent—we must have planned a way out of it—or else the program cannot ultimately be sustained. We otherwise would have sentenced tomorrow's private after-tax economy to perpetually shrink.

Meeting this standard requires that a portion of currently promised benefits be financed with something other than federal tax revenue. If a portion of future benefits are funded from another source, federal outlay liabilities in those distant years will consequently diminish relative to current law. The extent to which we advance fund those liabilities through such means is the extent to which future taxpayers will not be required to pay for them. We can plan and calibrate the extent and shape of this reduction in accordance with our values and priorities.

We encounter here a fortunate side effect. The extent to which we reduce future liabilities by advance-funding is proportional to the extent to which Social Security revenues today are diverted away from the Trust Fund and into the alternate financing system. We simultaneously have a financial need to reduce revenues to the program now (when we have an excess of revenues over outlays) and to reduce outlays later (when we have a grossly untenable excess of outlays over revenues). Both purposes are served by moving a portion of the payroll tax off of the federal ledger and into a system of advance funding.

The Social Security actuaries annually make 75-year projections of the program's finances. There is nothing magic about the figure of 75 years. Our standard for a solution should not be that it enables us to stagger along precisely to this date, after which we project more trouble. After all, there will be a trustees' report next year, too, which could state that we face insolvency all over again.

A practicable solution must be a somewhat permanent one, in that it projects no impending crash date to the extent of our ability to predict. The Social Security program should remain healthy throughout the wave of retirements by the baby-boom generation and should not be imperiled by any subsequently projected event.

In practice, this means that we should aim to produce a rising Trust Fund ratio at the conclusion of the valuation period. (The Trust Fund ratio is the measurement of how many years' worth of benefits can be funded by the remaining balance in the Social Security Trust Fund. Measuring the nominal dollar amount in the Trust Fund is of little consequence, for this may rise nominally yet be shrinking in real potency, if obligations of the program are growing still more quickly.)

Where does this leave us?

1. We must frankly assess and plan for all of the costs of the Social Security program and leave none of them unfinanced. Those who advocate the financing of benefits through the redemption of a Trust Fund should advocate and specify the tax increases that will be necessary to pay it off. Far preferable would be to bring outlays and revenues of the program, on an annual basis, into such proximity that such a resort to large-scale Trust Fund redemption is not necessary.

2. We must bring total outlays of the program to a level that is permanently sustainable, that is, not rising faster than economic growth in the long run.

3. Because this level of outlay reductions cannot be achieved without substantial reductions in promised benefit levels, a portion of promised benefits should be financed through means other than tax revenue.

4. Payroll tax revenues in the short run must be reduced so as to slow the accumulation of the debts that posterity will owe to the Social Security Trust Fund, and the excess must be used to advance-fund a portion of tomorrow's benefits. This portion would therefore no longer contribute to an untenable imbalance between revenues and outlays during the retirement years of the baby boomers.

It is also necessary to carry out these four steps if we are to produce a system that properly treats individual beneficiaries.

Ah, yes—the beneficiaries. They are, in fact, the whole point of this exercise. Before we get further carried away with the smooth functioning of the cash flow within the system, we had better look at what this means to the income of the individuals whom the system is designed to help.

First, let us review the system as it works now. The Social Security system is, on balance, a progressive one, which means that a lower-income individual receives a higher rate of return on his investment in the system than does a higher-income individual. Income is redistributed, through the Social Security system, downward along the income scale. Recall the progressive ("90–32–15") benefit formula that achieves this.

What this means is that your first $505 of income through the Social Security system buys you more benefits, proportionally, than do the dollars of your income beyond $505 a month. This is what we refer to when we refer to the social insurance character of the system. By turning the first few dollars of wages almost one-for-one into retirement income, a certain assurance is provided that retirement income will not fall below a basic floor of protection.

There are two main ways of looking at the benefits provided by the Social Security system: Replacement rates, and rates of return. The replacement rate relates an individual's Social Security income to the income that the individual was receiving in wages just prior to retirement. Consider the following figures taken from present law: A steady low-wage earner born in 1932 and retiring at the age of 65 received a "replacement rate" of 58.8 percent, an average earner 43.6 percent, a high-income earner 35.1 percent, and a maximum-wage earner 25.4 percent.[1] This means that the average earner retiring in 1997 at the age of 65 received a benefit that is 43.6 percent of the value of wages in his last year of work.

These figures show the progressive character of Social Security. High-income individuals get a comparatively worse deal on their investment than do low-wage earners.

Still, replacement rates only tell part of the story, for obvious reasons. A replacement rate essentially measures what is happening within benefits. It does not begin to touch adequately on the question of what was paid in contributions.

Consider the following example: Suppose you have two workers who were born 40 years apart. Suppose that each of them earned an exactly average wage for the time in which they lived. Suppose that one is taxed at an effective rate of 2 percent for his working life. Suppose that the other is taxed at an effective rate of 12 percent during his working life. Upon retirement, each receives a benefit that is 43 percent of earnings. Is this fair?

Of course not. One of them will have put far more into the system than the other, for a benefit that is no more valuable. And this also says nothing about the reduced standard of living that the second individual experienced throughout his working life as a consequence of facing much higher tax rates.

In order to give a complete picture of how the system treats individuals, the rate of return that individuals receive through the Social Security system must be evaluated. We will not provide posterity with an adequately functioning Social Security system if we tax them at an 18 percent rate in order to provide them with a 43 percent replacement rate.

It should be said that rate of return is also an incomplete measure of the fairness in the Social Security system. The Social Security system, it is acknowledged, is not a pension program in which an individual's contributions and the appreciation on those contributions are the sole determinant of the retirement income that the program will provide to that person. It is an insurance program, which protects individuals from poverty, and thus, many individuals will of necessity receive a poorer rate of return in order to help keep others out of poverty.

While this argument has some merit, its relevance is also limited by certain factors. First, it would be a misrepresentation of the ideological basis of Social Security to say that it is *purely* an insurance system or that it was meant to be only a poverty prevention program with no relationship between contributions and benefits. This is, in fact, the reason that the individual's contribution to FICA is kept separate from other government accounts. The Social Security benefit formula itself makes explicit references to an individual's wage history, the irrevocable core of the entire calculation.

Second, while the program is intended to function as social insurance, no insurance program is supposed to work in such a way that everyone loses. The various participants in an insurance pool join it in recognition that some of them will not get their money's worth for that decision, but that is the price that they pay for the security of making it. With health insurance, for example, some of us may not need to receive health benefits equal to the money that we paid, and others will require more, but we join the pool to shield ourselves against the cost of being unlucky enough to require an exorbitant cost in care. But if we all knew that we would lose money through the insurance program, then of course we wouldn't join it. It would no longer even have insurance value.

This is part of the problem with Social Security. Rates of return vary widely according to birth year, and we will eventually reach the point where all demographic and income cohorts are losing money through the program. This is because the program has been constructed so as to effectively transfer wealth not only from high to low income, but from later generations to earlier ones. With rates of return perpetually declining as a function of birth year, a point will be reached where no segment of working society is gaining from the exchange, and the political and philosophical basis of the insurance framework will collapse.

This would not be visible if we looked at replacement rates alone. We could perpetually raise taxes as needed to maintain an average 42 percent replacement rates, heedless of how much we were taking away from individuals in the process. Only by looking at the rates of return can this be seen.

Let us look first at Table 12.2, which shows the internal rates of return for average earners that would be received under current Social Security law if the system were solvent. There is a problem. This is a meaningless table. The system is *not* solvent. Unless it is restructured in some way, even these benefits cannot be paid. The rates of return shown assume that benefits beyond current payroll tax projections magically fall out of the sky and that no one has to pay for them.

Let us assume for the sake of illustration that we do not enact structural reforms in Social Security, incorporate no personal accounts or other advance funding, and simply try to patch together the current system.

We can do this in a couple of ways. One is simply to raise taxes as is necessary to keep the system going. If we consider the payroll tax increases alone, we can pretend that the top four rows in Table 12.2 have escaped into retirement without facing the tax increases. Then the deal for more recent birth years would look like that shown in Table 12.3.

Table 12.2
Internal Real Rates of Return, Average Earners, If Projected Taxes Were Sufficient to Fund Benefits

Birth Year	Single Male	Single Female	One-Earner Couple	Two-Earner Couple
1920	2.73%	3.65%	6.42%	3.43%
1930	1.94%	2.67%	5.05%	2.61%
1943	1.37%	1.97%	4.02%	1.90%
1955	1.45%	2.02%	3.92%	1.90%
1973	1.49%	2.01%	3.80%	1.88%
1985	1.60%	2.09%	3.85%	1.96%
1997	1.68%	2.15%	3.94%	2.05%

Source: May 14, 1998, memo from the deputy chief actuary of the Social Security Administration, based on 1997 trustees' estimates.

Table 12.3
Internal Real Rates of Return, Average Earners, with Projected Payroll Tax
Increases

Birth Year	Single Male	Single Female	One-Earner Couple	Two-Earner Couple
1973	1.21%	1.76%	3.62%	1.61%
1985	1.02%	1.56%	3.40%	1.39%
1997	0.78%	1.32%	3.14%	1.16%
2004	0.68%	1.20%	2.95%	1.04%

Source: May 14, 1998, memo the deputy chief actuary of the Social Security Administration, based on 1997 trustees' estimates.

But Table 12.3 significantly understates the problem. Remember that from 2014 to 2034, under current law, we will need to raise general taxes significantly in order to keep the benefit checks going, because we're redeeming the Trust Fund. In other words, though it doesn't show here on the ledger, the net deal should also take into account the multitrillion-dollar Trust Fund that these workers must pay off.

Look again at our workers born in the years 1943 and 1985. In order to deliver on the promised 1.37 percent rate of return for a single male born in 1943, the single male born in 1985 must first accept a lower 1.02 percent rate of return, plus the obligation to pay off his share of over $7 trillion in new general taxes in the years 2014–2034. The one born in 1943, on the other hand, has received the benefit of lower income taxes because Social Security surpluses were used to mask non–Social Security deficits during the time that he was paying income taxes. The differences in their reported rates of return don't begin to incorporate these effects.

Does it get worse beyond today's newborns? It does. Because tax increases are something of a delay tactic, they appear here too late to harm the near-term retirees, whether in terms of payroll or general tax increases. But note how the rate of return is dropping rapidly when you get to the 1970s birth cohorts and beyond. This continues, perpetually. For birth year 2004, rates of return are still lower than for 1997.

Before turning to other equity issues, let us explore the contrary option: benefit cuts. These can be effected immediately and thus the pain of them can be spread to include near-term retirees as well, instead of forcing rates of return to drop by 0.2 percent for every dozen years from the 1970s onward, as is the case with tax increases.

There are a variety of ways to simply restrain benefit growth to balance the system. One illustrative package, involving changes in CPI, retirement age, benefit computation years, and actuarial adjustment factors, would produce the result shown in Table 12.4.

A couple of caveats should be voiced here. First, although this picture appears even bleaker than the situation arising from tax increases, this impression ignores the following factors.

First, much of the burden of the tax-increase approach is not visible here, as it impacts rates of return for birth cohorts not in the table. Raising taxes causes rates of return to drop perpetually, whereas working through benefit cuts has stabilized its impact by the time we get to recent birth cohorts.

Second, because we have restrained benefit growth, the financing gaps that would need to be filled in to fund benefit promises are smaller than they are in the tax-increase illustration. While we see the toll that benefit cuts have taken on each cohort of beneficiaries, we don't see the differences in the toll that general tax increases take on those workers still employed in 2014, which would include the bottom three rows. This effect is more than considerable, it is enormous. For example, in the year 2030, the scenario shown in Table 12.3 would require an additional $666 billion in general tax revenues to keep the system afloat. In the "benefit cut" option shown in Table 12.4, this gap would be reduced by more than two-thirds. For the cohorts in the last three rows, the tax increase option is a far worse deal, much worse than the benefit restraints.

Third is the fact that the "benefit cut" option is sustainable in the sense of keeping benefit growth permanently no higher than the economy can han-

Table 12.4
Internal Real Rates of Return, Average Earners, If Solvency Is Achieved by Reducing Benefit Growth

Birth Year	Single Male	Single Female	One-Earner Couple	Two-Earner Couple
1920	2.71%	3.62%	6.40%	3.41%
1930	1.85%	2.57%	4.98%	2.51%
1943	1.27%	1.86%	3.90%	1.82%
1955	0.85%	1.41%	3.36%	1.61%
1973	0.68%	1.18%	3.04%	1.35%
1985	0.66%	1.13%	2.96%	1.35%
1997	0.70%	1.16%	3.00%	1.38%

Source: Based on 1997 Social Security trustees' estimates of NCRP DB plan.

dle, and the "tax increase" option is not. Thus there is a practical difference between them as well.

The picture resulting from the "benefit cut" option is none the less clear. It may be better than raising taxes, but it is still wretched.

Inequities abound in an unrestructured Social Security system. Inequities exist with respect to birth year, demographic group, and flawed work incentives.

Inequities according to birth year. The system treats individuals vastly differently according to when they were born. If we simply raise taxes to keep the system going, the difference between the rate of return for the average two-earner couple born in 1920 and that for the couple born in 2004 is the difference between 3.43 percent and 1.04 percent—a reduction of more than two-thirds every year, compounding over time. Again, this is the case before the discrepancy due to *general* tax increases placed on the latter birth cohort. If we wait until the deficits arrive, we will have bypassed the current opportunity to advance-fund some of our future obligations and to prevent some of this inequity.

Inequities according to demographic group. The system is far more generous to one-earner couples than it is to two-earner couples or to single individuals. This reflects the social views ascendant when Social Security was constructed, when it might plausibly be assumed that father would work and mother would stay home, in contrast to our economy today, in which roughly half of the workforce are women. These inequities are so great that they overshadow the program's progressive elements and cause many regressive transfers of income. A low-income single male born in 1943, for example, can expect a 2.39 percent rate of return under current law, which is less than the 3.08 percent rate of return enjoyed by a one-earner couple at the *maximum* taxable income! If the program is truly to function adequately as social insurance, these regressive transfers of income must be ameliorated.

Flawed work incentives. Though we as a nation are faced with a plummeting ratio of taxpaying workers to benefit-collecting retirees, the policies embodied in our Social Security system exacerbate, rather than mitigate, these trends. First, though life expectancy has soared, we have left the age for full eligibility for benefits at age 65 and for early retirement at age 62. The math is simple: if most of us live longer than previous generations and expect to receive annual benefits just as generous as they enjoyed, we cannot expect to start collecting them as early unless we are willing to impose much higher tax rates upon future workers.

Even though Americans are living longer and healthier lives than they were generations ago, they are retiring earlier, proof that retirement ages are established as much by economic and lifestyle considerations as they are by physical debility. And why not? For an individual at age 62, waiting until the age of 65 to retire makes little sense when computing one's Social

Security benefits. The extra benefits that are received by waiting until that age do not offset the extra payroll taxes that the individual would contribute in the meantime. Why continue to work and to pay taxes that one will never get back?

Disincentives to work do not stop there. There also exists the Social Security earnings test, which reduces seniors' Social Security benefits in proportion to other income earned in retirement. (In 2000, Congress repealed the earnings limit above normal retirement age, although the penalty still applies to those in ages 62–65.) Though seniors are sufficiently aware of this disincentive to complain about it, less publicized is another one, which has to do with the construction of Social Security's AIME formula. This formula only counts one's highest 35 years of earnings towards one's Social Security benefits. In other words, if one chooses to work part-time in one's mid-60s and if one's earnings are not among one's 35 highest years of lifetime wages, none of these earnings will be credited toward additional Social Security benefits.

A reformed Social Security system should remove these disincentives to work. It should see to it that individuals receive extra benefits if they postpone retirement, that they are not penalized for earned income that they receive after retirement age, that all years of earnings count toward one's Social Security benefit, and that retirement ages, both normal and early eligibility ages, are set so as not to create an incentive for Americans to spend larger and larger fractions of their lives receiving benefits.

Political dangers arise from pushing rates of return for high-income individuals below the breaking point. The preceding figures only apply to rates of return for individuals of average income. Because of Social Security's progressive benefit formula, rates of return for individuals of greater income are far lower. Consider the case of a single male of maximum taxable income. Table 12.5 shows the internal real rates of return in store for that single male if we simply raise taxes as necessary to fund benefits. Again, these figures count payroll taxes only, not the general tax increases required to redeem the Trust Fund, which would fall most heavily on high-income earners.

Although few shed tears for the maximum-income single male, these figures are troubling nonetheless. They threaten the ethic of a program in which everyone is in it for the common good, a contributory insurance system in which wages are related to benefits. (These figures presume that no changes are made to the current-law wage cap. Some proposals to restore Social Security to solvency would increase the growth of the wages subject to Social Security taxation more rapidly than does current law. If this is done, the figures will look even worse.)

The rates of return shown in the previous tables were bad, but at least they were positive. The average individual covered under Social Security would receive a poor rate of return, less than one might get simply by buying a certificate of deposit from the local bank or buying a government

Table 12.5
Projected Internal Real Rates of Return, Maximum-Income Single Males

Birth Year	IRR
1920	2.29%
1930	1.16%
1943	0.29%
1955	0.12%
1973	-0.25%
1985	-0.64%
1997	-0.72%

Source: May 14, 1998, memo from the deputy chief actuary of the Social Security Administration, based on 1997 trustees' estimates.

bond. But the individual cannot in most of those cases claim to be losing money outright.

For many individuals, however, outright losses are becoming real. The program is not only providing them with a poor rate of return, it is providing them with a negative rate of return. It is simply costing them money, period. The effect is first seen with maximum taxable earners, but it will be seen soon after that with high earners generally and ultimately with average earners. Eventually the program would experience the political unpopularity of welfare.

In summary, a reformed Social Security program must do all of the following with regard to beneficiaries, at the same time that it meets the fiscal criteria outlined in this chapter, if it is to remain sustainable.

First, it must simultaneously meet society's expectations in terms of both social insurance and in relating contributions to benefits. This requires both that absolute benefit levels for low-income individuals remain adequate and also that the current level of progressivity in the system be retained. However, benefit levels for individuals of all income levels, demographic groups, and birth cohorts must remain sufficiently tied to individual contributions. As this is impossible if changes are restricted to tax increases or benefit cuts alone, some advance-funded component must be incorporated into the system that promises a higher rate of return than does the basic system.

Second, it must eliminate disincentives to work that could make the reality worse than the already-dire projections of a plummeting ratio of workers to retirees. This means making adjustments to eligibility ages, to actuarial reduction factors for early retirement, to AIME formulas, and to the existing earnings test.

Third, it must reduce inequities between different demographic groups, focusing especially on those that create regressive transfers of income. A system that is in deep financial trouble cannot afford to engage in transfers from low-income single wage-earners to high-income couples. Rates of return for all demographic groups must be brought into closer proximity. Because these changes must be modest to avoid disruption, it is unlikely that such regressive transfers can be wholly eliminated, but they can be reduced.

NOTE

1. April 27, 1998, memo from the Deputy Chief Actuary of the Social Security Administration.

13

To Fund or Not to Fund? Personal Accounts or Government Investment

Two of the few conclusions to unite a sharply divided Social Security Advisory Council in its 1994–1996 report were: "The Council favors partial advance funding for Social Security,"[1] and "Any sacrifices in bringing the system into balance should be widely shared and not borne entirely by current and future workers and their employers."

The reasoning behind these conclusions is inescapable. Without some form of advance funding, the entirety of the burden of financing benefits must fall upon future taxpayers. The current structure of Social Security does not permit it to be otherwise. Benefits are either wholly funded from the sum of payroll tax and benefit tax revenue or supplemented by payments of interest and principal to the Trust Fund, funded through income taxes.

Previous chapters show what this would mean for future workers. By 2030, an effective 18 percent tax upon wages would be required for Social Security alone. Social Security and Medicare together would absorb more than 30 percent of the national tax base. It is not feasible to expect the nation's workers to finance benefits of this magnitude through their taxes and simultaneously provide for the nation's defense, educate their children, maintain the nation's transportation infrastructure, provide emergency assistance to the indigent, and meet any other unforeseen need of the twenty-first century.

We are indeed fortunate that previous Americans were neither so selfish nor so arrogant as to decide for us on which things we should spend our money. The nation was able to arm against the aggression of Nazi Germany and Imperial Japan because it had not been forced to devote those same resources to the spending preferences of an earlier generation. Americans were free in the 1950s to choose to develop an interstate highway system, and in the 1960s to plot a voyage to the moon. We have no earthly idea what will be the dreams and needs of future generations. It would be a peculiar form of compassion that would bind them to pay crushing tax burdens as a result of our decisions.

There are various means at our disposal to mess things up. We could leave the current system entirely in place and let matters play themselves out. Effective tax rates would skyrocket in the years from 2014 to 2034, and then the program would face insolvency anyway. Since we are unlikely to cut benefits for those already retired or on the brink of retirement, the economy will have little practical choice but to enact the virtual entirety of the tax increases we project as necessary to make the program whole. Simply by inaction, we can deprive posterity of our opportunity to pursue the American dream.

We could also go to the opposite extreme. Instead of financing these benefit levels as we do now, we could take today's payroll taxes, place them entirely into funded personal accounts, and issue new debt to pay current benefits. Here, too, posterity will bear the brunt of that decision, by paying off the interest and the principal associated with that debt. In such a scenario, future taxpayers would not be able to negotiate the size of that debt downward (through benefit restraints) even if they wished to. They would face nonnegotiable bills for payments of interest and principal.

No matter how one slices it, if we adopt a method of financing benefits that relies on tax dollars, future taxpayers will be sent our tab. We need to look very closely at the way that we fund benefits and how we distribute the burdens between today's and tomorrow's taxpayers.

The reason that the Advisory Council endorsed advance funding is that they recognized the simple math of the matter. Tomorrow's taxpayers cannot be given a fair deal if we do not today restructure the means of financing tomorrow's benefits.

This is not so hard to understand. Families know how to plan in this way. When you plan for your retirement, you put a little aside each year, starting when you're fairly young. You don't—if you have any sense—wait until you're about 60 and then wonder where the money is going to come from. If we wait until the baby boomers are well into retirement, we will be in the same situation as that family that didn't plan for retirement, and future taxpayers will bear the burden of that negligence.

Putting aside a little money each year—that's advance funding.[2] It is precisely what the current Social Security system does not do. Right now the entirety of Social Security taxes is used either to pay off current beneficiaries or to purchase the financial instruments that finance government consumption, which can be redeemed only through taxation. It is as if the family is taking its allocation for retirement savings each year and loaning it to itself to spend, promising to pay itself back at retirement. Not good.

In order to advance fund some of tomorrow's retirement benefits, a portion of the current payroll tax needs to be invested in other ways, in the production of goods and services that can be called upon in the future to provide the basis for retirement income. It could be placed in a stock index fund, but it need not be. It could be any asset of a type that you hold with a broker or with the local bank. You invest money in that institution, which in turn invests it in various economically productive enterprises, you are credited for appreciation on your investment, and when you need that money later as liquid income, it has grown and can be withdrawn. You may not know in advance exactly how much it will have appreciated, but it is a real asset to you nonetheless.

If we are to avoid the fiscally untenable situation that this book has attempted to illustrate, a portion of tomorrow's retirement benefits must be funded through the accumulation of assets that no one must be taxed in order to provide. This is not a controversial idea. Students of Social Security from the left to the right of the political spectrum recognize that investment reforms are needed if Social Security is to remain viable.

Bringing future tax burdens down to sustainable levels is only one of the many arguments for advance funding. But there are equally powerful arguments residing in the treatment of beneficiaries.

Go back to the rate-of-return charts in chapter 12 for a moment. Advance funding is essentially the only way to avoid the decline in return rates that will otherwise afflict the birth cohorts in the last three rows, as well as all subsequent ones. The ratio between the system's outlays and its revenues during their lifetimes is more daunting than for previous generations. Given this reality, it is imperative that these generations receive a better rate of return on the money that they invest in the system.

These younger generations—today's young adults and children—have been on the losing end of an intergenerational transfer of revenues. There is likely no reversing that without causing undue harm to current and near-term retirees. If the system's investment return is unchanged, we'll hit these generations with higher tax levels, which in turn would still only provide for less in the way of benefits.

Economists and sociologists alike are frequently troubled by a tendency toward inequality of wealth in this country. How serious a problem this is depends upon whom you ask, what their values are, what data they believe, and to what they attribute the phenomenon. But each of us has reason to be concerned if inequality of wealth is clearly related to an inequality in the opportunities to acquire wealth.

In the last ten years, the stock prices have risen rapidly. This rise has benefited millions of Americans who heretofore would not have been classed among the investor community. Small investors have flocked to mutual funds and have banked their retirement on the stock market. Roughly half of adult Americans have shared in the wealth through individual or pension investment in mutual funds and other stock purchases. Federal employees are among them, investing through the Thrift Savings Plan.

Why have these gains been limited to the top half of American families, exacerbating trends toward an inequality of wealth? That is not a tough question to answer: because the bottom half does not have the money to invest.

For lower-wage Americans, once 12.4 percent is deducted from their paychecks, their opportunity to invest that money is essentially lost. They are forced into a secure but low rate of return on that 12.4 percent, while those who are fortunate enough to have extra money to invest on their own are reaping the benefits of a boom market. How fair is that?

Every quarter of the year, I receive in my mailbox a statement from the federal government's Thrift Savings Plan. It tells me how much money I have put in, whether the total value has gone up or down, and by how much. It is one of the most splendid things that the government has done for me simply because I am a federal employee. Why I should be entitled to this but the rest of the U.S. public shouldn't be, is a question to which there is no good answer.

When we consider the question of advance funding in the Social Security system, we should not lose sight of this basic question of fairness and opportunity. If we balance the Social Security system without giving beneficiaries an opportunity to improve the quality of their investment deal, we are making a highly paternalistic decision for them, and one that will reduce income for most.

The $64,000 question, however, is how to accomplish the advance funding that might improve the situation. Here there is a parting of the ways.

One approach is literally to change very little else about the system but the way that surplus money is invested. Instead of loaning surplus Social Security taxes to the federal government, the program will invest them in the equities market. Once there, they will earn, on average, a higher rate of return, it is said, than the T-bills that the system currently buys; thus, when the Trust Fund must be redeemed, there will be more there, and the system as a whole can stay afloat without major changes in either tax or benefit levels.

Voila! No muss, no fuss. No nasty benefit cuts, no tax increases. We invest the Social Security system in the private market, and all of our problems are solved.

A similarly pollyannaish rendition can be given of the personal account option, going something like this: Instead of investing the Social Security surplus in T-bills, it will be given to individuals to invest in their own personal accounts. Placing this money into personal accounts will allow individuals to receive a higher rate of return, which will ultimately allow the financing of larger portions of Social Security benefits as the years go by, and soon enough, our financing gap will be closed, again without either changing tax or outlay levels. Presto!

Every plan that promises that we can shuffle investment from here to there and watch the system fix itself is selling snake oil. But it is not always easy to detect—and is one reason that this book is being written.

Here, let us simply consider the finding that some form of advance funding is necessary if we are to maintain a viable system, one that gives different generations comparable treatment and holds tax burdens to a sustainable level.

What are the arguments for government investment versus individual ownership? Let's review the policy concerns in each direction: having the government invest the Trust Fund in the equities market or placing the taxes into personal security accounts which the individual would own and control. Before proceeding to the mechanics concerning whether either approach can, technically, "work," let us first address the philosophical questions that arise.

The concept of federal government investment of the Social Security Trust Fund in the equities market sets off alarm bells in the minds of many students of U.S. democracy. It is viewed as socialism of a quite literal sort, in that the largest federal program, the single largest accumulation of financial assets in the history of the U.S. government, would literally "own" a sizable portion of the private equities market. Though we have, in moments of weakness, countenanced ill-advised admixtures of government power and private enterprise in the past, this would be an unprecedented step.

Proponents of this approach believe that the necessary "firewalls" can be constructed to ensure that the government does not use its coercive power to distort the private marketplace. They urge that the investment be made in passively managed funds, directed by an investment board that remains independent of immediate congressional control. Thus, it is claimed, political entities in government will exert no direct power in voting shares of private companies or otherwise interfering in the operation of the market.

It is difficult to conceive that government can exert such leverage in the private market and yet perpetually resist the urge to meddle in such investment decisions. In fact, we see no such lack of restraint even when it comes to wholly private investing. The Department of Labor has promoted "economically targeted investments" by the pension funds of private companies. ETIs, as they are called, are investments in certain enterprises that are deemed to foster a social or political good. Though opinion is divided on whether such "economically targeted investments" have in fact been good investment choices for pension funds by the measure of rate of return, the lesson is nonetheless clear that the federal government was willing to spend resources to identify and to promote worthy recipients of investment.

The World Bank has conducted a study that shows that governments are generally unable, in their investment practices, to remain free of political and social considerations. That is, after all, what government is for, to enforce political will. The statistical evidence is that the inability to resist such temptations results inevitably in the choice of political considerations over fiduciary ones. This is why privately managed investment almost always, in the end, produces a higher rate of return than publicly managed investment.

The World Bank put it thus:

If the publicly managed funds are partially invested in the private sector then another problem arises: fund managers may be motivated by political rather than economic objectives. In general, central planning has not been the most efficient way to allocate a country's stock. Pension funds hold a large part of the financial assets in a country, especially if the funds are mandatory. The net impact on growth may be negative rather than positive, if public fund managers allocate this large share of national saving to low-productivity uses.[3]

And the evidence is that this is what they tend to do.

Though no imagination is necessary to conjure up disturbing scenarios, let us imagine nonetheless. For the past few years the federal government, various state governments, and the tobacco industry have been engaged in a protracted legal struggle. Many politicians have sought to curry favor with voters by positioning themselves as crusaders against "big tobacco." How long do you believe it would be before ABC News or CNN does a story on how Social Security is investing money in the tobacco industry at the same time that the government is fighting a legal action against it? How long after that would it be before a Senator arose on the floor with an amendment requiring the government to direct the Social Security Investment Board to divest itself of its shares in tobacco companies? or companies involved in racial discrimination lawsuits, or implicated in oil spills, or refusing to permit unionization of their labor force.

In fact, it was precisely the possibility of such investment taking place that prompted several unions to write to Congress in early 1999, declaring their intention to oppose any direction of investment towards union-opposed objectives. The political struggle over such investments is not hypothetical. It has begun even before such measures are enacted.

The end result of such investment by the federal government is that a permissible investment will be whatever an electoral majority decides that it can be. When access to investment dollars for the private sector becomes contingent upon satisfying the majority party in Washington, no possible good can ultimately arise.

It is said that the investments in the federal employees' Thrift Savings Plan have not been politicized in such a way and that this proves that the federal government can succeed in passively investing, without exerting political leverage.

But there is a difference there—a big difference. Saving through the Thrift Savings Plan is conducted on behalf of and under the ownership of individual account holders. Individuals, not the government, decide whether they wish to have money in the TSP's "C" Fund, a stock index fund. It is their desire to maximize their investment return, not the government's political purpose, that is the controlling influence upon investment decisions.

This concern is really just the tip of the iceberg. While it may ultimately be impossible to prevent government investment in the private sector from being subject to political considerations, firewalls may hold out in the short term. We could establish a certain degree of independence for the investment board, and for the time being at least, Congress might respect it.

But, having the federal government invest the Trust Fund in the private equities market introduces other conflicts of interest much more immediate than those associated with the politicization of specific investment decisions. The problem is this: the government would then make the solvency of the Social Security system explicitly dependent upon the rate of return in the stock market.

During the program's deficit years, gaps would be made up in a combination of ways. Part of it would be made up, as before, by the federal government's redeeming the T-bills held by the Trust Fund and raising taxes as necessary to do that. But part would also come from another source—the government would sell off stock by the bushel to get the cash to pay promised benefits.

Remember—this option leaves defined benefit levels fixed. Instead of fluctuating as any 401(k) plan does, where your total balance and ultimate benefits depend on how much your investment has appreciated, the government has guaranteed that it will pay out certain defined benefits, come hell or high water.

What if something goes wrong? Suppose that in, say, the year 2025, a year in which hundreds of billions of dollars of stock must be sold in order to meet benefit payments, the stock market takes a dive. Now, that stock is worth a lot less, and the government doesn't get its hoped-for price. It's in a real bind.

This is not a mere hypothetical. Some believe that the withdrawal of millions of baby boomers from the workforce and their heading into retirement might well have a depressive effect upon the economy and upon stock prices, too, as many baby boomers sell the shares accumulated in their private pension plans.

If the stock market dips in a particular year, it is not likely to significantly cut into the benefits of stock market investment over the long run, and thus the overall position of the federal government will likely not become grossly untenable. In the short term it would simply have to redeem more of the Trust Fund through T-bill purchases and raise taxes enough to cover the shortfall.

The point is not the severity of the math, it is the conflict of interest at work. Government policymakers in the years 2020, 2025, and beyond will be calculating how the books will look if the stock market goes up by 10 percent, by 20 percent, or down by 5 percent. They will figure out how they will raise extra taxes if the market index goes down, because otherwise promised Social Security benefits will not be payable. They will have before them a clear and explicit relationship between stock market indices and the federal balance sheets.

Is there any way in the world that this will not ultimately distort federal economic policy? It will become part and parcel of the president's job to see to it that the stock market index is manipulated so that it goes up, up, up, forever upward. Anything that the government can do to inflate stock prices, it will do. It will have to do it, as a consequence of its own fiscal needs. This may work for a while, but then there will be a price to pay for that manipulation. Japan is discovering this now, through the havoc created by the distortion of its own financial markets.

Of course, government finances even under current law are not wholly independent of what happens in the stock market. As various forms of private income goes up, so does the federal government's revenue go up, from a larger tax base. But here we would be taking the explicit dependence to another level entirely. The federal government would explicitly be budgeting for Social Security *benefits* according to how much the market went up. The corruptive influence upon federal policy cannot be missed.

Another problem with investing the Trust Fund in the equities market is more a question of distorting the debate, or of accounting, than it is of substantive effect. But it is a very real problem in terms of its implications for how policymakers and the press think about these issues, and it is a frequently misunderstood point.

Opponents of personal accounts often claim that putting money into personal accounts requires "benefit cuts" in a way that government management does not. The representation is actually made that the same money, invested in the same way, either is a benefit or is not a benefit depending on who controls and directs it.

Suppose, hypothetically, that we were to invest an amount of money equal to two percentage points of this year's payroll tax base in private equities instead of Treasury bills. We could put it in the form of savings accounts for individuals, or we could simply have government do the investment en masse.

To Fund or Not to Fund?

For the purposes of illustration, let us assume various simplifications. Let us assume that exactly the same investment choices are made in each case, and let us assume the administrative costs are the same. Neither assumption is a reflection of real life, but let us make them for the purposes of demonstrating a point. We will assume that the only difference is the name associated with that investment—the names of individual beneficiaries or the name of the OASDI Trust Fund.

Economically, what is happening is identical and has an identical impact upon net national savings, on outlay obligations, and total benefit levels. But they are not accounted for in the same way by the federal government. If the money is in personal accounts, it is not counted as being part of the "Trust Fund," whereas if it is invested by the government, it is.

Moving benefits into personal accounts and away from an impractical Trust Fund financing mechanism is not bad news; that is precisely the point of creating personal accounts—to create a method of financing benefits that does not depend wholly on crushing tax levels or on government sales of stock. It is not a "benefit cut," but a change in the financing mechanism.

The only difference is that in a personal account system, proponents must explicitly total up the benefits that are coming *separately* from the two forms of investment, whereas in a Ball-style plan the proponents get to mix the two together invisibly and to pretend that the whole thing promises higher benefit levels by comparing it only to one piece of the personal account plan. This enables proponents of a government investment approach to play a little fast and loose with the analysis of results. Advocates of government investment of the Trust Fund will frequently say that they oppose personal accounts because they make the financing problem worse by taking still more money out of the Trust Fund and require deeper "benefit cuts." This is said even though there is often no difference, in terms of assets purchased and benefits promised, between a particular personal account plan and one with investment of the Trust Fund in equities.

Even knowledgeable individuals who know better will often ask, "Why make the actuarial problem worse by taking money out of the Trust Fund and putting it in personal accounts?" This is a nonsensical statement for someone who is advocating a Ball-style plan, in which money will just as surely be directed into other investment. The implication is that somehow the problems have been solved through government investment without tough choices, whereas personal account proposals introduce those choices unnecessarily. This argument is not constructive.

Though not purely a substantive point, it is a real one, which affects the way that policymakers think about these problems. Politicians are susceptible enough to the temptations to push good news only, to promise benefits that, seemingly, no one is paying for. Investing the Trust Fund in the equities market, though it accomplishes nothing in a total sense, feeds that illusion and encourages public servants to yield more easily to the temptation of promising a free lunch.

Now let's move from the problems with the Ball approach to the frequently cited concerns about personal accounts.

One is the question of administrative costs. Proponents of government investment of the Trust Fund often cite the comparatively higher administrative costs that would be associated with personal accounts. The quite straightforward observation is made that the government would have less difficulty investing in the aggregate in the private market than setting up an entirely new collection, recordkeeping, and investment structure in which every individual's specific contributions, investment decisions, appreciation on investments, and various other factors are tracked on a timely basis.

Estimates of administrative costs vary according to the structure of a personal account system. During the deliberations of the Security Advisory Council, estimates were produced by the Social Security system of the administrative cost associated with a number of different approaches. Under the approach developed by Carolyn Weaver and Syl Schieber, administrative costs were assumed to subtract roughly one percentage point from the net real yields in personal accounts. This was the approach that gave workers more freedom to invest their personal accounts as they saw fit, within regulatory guidelines, without being tied to a limited selection of investment funds approved by the federal government, as is done with the Thrift Savings Plan.

Schieber and Weaver were willing to accept higher administrative cost estimates for their plan because of its other characteristics. They had larger personal accounts than many alternatives, and thus administrative costs were smaller relative to balances and yields.

Administrative cost estimates for other types of personal accounts, for example, those developed by Ned Gramlich and by the National Commission on Retirement Policy, were much lower—taking roughly 0.105 percent out of net yields from personal accounts, according to estimates provided by the Social Security actuaries. The reason for the lower estimates is that these plans adopted the model of the Thrift Savings Plan provided to federal employees. Under such a model, an investment board within Social Security would approve a number of funds from which wage-earners could select.

Because the record-keeping and the actual physical investment of the funds would be handled through SSA, administrative costs would be greatly reduced on a per-capita basis, rather than having administrative costs arise separately in accounts established by people on their own. The relationship between the employer and the federal government would not essentially change.

Nonetheless, administrative costs will be higher under a personal account plan than they would under the approach favored by Ball and Aaron. We can strive to minimize the administrative costs, and we can also raise arguments as to why the benefits of personal accounts outweigh the negatives, such as the cost of administration. But this is a factor that must be acknowledged and considered in moving to any personal account system.

In addition to administrative cost, there is the question of risk. All investments have associated risks, and the question is raised as to who should assume the increased risk that would come from moving to higher-yield investments. Most advocates of investment-based reform argue that in the long term, the benefits of higher yields will outweigh the detriment of increased risk, but this does not obviate the question of who absorbs the results of such deviations as do occur.

The risk question is not as cut and dried as may first appear. It is not simply a question of whether individuals or government bears the risk. Government cannot eliminate risk on behalf of anyone, because to the extent that the risk is incurred and to the extent that government takes a hit as a result of it, the payment for the consequences will come out of the pockets of taxpayers. A better way of phrasing it might be whether it should be individual beneficiaries or beneficiaries and taxpayers as a group who bear the risk associated with investment in the equities market.

All that government is able to do is to pool risk, to distribute it among a larger group of people. Whether this is more or less risky in the end is in the eye of the beholder. Consider, for example, the situation that would result from the plan put forward by the National Commission on Retirement Policy, which contains a small personal account supplement to a defined benefit system. Let us assume that the market suffers a huge downturn just before the year of retirement of a particular birth cohort—so severe as to bring its net yield from a lifetime of investment down to, say, 3 percent. This would be troubling in that those retirees would have less income than if they had invested well and received an 8 percent real rate of return. But our consciences could be clear, in that even for a majority of those beneficiaries, they would still receive more money than had we simply raised taxes or cut benefits in order to fix the system.

But if, on the other hand, a massive downturn in the market occurs in a year that the government has to sell stock at a given price to meet benefit promises, than the consequences fall on everyone and are magnified, not mitigated, by government's involvement. Instead of some unlucky people getting a little bit less money than they had hoped for—and being fully protected by the basic defined-benefit protections in the traditional Social Security system—the system's solvency would be threatened.

Which do you think is riskier? A system in which some people, if they are unlucky and get a small rate of return, still do better than under the traditional system, although not as well as they could have done with a higher rate of return, or a system in which the whole program becomes insolvent if government invests badly?

This is not a hypothetical scenario. The Congressional Research Service conducted a study of various plans in which the rates of return assumed for each plan were the same. What they found was that when the conservative assumptions used for the investment in personal account plans were applied to the Ball plan to invest part of the aggregate trust fund in the equities market, it didn't work. The Social Security program would be insolvent.[4] In other words, unless a high rate of return came in, benefits couldn't be paid as promised. That doesn't sound very risk-free.

Nonetheless, risk is an issue that must be dealt with in evaluating all personal account proposals. Proponents must show what happens not only when individuals get high rates of return, but what happens when individuals get low ones. Analysts must consider what proportion of individual risk is tolerable within the system and what proportion of defined benefit guarantees (themselves susceptible to the political risk that the government may be ultimately unwilling to tax sufficiently to pay them) is appropriate.

This last point is significant. Even the current system is not free of "risk." It is known that the current benefit promises are untenable. T-bills may be a safe investment, but there won't be enough of them there to finance benefit promises. It is not known with certainty how society would react to that, whether by increasing taxes or cutting benefits. One of those would have to give under current law. Beneficiaries won't feel very shielded from "risk" if they head into their retirement years without that question settled.

There have never been significant protests against the risk in the Thrift Savings Plan (TSP) by any of the fervent opponents of personal accounts, nor any suggestion that the hard-earned contributions of federal employees were in danger of being frittered away, a great inconsistency in their position. In fairness, it's not exactly the same thing—one might tolerate a higher degree of risk within TSP only if the same is not present in Social Security—but the fact remains that the literature on TSP remains relatively barren of the alarmism sounded about Social Security, and none of the doomsday scenarios about investors losing their shirts have come to pass through TSP.

Senator Robert Kerrey said it well at a Finance Committee hearing in September 1998; when asked whether the recent stock market plunge had made him rethink his proposals about Social Security, Kerrey turned the question around and invited the questioner to ask participants in TSP whether they felt that program should be abolished as a consequence of the market downturn. These fluctuations do not change the reality of whether it is more desirable to have the investment opportunity or to lack it.

Risk will exist in new forms under both a personal account approach and under a collective approach. Our nation must come to grips with what types and levels of risk we are comfortable.

Other considerations, however, are unique to personal accounts in a positive way. One is the matter of personal ownership and property rights. Money in a personal account would belong to the individual and would be his or her nonforfeitable property. This has a number of consequences.

One is that this portion of the individual's benefits could not be taken away. If the federal government passes a law tomorrow that cuts your traditional Social Security benefits in half, there is not one blessed thing you can do about it. Supreme Court ruling has established this principle (*Fleming v. Nestor*[5]) and indeed, it can hardly be otherwise. No one has an inherent right, regardless of how one has been taxed in the past, to require someone else to provide them with a benefit through their taxes.

But the question of your own property is quite different. If your contributions have been collected and placed in an account with your name on it, if you have ownership over those assets and can direct how they are invested and ultimately how they are distributed to you, then they cannot be taken away.

Another point of comparison between the two options is whether they can facilitate an increase in net saving. Investment of the Trust Fund in the equities market, without other changes, would not produce such a net increase in saving.

By contrast, however, personal accounts *can* create a vehicle for new saving—and likely would. The degree to which we simply divert payroll taxes into personal accounts and do not change contribution or benefit levels does not add to aggregate saving. But to the extent that additional voluntary contributions are made, new saving can occur.

It is unlikely that the opportunity to create additional tax-sheltered savings growth would find no takers. Roughly half of workers have no pension plan, and many have not taken the trouble or felt themselves to have the disposable income to set up IRAs. But once everyone in the United States started receiving annual statements showing how savings were accumulating in their name through personal accounts, this would be a vivid and visible reminder of where their retirement income would come from. Rather than a vague description of future Social Security benefits, which the individual would have no opportunity to affect with his own behavior, a statement would be provided showing the income accumulated to date, and the message would be obvious: additional contributions to this account will mean additional security in retirement. To the extent that individuals act upon this, national savings will increase, and thus future income for seniors will as well.

It is notable that even some of those who have sought to prop up the old Social Security system seem to be recognizing the necessity of such a feature within Social Security. The latest Ball plan includes voluntary personal accounts, in recognition that a vehicle must be created to allow for new savings, not present in the underlying Ball-Aaron plan. The Clinton plan also includes supplemental "USA accounts" as a new entitlement on top of Social Security. Note that every objection about administrative costs and impracticability that applies to personal accounts would apply to these voluntary accounts. So we see that even the traditional defenders of the system do not see these administrative questions as insoluble.

In sum, government investment of the trust fund is an attempt to bypass the measures—such as reducing the dissaving in the traditional Social Security system—that are needed to add to net national savings. By contrast, personal accounts provide a vehicle to add to those savings levels. This is an enormous and positive difference.

One factor that does not differentiate between the two options is the "transition cost." This concept is frequently misunderstood. "Transition costs" arise not because of the *method* of advance funding but from advance funding itself. If we decide that we must put aside additional savings today in order to be able to reduce unfunded liabilities later, then that first decision to use advance funding places on us a "transition cost" in proportion to how much we must increase saving in the near term.[6]

Let us return again to the analogy of the family planning for retirement. The family decides that it must begin to fund for tomorrow's retirement income by putting aside additional savings today; it then faces a similar kind of "transition cost." It has to make room in its budget for that funding.

It should also be noted, however, that if the family wants to have a given level of retirement income later on, failure to accept those "transition costs" does not make everything work out more easily. The family simply has more money to spend today, but a much bigger problem coming up with the money tomorrow.

What is critical to understand is that the question of transition costs is *not* predicated upon whether government invests the trust fund or whether it creates a vehicle for investment through personal accounts. If, in a given year, $65 billion that would formerly have been invested in Treasury bills is instead invested in personal accounts, then that is $65 billion that the government no longer has available to spend or to reduce its borrowing, and it must tighten its belt to that extent.

Were we to take an equivalent amount of payroll taxes and invest that portion of the Trust Fund in the stock market, instead of refunding to individuals through personal accounts, the transition cost to the government would be exactly the same, because it would no longer have access to that money in the form of purchases of Treasury bills.

Advance funding requires a transition cost either way, and it does not ultimately introduce any costs that the federal government would not otherwise face. It simply changes the timing of those costs in an effort to secure the advantage of compounding. Again, return to our family. Why does it agree to give up a little income this year and next, to put into saving? Because it's less costly that way in the long run. That is all that a transition cost is.

To Fund or Not to Fund?

Let's review the arguments on either side. If the government does the investing, we have the conflicts of interest associated with government ownership of private corporations, we have the temptation to steer investment for political purposes, we have the corrupting influence upon government decisionmaking that arises from the tie between stock prices and the government's balance sheets, we have the comparatively poor track record of public investment relative to private investment, and we have not done anything to increase net national savings.

If the individual owns the investment, we have the potential to increase net savings through additional voluntary contributions, we have benefits that cannot be taken away from beneficiaries through the political process, we retain the right for individuals to be as risk-averse as they choose, and we give individuals a modicum of additional control over their own economic future.

In either case, we have a transition cost, and we have a new mixture of assets that finance future benefits. However, the benefit levels and the risks underlying them are the consequences of the specific design elements of each plan, not inherently a result of the decision to invest privately or through the government.

Essentially, it comes down to whether the administrative questions surrounding personal accounts are so great as to outweigh all of the other considerations that make government investment of the trust fund an impossible proposition for reasons of both policy and political tradition.

The choice is straightforward. If it's unacceptable to operate through benefit cuts and tax increases alone, then we must advance-fund. And if we advance-fund, it must be through personally owned and directed investment, because the alternative—government control of the private equities market—would be intolerable to our free economic traditions and to our political tradition of seeking to avoid corrupting admixtures of political and economic power. If the administrative questions with personal accounts are prohibitive, then we will have to fall back on various undesirable alternatives. But if they can be resolved and minimized, there is no other sensible policy choice.

NOTES

1. Report of the 1994–1996 Advisory Council on Social Security, p. 16.
2. This illustrative analogy may be resisted by some economists, who argue that a nation cannot "save" for retirement because all goods consumed by the elderly must come from the productivity of workers at the same time. The analogy does yet apply, however, with respect to the budgeting of the federal government, which can "advance-fund" in the sense of foregoing tax revenues today in exchange for reduced outlay burdens tomorrow.
3. World Bank, *Averting the Old Age Crisis: Policies to Protect the Old and Promote Growth* (New York: Oxford University Press, 1994), pp. 94–95.

4. Congressional Research Service, *Social Security Reform: Projected Contributions and Benefits Under Three Proposals*, Report for the U.S. Congress, December 3, 1998.

5. 363 US 603.

6. Moreover, there is the "transition cost" of any solvent plan relative to an insolvent one. The mere act of reaching actuarial solvency, even without personal accounts or another form of advance funding, means that the reform plan has needed to fill in a $3 trillion hole relative to current law, and additional "transition costs" must be borne on top of that expense.

14

The Top Ten Tricks in the Social Security Debate

Electoral politics is not always conducive to constructive, analytical debate. Politicians run for office asserting that their election will mean wonderful things for the voters, whereas their opponents are venal, heartless troglodytes who want only to feather their own nest and to cruelly mistreat their constituents.

Practitioners of politics routinely demonstrate their conviction that Americans will believe, based on 30 seconds of advertising, that the person paying for the ad is virtuous and his opponent a corrupt thug. And so they turn discussions of the great issues of our time into contests between unmitigated good and irredeemable evil.

When the issue at stake is one of vital importance to the health and welfare of a group of Americans for whom we, as a general rule, feel reverence and affection—such as our senior citizens—this tactic is particularly effective. If someone who disagrees with one's own prescriptions for action on Social Security can be made to seem like a heartless senior-hater, one has a sure-fire political winner.

Unfortunately, this game is not particularly constructive when we are faced with a program with an unfunded liability of $3 trillion, by the most conservative estimates. Closing a $3 trillion gap between *projected* tax revenue and federal payments requires more than a little careful thought, as to how best to spread the burdens of filling it.

Small wonder, then, that public servants are reluctant to recognize the real trade-offs involved in fixing the system. The honest work and analysis

that many legislators have engaged in is too often drowned out by a ca-
cophony of partisan voices.

On the last day of the 1998 congressional session, a Democratic colleague
of mine shared with me some information churned out by various politicos
for use in the autumn campaign. One sheet was entitled, "Questions and
Answers about the Republican Raid on Social Security." In this missive, it
was asserted that Republican plans for a tax cut would "steal approximately 15 percent of the Social Security surplus." Not content with this, the
flyer went on to state that "Republicans want Social Security to go broke."

Republicans are not the only victims of these games. Democratic Congressman Charles Stenholm cosponsored the NCRP plan to restore Social
Security to solvency. He squarely faced every one of the tough choices to
bring the program into balance and fought every step of the way to make
sure that the proposal was sufficiently progressive to give adequate protection to low-income retirees. He was attacked for his trouble, and representations were made about Stenholm, as about the rest of the sponsors, that he
was inflicting unnecessary pain, that the problems in Social Security could
be solved without any of the cost restraints that Stenholm had backed.
Given the choice between heartless Charlie Stenholm and an opponent offering a pain-free solution, who you gonna pick?

Interestingly, voters picked Charlie Stenholm, as they did most of the reformers subjected to such attacks. The public rewards courage more often
than campaign advisors give them credit for doing.

This is how the debate gets cast. People who want to capitalize on Social
Security as a political issue are fond of issuing circulars and press releases
characterizing reformers as senior-haters and offering instead mystical an-
tidotes for Social Security's problems, in which benefits will materialize
from nothing.

So many different methods are used to disguise the costs of the various
free-lunch approaches that a review of the more popular tricks takes up an
entire chapter. These elements of proposals are so tempting that they se-
duce even the most well-motivated individuals.

1. SHUFFLING INVESTMENT AND CALLING IT PROGRESS

We have already reviewed this trick to a degree in describing the Ball
plan. This temptation will dangle tantalizingly in front of Social Security
policymakers every step of the way. Its essence is that because Social Security will seek a higher rate of return on its investments, the need to address
the current-law imbalance between revenues and outlays will be reduced.
We don't want to raise taxes, and we don't want to cut into benefit growth,
so we'll say that Social Security will get a higher rate of return on its invest-

ment after we invest Social Security contributions in a different way. It's about as straightforward an appearance of a free lunch as one can find.

Think this through for a moment. The government would no longer have access to as much T-bill investment from Social Security. Social Security—or individual Social Security investors—thus buys private equities, while the federal government, deprived of access to that amount of T-bill purchases, must therefore borrow more on its own. But everything works out swimmingly because the new borrowing of the federal government is done through low-yield T-bills, whereas higher returns are gained from equities. The system as a whole borrows at low cost and invests with a high return. You do enough of this, and all the solvency problems vanish.

But of course, someone else is paying for that. The government is now getting the benefit of doing new borrowing at lower cost and doing more investing at a high rate of return. So someone else, somewhere, is facing the reverse mix: a lower rate of return on investments and a higher cost associated with borrowing. That "someone" is basically the entire private savings system of the United States. Note that this would not be true if we actually created new saving. But to the degree that we are simply engaging in this maneuver to avoid any tough choices, we are simply *redistributing* the returns from existing saving, improving the return to Social Security, and reducing it for everyone else.

Don't misunderstand. Everyone can indeed win in the savings/investment game. It needn't be zero-sum, if we reduce net consumption. But the investment shuffle itself doesn't create new saving or new income.

A net increase in saving can be accomplished any number of ways, but a good start is to reduce the *dis*saving in the current Social Security system, reflected in the imbalance between its revenues and its outlays, as the NCRP plan does. But what some plans seek, by contrast, is to use the investment shuffle as an attempt to *bypass* those other decisions and thus, in effect, accomplish nothing.

The way that we tabulate the costs and benefits of different reform options is quite misleading. When analysts provide a little menu of options to strengthen Social Security, they often present each option together with a number showing how much of the overall actuarial problem it solves. The option of shifting investments of the Trust Fund is often assigned a pretty big number. It ought to have a zero next to it, because it accomplishes nothing in and of itself.

2. RELYING ON POSTERITY TO PAY OFF THE TRUST FUND

Relying on posterity is the easiest bit of slight of hand to identify, and yet it is astounding how willing journalists are to swallow it. The problem is basically this. You can get to actuarial solvency, on paper, in any one of a number of ways. You could, for example, simply make huge credits to the Social Security Trust Fund in the near term, building up not $4 trillion, but perhaps $5, $6, $7, or even $10 trillion, or whatever amount will get you through the 75-year period without the Trust Fund dipping to zero.

What does that solve? Not a blessed thing. It does future Social Security beneficiaries not one whit of good if Social Security is sitting on a $10 trillion Trust Fund and is seemingly solvent, if the amounts that have to be paid *to* the Trust Fund and to beneficiaries each year can't be found unless the government starts hiking taxes radically.

As we have already discussed, any proposal that leaves an enormous Trust Fund to "buy down" in this way is perpetrating a fraud. It's just the same thing as telling posterity that the problem is theirs and that we have no intention of doing anything about it. Every plan should be scoured to see how much it relies on such a Trust Fund "drawdown" and thus leaves a huge portion of the problem essentially unsolved.

3. COMPARING REFORM PLANS TO "CURRENT LAW"

The essential problem with comparing reform plans to "current law" is that "current law" allows the system to go bankrupt. Whether or not you believe that we *will* allow Social Security to go bankrupt, that is what *would* happen under current law, by our best available projections. If you believe that we will raise taxes or cut benefits to make the system whole, then you should compare reform plans to that alternative.

Tables are forever being constructed in which reform plans are compared unfavorably, in terms of benefit levels or rates of return, to "current law." This is nonsense. "Current law" can't pay those benefits. "Current law" is even a misnomer. When the funding runs out, Social Security does not have the borrowing authority to continue to send checks. Literally, if we did not change the law, then benefits could not be paid on time starting in 2034. The system would just have to wait until the money came in, effectively cutting people's benefits by about 25 percent.

Anyone's plan can show a great rate of return, if it promises a benefit level without coming up with the funding for it. By that logic, we should all simply author plans with absurdly high benefit levels, no taxes whatsoever, and claim victory. You can't beat an insolvent system for a high rate of return.

"Current law" tables are *literally* meaningless unless they factor in the tax increases or benefit cuts that are needed to make the existing system whole. They refer neither to what current law could provide if fixed nor to what will happen if it is not fixed.

4. MY BENEFITS COUNT, BUT YOURS DON'T

Many analyses—seriously—only count part of the benefits in reform proposals that they don't like. An example of such a study, and a push-poll conducted in the wake of it, will be examined in a later chapter.

This tactic was alluded to in the previous section describing the comparisons between personal account plans and Ball-style plans. Even if the money is invested in exactly the same way in both plans, some will only count the portion that is controlled and directed by the government and not the portion controlled and directed by individuals. The policy merits of each approach can be debated, but it is not reasonable to count the benefits from one another's plans that we agree with and not count those that we don't.

The lion's share of the "studies" done by the anti–personal-account groups do this. More often than not, "benefit cuts" referred to in these studies are simply the result of their refusal to recognize the benefit components, specifically the personal account income, that they disagree with. Instead of projecting a range of possible outcomes, they pretend that the benefits wouldn't exist. One could do this just as easily in reverse. You may happen to oppose government investment in the equities market and could refuse to count the benefits funded by that investment. It doesn't advance the debate, but it is no sillier than what has been done by a number of anti–personal-account groups.

5. REIMBURSING THE TRUST FUND WITH GENERAL REVENUES

The option of reimbursing the trust fund with general revenues will remain on the table throughout the Social Security debate, and it is seized upon by personal-account proponents as much as anyone. This maneuver, however disguised, would increase costs to future taxpayers, and this should be recognized.

Proponents of personal accounts have a political problem. They would put some of the money that under current law would go into the Social Security Trust Fund, into personal accounts. On policy grounds, this makes perfect sense—the personal accounts are a more direct and tenable method of funding the benefits than sticking future taxpayers with the bill. But we measure actuarial solvency as lasting until the point where the Trust Fund runs dry. If less money is going into the Trust Fund, then it projects to run dry earlier.

The right answer to this conundrum is to gradually phase down the liabilities that are to be paid out from the traditional OASDI system—not to phase them out, not even to decrease their value in dollar terms, but to slow the increase in those annual outlays and move the payment of some of those benefits into personal accounts. That is, after all, the whole point of setting up personal accounts: to give retirees benefits that are not contingent on unrealistic levels of taxation. If those benefits come from the personal accounts, then less of them need to come from the tax-financed side.

But many proponents of personal accounts don't want to have to live within the tighter restriction of a Trust Fund that is not growing as rapidly as under current law. They want to promise the gains from the personal accounts, but they don't want to be seen as reducing the benefits that come from the traditional system. So they pull a clever maneuver: They take a portion of the payroll tax and put it in personal accounts, but then they reimburse the Trust Fund by an equivalent amount.

Why do this? Because now there's more money in the Trust Fund than if it had simply lost the extra revenue to the personal accounts, we don't have to cut benefit growth back nearly as much to fit within projected Trust Fund revenues. What this does, in practice, is to increase the effective tax rate imposed on everyone through the Social Security system.

Pretend that the federal government is a family and that Social Security is a child in that family, a kid who takes a job that helps to make ends meet. Suppose the kid is bringing in more money than he is consuming. The family as a whole brings in $100 and spends $100. The child is bringing in $40, but only costing $30 to feed and clothe.

So the family says to little SS Junior: Look, we need the extra $10 you're bringing in to help make ends meet. But we'll keep track of everything we've borrowed from you, and some day we'll pay it back with interest.

We see how this is like the current setup. The federal government is helped to balance its books by receiving the surplus coming through Social Security. It keeps track of how much has been borrowed and promises to pay it back some day with interest.

Now, one day, the parents get their act together, Dad gets a raise, and now they can balance the books on their own. Suddenly the fact that the kid is bringing in $10 more than is being spent on him means a $10 surplus for the family. (This is equivalent to what we are on the verge of doing in the federal government. We're almost at the point where we've balanced the non–Social Security books. We may have a surplus soon that is greater than Social Security surplus alone.)

The family says to Junior: Look, we don't need your extra $10 anymore to help make ends meet. Why don't you put it in the bank for yourself, and then some day you'll have a lot more.

Now comes the critical decision: If the family followed the NCRP model, since the family is no longer borrowing the extra $10 from Junior each year, it would stop giving the kid credit for $10 borrowed each year. They'd take that $10 and put it right in the kid's account. Makes sense, doesn't it?

But under some Social Security reform plans, the kid would get the $10 for his account and the family would keep crediting little Social Security Junior for the extra $10, as if he were bringing it in. At the end of the story, not only would he get the money he put into the bank, but the parents would pay him back just as large an amount as before.

Why would we do such a thing? Because we don't want to be accused of "cutting benefits." Even though Junior is putting the $10 now in his account, we want to be able to tell the world that the family isn't backing off of what it previously promised to pay him.

If you want to know how some plans seem able to make ends meet without making the tough choices contained in the NCRP plan, that's how. People today face the transition cost associated with putting the money in personal accounts, and then we credit the Trust Fund as if that money had never left—so taxpayers tomorrow get to pay off the $4.46 trillion Trust Fund anyway. When you stick taxpayers with that burden at both ends, it's not hard to promise higher levels of benefits. It's simply a way of effecting the tax increase in disguise.

The following chart should make it very clear. Consider four different ways of doing things: (1) current law; (2) taking 2 percent of the payroll tax and putting it in personal accounts, as in the NCRP plan; (3) requiring a 2 percent payroll tax increase used to fund personal accounts, and; (4) taking 2 percent of the current payroll tax and putting it in personal accounts and then reimbursing the Trust Fund for the money taken out. The different scenarios are shown in Table 14.1.

As you can see, the net tax obligations of the last two options are exactly the same. It may well be that the body politic, in its wisdom, will decide that it is not willing to live within the 12.4 percent net payroll tax rate that exists for Social Security and that net taxes will need to be increased. But we should be aware of what we are doing when we employ such a maneuver: if we use non–Social Security money to reimburse the Trust Fund, the bill will eventually be sent to the U.S. taxpayer. It may be the right decision, or it may be the wrong decision, but it will not be a cost-free decision.

Table 14.1
Effective Tax Rates for "Add-on" versus "Carve-out" Proposals*

	Amount to OASDI Trust Fund	Personal Accounts
Current Law	12.4	0
2% Carve-Out	10.4	2
2% Add-on	12.4	2
2% Carve-Out with Reimbursement	12.4	2

*As a percentage of taxable payroll

6. ASSUMING THE FRUITS OF INCREASED SAVING WITHOUT PRODUCING IT

It is much easier to produce a package that purports to guarantee a solvent system if one uses optimistic economic projections. The reasons are clear. More economic growth means more wage growth, and more wage growth means more payroll tax and income tax revenue. The GDP grows relative to the size of promised benefits, which is another way of saying that benefit outlays shrink relative to the tax base that is supporting them and thus become more affordable. Consequently, fewer additional changes to the benefit structure are required to bring the program into balance.

All who work on Social Security reform have an incentive to limit the bad news that must be delivered, something that can be accomplished by positing higher economic growth. This is not to say that higher economic growth will not make our problem easier. Nor is it to disdain dynamic economic models that project higher economic growth as a consequence of an upturn in national savings. Economic growth can be increased with the appropriate increases in savings and investment, and indeed, the policy recommendations made in the NCRP plan are in the service of that ideal.

We cannot, however, assume the benefits of policies that we have not created. We cannot duck the choices that are required to increase net national savings and then claim the improved economic results of having made them. As is typical, both the political left and the political right succumb to these temptations.

The left is fond of using the assumption of faster economic growth as a way of saying that the current problems in Social Security will go away of themselves. This was shown in chapter 7 to be a double-edged sword that may reduce long-range actuarial deficits without cutting significantly into the real problem, the size of future annual gaps between revenues and benefit payments.

Further, the left is mum on the question of just how that increased economic growth is to be achieved. A great deal of the reason for actuarial projections of relatively slow economic growth over the 75-year valuation period has to do with the decline in the working population relative to the proportion of the retired population. Many scholars believe that the wholesale departure of millions of baby boomers from the workforce will have even more extreme effects in reducing economic growth than are projected by the actuaries.

In order for the economy to grow, U.S. workers must be productive, and in order to be productive, they need to work. And yet the various things that we could do to deter the drive into retirement for those hitting their early 60s are opposed by labor. Examples would include shifting up the eligibility ages for Social Security, fixing the actuarial adjustment formulas in Social Security benefits to relieve incentives for early retirement, and making it more affordable for employers to retain long-serving employees by restricting the growth of their burdens to finance retirement and health benefits.

One cannot sincerely bemoan low economic-growth estimates that are based on the departure of millions from the workforce and then defend the very policies that drive those individuals out of the workforce and into retirement.

It is not only the left, however, that seeks to "estimate" the problem away by using rosy economic projections. The right uses such techniques to paper over the costs of transition to funded Social Security accounts.

Recall the personal account approach outlined earlier in this chapter. Here, the OASDI Trust Fund would be reimbursed from general revenues for the payroll taxes that have been moved into the personal accounts. The federal government will thus face the same financing problem that it has already—a Trust Fund of the same size as today's to pay off—plus the obligation to fund personal accounts through payroll tax collections simultaneously. If total benefits are the same or higher, our net liabilities have actually gone up.

No one would make such a proposal unless they retained a belief that the establishment of such accounts would ultimately alleviate federal fiscal liabilities. In this illustration, as benefits build up in personal accounts, they would replace the benefits that would be paid from the traditional OASDI system—not dollar for dollar, but a significant amount of them—and thus the liabilities to be made good through redeeming the OASDI Trust Fund would ultimately be lessened.

Unfortunately, under many of these proposals, liabilities under the OASDI system would not be reduced before 2030 to an extent greater than the required new investment in personal accounts. In other words, we would still be in the phase of the system where net cost has increased. What do we do?

We are told that we will be rescued by an enormous increase in tax receipts, especially corporate tax revenue, which we can collect and earmark specifically for the Social Security system. The old financing gap between payroll tax revenues and benefit obligations is still in place; thus, so is that enormous "asterisk" that represents the fact that somehow government will collect the necessary tax revenue to pay off the T-bills it must redeem for the OASDI Trust Fund.

Now, however, the asterisk has changed its form. Instead of needing several hundreds of billions of dollars to redeem principal and interest from the Trust Fund in, say, the year 2025, we only need to plug about half of that gap with such redemption. The other half comes from increased corporate taxation that has resulted from higher economic growth. The amounts are considerable—more than $100 billion in new taxation annually from 2023 onward, and rising fast.

Reforming Social Security

Since we don't have to redeem nearly as much of the Trust Fund each year thanks to plugging the gap with more corporate taxation, the Trust Fund lasts a lot longer—in fact, never depletes! No problem. No benefit cuts, no tax increases, just a different financing system and then a spurt of increased economic growth.

There is a flaw here. No element of the proposal takes concrete action to increase the net saving provided through the Social Security system. Consumption by the system is not restrained, nor are mandated contributions increased. The net investment of the system in the economy of the United States is unchanged. From where comes the assumption that net economic growth will increase?

The answer is very simple. It lies in the belief that government wouldn't lock in that surplus and save it and thus contribute to net national savings in that manner. And 1998 is one of many episodes in Congress's long and distinguished history that seem to prove this belief to be right. In 1998, the Congress faced a unified budget surplus for the first time in a generation, but it was a surplus created only by Social Security surpluses, not by surpluses in other parts of the budget. Even though Social Security desperately needed attention to ensure its long-term stability and even though that money by right "belonged" to Social Security as much as to any other obligation of the government, President Clinton and the Congress engaged in a spending spree of more than $20 billion in "emergency" supplemental appropriations above and beyond the normal appropriations allowances.

Actions such as these may be evidence that Congress wouldn't run such a surplus and thereby produce the savings and growth. Though rhetorically it's a persuasive argument, it is still double counting. You can say that you believe that personal accounts would produce more growth because the surplus would otherwise be spent. But one can't use a surplus to finance personal accounts unless that surplus is there. If one assumes it wouldn't be there, one can't use it to create personal accounts.

In order to make a projection based on moving a given level of investment from one place to the other, one has to compare the situation you're moving *from* to the one you're moving *to*, which in this case, has the same level of net investment. You can't take an action that by itself doesn't add to net savings and then claim the higher economic growth resulting from higher savings, on the basis of a belief that the Congress would otherwise fritter it away.

If that were the case, then this problem really becomes easy. We just have to move existing investment around from one place to another, and then each time we move it, we claim all of the fruits of that investment, not relative to each other, but relative to zero.

7. DRAWING DOWN THROUGH YEAR 75

A reformed system must be set on a permanently sustainable course. You haven't fixed anything if you are simply building up the Trust Fund just high enough that it will be depleted in the 75th year of a 75-year projection. This is called the "cliff effect." One year after enactment, such plans no longer work.

This problem was a feature of many past Social Security rescues and of versions of Ball-style plans today offered by several members of Congress.

8. MINIMIZING COST ASSUMPTIONS BY ASSUMING AVERAGES

Minimizing cost assumptions by assuming averages is fairly specific to "clawback" proposals, in which the federal government agrees to continue to guarantee a defined benefit, but will fund that defined benefit through the buildup of an investment in a personal account.

Many personal-account proposals attempt to make the new accounts a "can't lose" proposition such that no risk falls on the individual of doing worse than under the previously guaranteed deal. This temptation is an understandable one. Instead of accepting the burden of proof that a personal account plan will perform better than the old system even if a conservative rate of return is gained, the personal account proposal simply guarantees that the individual will do no worse.

These types of personal account proposals work in a number of ways. Some would give an individual no new Social Security benefits until the personal accounts themselves had grown to a level where they could produce the old promised Social Security benefit. If your old benefit was supposed to be $1,000 a month, and if the new personal account could give you $500 a month, then you still get only $1,000 a month, although $500 would come from the new account and $500 from the old system. In such a form, traditional Social Security benefits are basically lost dollar for dollar as personal account benefits build up, creating almost no incentive for additional saving by the individual.

Most such proposals don't go to this extreme, but instead allow the total summary benefit to grow a little bit as the personal account benefit grows. One might create a swap of 75 cents off the traditional account benefit for each dollar building in the personal accounts, up to the point where the individual has beaten the old deal by 25 percent, after which the system will no longer owe them a traditional benefit. In such a plan, if the personal account built to $500 a month, mean that the total benefit would have grown by $125 a month, for a total of $1,125 per month. The old system would pay $625 and the new system would pay $500. Incentives to save are somewhat dampened, because the individual does not get a dollar back for every dollar put in and would be better advised to put the money in a different investment.

Unless individuals assume some of the risk, they cannot be given the full investment potential, and thus the incentives, that come from the gain. If they put more money in or if their investment does better, they should get all the extra income that comes with it. A penny saved should be a penny earned. It is much better as a savings incentive and much better in terms of federal fiscal policy, because the federal government is not on the hook if the investment returns come in low. An individual's total risk can be minimized through the defined benefit portion of the system.

But that is not the issue here. Rather, there is a consequence of averaging projected rates of return for individuals. In a proposal in which the personal account investment risk falls on the individual, government liabilities don't change as investment performance deviates from the mean. One investor may earn 3 percent on investments, and another 6 percent, which will cause a deviation in their total income (only a slight deviation if most of the benefit is still defined by the traditional OASDI system), but the liabilities of the government don't change as that deviation occurs.

If, however, the government is guaranteeing the benefits through a "clawback" mechanism, in an attempt to spare the investor from risk, the consequences of the assumption of averaging are significant. To take a case in point: Suppose you have a plan that has a 75 percent clawback offset, as cited earlier. And say that we originally had a $1,000-a-month benefit to guarantee. Consider the case of a birth cohort in which an average rate of return is expected to produce a personal account that would provide a $1,000-a-month benefit. Here's how the scoring would look:

Original Benefit, Old System: $1,000

Projected Account Benefit, Average Return: $1,000

Amount from Account to be Added to Benefit: $250 (25 percent of $1,000)

Total Benefit: $1,250

Total Paid from Account: $1,000

Total Paid from Tax Dollars: $250

If you assume all individuals in this birth year and income level get an average rate of return, the government has to shell out $250 a head at this point from tax dollars.

But consider the problem introduced by variation. Let's say that these folks have generated these account balances by participating in the new system for 30 years. Over 30 years, a gain or loss of a percentage point in average return can make a huge difference. If one investor gets a bond rate of return, one gets an average rate of return, and another gets a high rate of return, then that $1,000 benefit could vary greatly—let's say from $600 to $1,400. Now consider the case of the unlucky and the lucky individuals.

Joe Unlucky

Original Benefit, Old System: $1,000

Projected Account Benefit, Bad Return: $600

Amount from Account to be Added to Benefit: $150

Total Benefit: $1,150

Total Paid from Account: $600

Total Paid from Tax Dollars: $550

Joe Lucky

Original Benefit, Old System: $1,000

Projected Account Benefit, Good Return: $1,400

Amount from Account to be Added to Benefit: $350

Total Benefit: $1,350

Joe Lucky has more than this amount from his personal account alone, so the system owes him nothing.

Total Paid from Account: $1,400

Total Paid from Tax Dollars: $0

We have three individuals whose personal accounts accumulated to be $600, $1,000, and $1,400 respectively. Were they all at $1,000, the government would owe them a payment each of $250, or $750 for all three. But because of the variation, the government owes them, in the three cases, $250, $550, and $0 from tax dollars. Total liabilities are $800. The deviation from the average has increased the total liabilities of the government by 6.67 percent.

This is hardly the most important factor when it comes to evaluating proposals. But if the proposal considered has a "clawback" feature, it is important to note that deviations from the average will drive liabilities up, especially when you get to the birth cohorts that the projections involving groups that are assumed to be off the ledger.

For the preceding example, assume instead that you have three individuals with payment levels of $1,000, $1,400, and $1,800 from their personal accounts. If you assume that the amounts are averaged, such that each has earned $1,400, then one would assume that total payments to this group would be $0. But because of the deviation, the government would owe $250 to one of them. The closer that a birth or demographic group is to falling out of the government liability estimates, the more that deviations from the mean will drive actual costs to be higher than projections based on averaging. This cost must be factored into the evaluation of any such proposal.

9. ESTIMATING THE PROBLEM AWAY WITH RATES OF RETURN

The larger the gap that one assumes between the rate of return at which the system invests and the rate at which it borrows, the more the problem appears to vanish, even though in a national sense, nothing has happened to cause it to.

High-rate-of return assumptions should of course warrant scrutiny in and of themselves, even if not assumed to bridge the government's own financing problems. Clearly, one must be cautious in assuming that all individuals will receive stock market rates of return or that the Social Security system, either collectively or through individual investments, can base its solvency based on such an assumption. Such projections are enormously sensitive to return rates. If the whole package, in order to hang together, requires a consistent and impressive rate of return, this is grounds for great concern.

This issue is much more relevant to "clawback" proposals than those such as the NCRP plan. Under the NCRP plan, projections were run assuming 2.6 percent, 4.2 percent, and 5.9 percent real rates of return, and the results were examined. The system would remain solvent under all three. But if a proposal is no longer solvent once an intermediate or poor rate of return is plugged in, it ought to be scrapped. To do otherwise is to force taxpayers to be liable for any disappointment in investment returns. Proposals that fail this test would include the Ball plan for aggregate investment of the Trust Fund in the private market, as well as several personal account proposals in which liabilities are assumed to phase down based on everyone receiving a stock market rate of return.

10. NOT PAYING YOUR OWN WAY

The ethic of Social Security is that it is supposed to be self-financing. No one asks whether welfare recipients have paid enough taxes to finance their welfare benefits. The society as a whole deems the emergency assistance necessary and budgets for it as it deems appropriate. We could do the same thing with Social Security: forget about trying to balance it on its own terms and use whatever other federal resources are available to pay for it.

It's not difficult to promise an attractive Social Security program if you can fund it with all the money that would otherwise be spent on the national defense. But the country does need to defend itself, and if we are going to make Social Security benefits a top national priority, we ought to be able to find a way to pay for them within the Social Security system. Give me all $1.6 trillion in the current federal budget, and I'll give you a great Social Security system with enormous benefit levels that will beat any other package out there.

Any plan that claims not to raise taxes but then proposes that we devote other general revenues to Social Security is doing a bit of a shuffle. All that means is that we use different tax money to pay the rising costs of Social Security. We're simply choosing not to count those taxes when figuring how good a deal it all is, because they weren't Social Security taxes. But if we're maintaining every dime of the old spending obligations, the taxpayer will have to pay for them.

Besides, this job is being done already. Social Security and Medicare, left on their own, would eliminate all of our other appropriations in due course. One reason that we need to reform Social Security and Medicare is to prevent the nation from losing its sovereignty over the allocation of its own resources. We don't solve that problem by giving in to it.

15

Tackling the Policy Challenges of Personal Accounts

It is possible to believe on philosophical and policy grounds that personal accounts should be a component of a Social Security solution and yet to be daunted by the numerous policy questions that they introduce into Social Security. What follows discusses a few issues that must be addressed.

RISK

Those who defend the traditional structure of the system often cite the argument that current benefits are free from risk in a way that personal account benefits would not be. The benefit formulas are written into the law and are funded by the purchase of Treasury bills, which are backed by the full faith and credit of the U.S. government and thus are sound for as long as the government can meet its debts. Since the government has the sovereign power to tax as necessary to fund benefits, beneficiaries can sleep soundly in their beds, it is said.

This is true to an extent, but it overstates the case. True, Treasury bills have always been a secure investment, but this does not mean that the levels of Social Security benefits are guaranteed for any period longer than that before the next vote of Congress. If beneficiaries truly were shielded from all risk of changes to benefit levels, various senior-exploiting organizations would not be able to send out the scare mailings that charge that Congress is about to cut their benefits, contradicting their own claims that Social Security benefits are "guaranteed."

This becomes more than a theoretical issue as the program evolves and pressure increases in the directions of both tax increases and benefit cuts. Though historically, Congress has tended to move in the direction of tax increases, there is undoubtedly a limit to how far they will go, which will bring benefit levels into jeopardy.

Plus there is a very real deadline out there: the date at which Social Security becomes insolvent. It is a misnomer to say that Social Security benefits are risk-free and "guaranteed" when they statutorily are not. If in 2034 the amount of T-bills held by the Trust Fund is depleted, the program does not have any legal means to keep sending out the checks on time. The program does not have borrowing authority.

The Congressional Research Service (CRS) believes that the only way that the program could continue to operate would be to simply delay the issuance of checks until payroll taxes came in, slowing payments and effectively reducing the payout to cut benefits by about 25 percent. While it is difficult to imagine that the government would reach this point, it would require an explicit change in law to prevent it. The "guarantee" is somewhat overstated.

There is some uncertainty in personal accounts. Benefit levels are not set by formula, but will be determined as a consequence of the contributions made by individuals and of the appreciation on those contributions. These results will vary from investor to investor within a birth year, and from birth year to birth year depending on the performance of the market as a whole.

This raises the question: How much will we, as a society, tolerate differences of result among beneficiaries?

This is not a question that can be answered glibly, in accordance with a reflexive political view. Those who are more free-market oriented may be quite content with different people achieving different results on their investments and living with the consequences of those decisions.

But Social Security is somewhat unique. We're required to put into this system. Perhaps we don't want to compete with our neighbor, who was born the same year and earns the same income, to see who can get the better rate of return on his or her investment.

Still, let us not forget the vastly different treatment that the *current* system delivers to individuals according to when they were born, as depicted on previous charts. These differences are scarcely more tolerable simply because they are familiar. One might even prefer that lower benefits, when they occurred, bore some relationship to individual actions, other than the accident of simply being born in the wrong year, when the current system funneled money away from one's birth cohort. Curiously, many of those who speak most sternly against tolerating differences in rate of return in personal accounts are blithely indifferent to the fate of individuals who simply have been born in an unlucky year in the lottery of the pay-as-you-go system.

It is often alleged by traditionalists that those who favor personal accounts are advancing the notion that these accounts would free individuals to chase gaudy rates of return in the market, at the price of significant risk. That is not the case. Many who have come around to embrace personal accounts did so through a roundabout way, after realizing that no alternative was viable, that the system cannot work without advance funding, and that this funding can only be plausibly achieved through personal accounts. Many accept the principle that individuals should not be exposed to significant new risk through Social Security relative to current law.

Critics of personal accounts often display charts that show the wide divergence of results that would have come from investing Social Security payroll taxes in the stock market over the past several decades. Of course, such an argument loses its relevance when it is understood that very few suggest complete privatization of the Social Security system. Most actuarially sound personal-account proposals would only allow a small portion of the overall payroll tax into the personal accounts—two or three percentage points. Even fairly wild swings in the rates of return on these accounts would not produce vastly different outcomes in overall Social Security income, because the majority of the income would still be from the defined benefit system.[1]

For the proposal developed by the National Commission on Retirement Policy, computations were performed by the Social Security actuaries, showing what would come from beneficiaries receiving high, intermediate, and low rates of return from the personal accounts.

The results were instructive. In the near term, the personal accounts did not have enough time to appreciate significantly, and thus the total benefit levels were largely defined by what was provided through the OASDI system and much less dependent on the accounts' rate of return. But over the long run, the situation reversed. For those retiring in, for example, 2030 and beyond, the personal accounts, even with conservative rate-of-return assumptions, had grown so as to compete with the traditional OASDI system in terms of total benefits delivered. By this point, the fluctuations do become more significant, but they have also had enough time to appreciate, such that even with low rates of return, most beneficiaries are doing better than with a traditional fix.

In either case, the fluctuations from the mean do not become an argument against personal accounts. In the short run, the fluctuations are too small to matter significantly, and in the long run, most everyone benefits from reform anyway.

That being said, there are still additional measures that can and should be taken in order to protect low-income individuals from any new risk introduced by personal accounts. The most obvious way is to fortify the safety-net features contained within the traditional defined-benefit component of the OASDI program.

Consider the 12.4 percent payroll tax rate. Suppose that a given amount—two percentage points—is moved into personal accounts. We would need to make sure that the remaining 10.4 percent does not provide less of a safety net for low-income people than did the original 12.4 percent.

This can quite easily be done. The NCRP studied various approaches to Social Security reform, some containing personal accounts, others without them. Each of the packages had identical provisions in most respects. The essential difference between the personal-account packages and others was the way in which liabilities and benefits in the personal-account plans were transferred from the traditional OASDI system to the personal accounts by gradual and phased-in changes to the Primary Insurance Amount (PIA) formula that determines benefit levels. These changes can be phased in via means that can be as progressive as the designer chooses. In the case of the NCRP plan, this was done by making changes to the 32 percent and 15 percent factors only and leaving the 90 percent factor untouched.

Additional features in those packages acted, however, to make doubly sure that low-income people were protected from the introduction of new risk by personal accounts. In the NCRP proposal, the plan included a new "minimum benefit" provision that guaranteed that an individual who worked a full lifetime would receive a poverty-level OASDI benefit at the very least, even before any income from the personal accounts.

In practice, this feature not only preserves but would actually strengthen the existing safety net features of Social Security. In the case of the NCRP plan, literally no new income risk would be created by the personal accounts. The income guaranteed to low-income individuals would increase, because for most low-income individuals under current law, Social Security does not guarantee a poverty-level benefit. The income from the accounts would be a pure bonus for low-income individuals.

Some figures from the Social Security actuaries that illustrate the point are given in Table 15.1. What do these figures mean? The first two columns are identical, reflecting the fact that low-income people would get exactly the same benefits from the OASDI program in the plan that has the personal account component as they would from a plan without one. But the third column is higher, reflecting the fact that the personal accounts provide bonus money to these individuals. Their basic guarantee is just as strong as before, but they have additional money coming in now. These figures subtract administrative costs estimated by SSA.

The diminishing return rates shown for later birth years reflect the fact that these figures are taken at age 67 rather than at normal retirement age, which is gradually increasing both under current law and under these proposals. You may be wondering how these figures measure up to cur-

Policy Challenges of Personal Accounts

Table 15.1
Replacement Rates,* Low-Income Earners Retiring at Age 67

Birth Year	Traditional Solution without Personal Account	Personal Account Plan Not Counting Account	Personal Account Plan Including Account
1948	59.2	59.2	62.2
1958	52.6	52.6	58.6
1968	45.1	45.1	55.5

*As a percentage

Source: Table provided by Social Security actuaries based on 1997 assumptions.

rent-law benefits. "Current law" under the estimates used at the time of NCRP deliberations projected to require a 2.2 percent payroll tax increase plus the redemption of a multitrillion dollar trust fund to pay out the benefits. If we come up with an additional 2.2 percent of payroll to fund the two systems, the figures look as shown in Table 15.2.

If we raised payroll taxes today permanently by 2.2 percent, replacement rates would still go down at age 67, as a consequence of current-law changes in the retirement age. But even with a faster acceleration in the normal retirement age under the NCRP plan, replacement rates at age 67 would be higher if that extra 2.2 percent were contributed to the plan's accounts instead. Moreover, the permanent diminution in replacement rates by birth year would be alleviated, even if subsequent generations desired to retire at the same age. It is not often understood that a plan such as this may contain changes in the normal retirement age and still offer a better deal for those who retire early.

This is not the only approach taken to the risk question. Others have suggested offering risk protection of a sort provided by the Federal Deposit Insurance Corporation (FDIC), where account investors would contribute a small portion of their account balance as insurance against loss.

Others have suggested making the personal accounts a "can't lose" proposition. Individuals would be guaranteed a given benefit level whatever happens in their personal accounts, and the government would fill in any gaps in benefit levels arising from inadequate appreciation in account balances. One problem with this approach is that it duplicates the conflict of interest in the Ball plan, in that the federal government's benefit obligations would explicitly depend on the rate of buildup in the personal accounts, and thus incentives for the government to manipulate stock market prices would be newly great.

157

Table 15.2
Replacement Rates,* Workers Retiring at Age 67, Alternative Social Security
Systems Provided with Additional 2.2 Percent of Taxable Payroll

Birth Year	Current Law with 2.2% Tax Increase (Low-Wage Earner)	NCRP Plan with 2.2% Tax Increase (Low-Wage Earner)	Current Law with 2.2% Tax Increase (Average Earner)	NCRP Plan with 2.2% Tax Increase (Average Earner)
1948	60.9	65.6	45.4	45.8
1958	57.9	65.2	43.2	43.4
1968	56.4	66.9	42.1	48.2

*As a percentage

Source: Extrapolation based on Social Security actuaries memo of April 27, 1998.

Total risk must be kept in perspective. Large deviations in income through Social Security could only occur if the personal-account sizes were large enough. The personal accounts that have been described in most politically credible proposals have not been large enough to contribute significant new risk to basic retirement income security.

PROGRESSIVITY

Personal accounts would differ from the traditional Social Security system in one very important respect. They would in and of themselves have no progressive or redistributive character. As a consequence, the net amount of progressivity of the system would be reduced if nothing else about it were to change.

The first method of dealing with this problem is simply to conclude that it is not a problem. One may develop a system involving personal accounts in which individuals at all income levels do better than they would under a traditional system. If everyone has more money than under the projections of the old system, one may choose not to worry about levels of progressivity, because the safety net for low-income people would have been strengthened, even if they seem to have lost ground relative to those on the high end.

However, it is difficult to draft a credible plan in which "everyone wins" relative to current promises. It is *quite* possible to draft a plan in which most everyone does better than what current law can actually buy. But many people compare plans not to what current law can provide, but to what current law is promising, funded or not. That's a higher standard, and it can't be met without bridging a multitrillion dollar financing gap. Bridging that gap will involve trade-offs, and someone has to pay up somewhere in those trade-offs.

Progressivity has to be a concern. If you desire a plan similar to the NCRP plan, one that makes the total costs of the program affordable over the long term, the personal accounts will need to be "carved out" of the existing tax rate, not collected through an "add-on" contribution or subsidy. This means reducing the amount of tax going into the traditional OASDI system. The contents of that "carve-out" will not be progressive. Thus, the remaining OASDI system must be made more progressive.

This can be done, and in the NCRP plan it is done. In fact, one can choose to be as progressive as one likes. What we did was to *increase* the net progressivity of the whole system in the short term, so that in the distant future, when the personal accounts build up to large levels, the net progressivity in the system would be comparable to today's. We sought retaining the current level of progressivity as a long-term goal.

One needn't, however, go as far as we did. One could simply attempt to ensure that the net level of progressivity is met in the short run, which would require less in the way of added progressivity to the traditional OASDI benefits. Then, as the personal accounts build up, overall progressivity might diminish somewhat, but it would come not at the expense of low-income workers, but rather through the appreciation on the high end, and all would be participating in that appreciation.

A number of thinkers have invested time and energy into these questions of progressivity. "Matches" have been suggested for the personal accounts of low-income people, to multiply their contributions and to add a progressive element to the accounts. Senator Rick Santorum has developed the idea of determining the personal-account sizes by graduated marginal rates applied to the taxable wage base. Under his plan, the number of percentage points going into the personal account would be higher, the lower one's income. Still others have suggested making the personal account a flat minimum amount rather than a percentage of taxable payroll, for example, $500.

The NCRP approach is most likely to be palatable to traditionalists, for the simple reason that they are more skeptical about personal accounts altogether and thus will not believe that the safety net is adequately upheld except through the traditional OASDI benefit. However, if one chooses instead to pursue progressivity within personal accounts, the Santorum idea is interesting. It avoids the compliance problems created by a flat $500 personal account minimum, because even with its progressivity, it retains a relationship between wages and personal account credits and thus retains the incentive to report covered earnings.

159

TRANSITION COSTS

Perhaps the single largest issue with regard to personal accounts is the subject of transition costs. In the long-term, there is no transition cost of personal-account plans relative to any other kind of plan. We have trillions in benefits to pay. We have to raise all that money from this point forward, because the system has not saved anything. Now we choose how we are going to go about it. Do we simply raise money through the tax system as is necessary to pay benefits? That's current law. Or do we put some savings today into accounts that will fund some of tomorrow's benefits? One way or the other, we still have to raise the money from this day forward.

In a sense, the concept of a "transition cost" is a bit of a misnomer. If we don't change the benefit levels that the federal government is guaranteeing, it has exactly the same amount of work to do to fund those benefits, one way or the other. More technically, the concept of a "transition cost" has slightly different meanings for the Social Security system and for the federal government as a whole.

From the standpoint of Social Security, creating personal accounts can literally mean no transition cost at all. Consider a very modest reform such as the original Gregg bill, S. 321. This legislation would have simply refunded 1 percent of the national payroll tax into personal accounts and, according to the age of the wage-earner, would have made slight adjustments in the Social Security benefit formula so as to transfer a portion of the liability for benefit payments from the tax side to the personal-account side.

From Social Security's perspective, there would be literally no transition cost. The 1 percent tax refund was less than Social Security's annual surplus in tax revenue. As that extra revenue was being loaned to the federal government anyway, Social Security would experience no cash crunch. Its out-year liabilities would have been reduced as a consequence of some other changes in the bill. By the time that the extra cushion of the surplus would otherwise have evaporated, these changes would hold down the spending side enough that Social Security's first annual cash deficits would be delayed by a few years. This is an example of how the cash-flow curve of Social Security could be smoothed out by creating a small personal account, slimming the near-term surpluses, and reducing the out-year deficits.

If one wished today to enact a 2 percent account plan, such as the NCRP plan, Social Security would experience only a mild form of transition cost. That 2 percent would still be less than its annual surplus, and so the Social Security program would still have enough each year to pay benefits. However, the size of Social Security's annual surplus comes only partially from surplus tax revenue—and partially from interest credited to it by the federal government. This makes the cash-flow situation a little more complex.

Let's be specific. Take, for example, the NCRP plan. In its first year of enactment, outlays of Social Security would be approximately $409 billion. A 2 percent tax refund into personal accounts would reduce non-interest income of Social Security to roughly $405 billion, and total income to $463 billion. As Social Security would still have enough in total annual income to pay benefits, this 2 percent could be placed in personal accounts without cutting into the Trust Fund. However, the federal government would have to make an immediate payment of $4 billion in interest payments to keep the benefits flowing to individuals.

However, at the same time that the plan introduces this cash-flow challenge in its first year, it would vastly reduce out-year liabilities by changing the method of paying out benefits. Under current law, for example, Social Security would face an annual deficit of $666 billion in the year 2030. Under the NCRP plan, the deficit would be reduced to $145 billion. The government would accept the need to pay a $4 billion payment today, in order to reduce liabilities by more than $500 billion a year by 2030.

From Social Security's perspective, a 2 percent plan can be enacted immediately without any "transition cost" to Social Security. Or, if you do not wish to count interest payments as part of Social Security's revenue flow, we say that there is within Social Security an immediate "transition cost" of $4 billion in the first year.

From the federal government's perspective, however, the transition cost is more significant. Prior to reform, it enjoys access to capital from surplus Social Security taxes. It would have to give that up and also pay an additional $4 billion. In sum, the federal government would face a transition cost in the first year of $63 billion for a 2 percent plan.

With this particular 2 percent plan, transition costs, even from the federal government's perspective, would hover between $50 billion and $100 billion annually during the 2000–2010 period, and then begun to plunge dramatically. By 2015, the paths have definitely crossed, and the transition is effectively over (meaning that the path of the new law is less expensive than the old). The extra interest paid if the transition were wholly financed with new debt would be paid off by 2017. By the 2020s, savings would be on the order of several hundreds of billions per year.

This information is peculiar to the NCRP plan. If a 2 percent account plan did not address benefit growth in the way that the NCRP plan did, then transition costs would be higher and the transition period last longer.

We could, on the other hand, if we were willing to raise effective tax rates, create larger personal accounts by requiring additional contributions and thus not create any new transition issues whatsoever. If one does not believe that payroll taxes are already too high, this is a quite plausible solution to problems of transition. We could fund a 3 percent account, or one of a larger size, simply by requiring a net contribution that is higher.

We can also play with the distribution of transition costs between portions of the government. Senator Gramm's plan, for example, seeks to avoid a cash-flow problem as a consequence of moving 2 percent or 3 percent of the payroll tax into personal accounts, so it taps non–Social Security revenues to reimburse the Trust Fund to that extent. As a consequence, Social Security itself would have literally no new transition problem. It is acquiring assets just as rapidly as before the accounts were established, and no *new* short-term imbalances are created within the Social Security system.

Reimbursing the trust fund in this way displaces the transition problem out of Social Security into other parts of the federal government. The annual transition cost would be the federal government's fiscal challenge, not Social Security's. Social Security's ability to write checks would face no new constraints. In coming decades, we would have the simultaneous tasks of funding the personal accounts and repaying the Trust Fund as previously scheduled. It is during those Trust Fund redemption years that the transition costs of this plan to taxpayers would begin to be felt most acutely, but not because Social Security itself faced a new cash crunch that it doesn't now.

Once one moves beyond 3 percent, it is difficult to create a personal account plan that does not in and of itself involve substantial transition costs, whether viewed from the perspective of the federal government as a whole or narrowly within Social Security. If we put more than $129 billion in the year 2000 into personal accounts, then Social Security simply would not have enough coming in, even after interest payments are made, to pay current benefits, and it will have to start calling in Trust Fund principal to do it. On the other hand, it is no more difficult for the federal government to repay principal than to pay interest. However, Trust Fund assets would be depleted, and some other means would have to be found to fund benefits before it ran out.

None of these matters are prohibitive. Nothing says that we cannot make whatever decisions we choose—whether it is floating new debt, requiring additional contributions to FICA, cutting other spending and using non–Social Security surplus revenue that materializes as a result, or cutting into traditional benefit growth—to fund a transition to personal accounts of whatever size we want. We simply need to recognize and plan for the costs associated with those goals.

ADMINISTRATIVE QUESTIONS

It is not an exaggeration to say that administrative questions are the only plausible objections remaining to the incorporation of a personal-account component within the Social Security system. All of the other standard objections either do not hold water substantively or can be resolved with a minimum of exertion. The only "advantage" that collective investment of the trust fund can seem to have over personal accounts is the relative lack of administrative cost.

This is not an ideological concern. It is real. If the government invests the trust fund in the equities market but does not allocate specific gains to specific investors, the whole system is spared a certain amount of administration and record keeping. Part of the price of creating individual benefit ownership within the system will be how to track and credit that ownership. Those issues must be accounted for.

The arguments in favor of individual ownership over aggregate investment of the trust fund are overpowering. The latter is simply not plausible, for reasons already outlined. The nation will not adopt a socialistic approach (the Senate in 1999 condemned the idea on a 99–0 vote). Either we figure out solutions to the administrative dilemmas or else we start gouging benefits. That's the real choice.

The National Commission on Retirement Policy (NCRP) opted for an administrative structure much like the Thrift Savings Plan for federal employees, for various reasons.

It would be wonderful if we could promise each of millions of Americans that they would receive the sort of service on personal accounts within Social Security that some get from their company pension plans. But the administrative estimates received for such services suggested that any chance that low-income people would have of receiving positive appreciation on small accounts would be lessened by administrative costs in such a structure. Someone who is making $15,000 a year would only put $300 annually into a personal account under a 2 percent plan. If annual administrative costs for such an account approached, say, $30, then the account would need to appreciate by 10 percent annually just for the investor to stay even. That's not going to help anyone.

Moreover, we do not want to create a structure that fundamentally changes the relationship between the employers and the system as a whole. Small employers in particular have a substantial burden when it comes to record keeping and forwarding FICA taxes. Though the FICA taxes on the paychecks are sent throughout the year, only at year's end does the employer reconcile the amount put in on behalf of each employee. In order to minimize new administrative burdens, we would want to work within the structure that is already in place, through a simple and streamlined process.

The Thrift Savings Plan provides a model. A number of investment choices would have been screened by the federal government, and wage-earners would simply do what federal employees do now—check a box indicating the combination of funds in which they wish to invest. For purposes of maximizing investor choice and also to diversify the impact upon the investment market, we should offer as many funds as practicable that meet the tests established by the Personal Investment Account Board. The taxes would be forwarded to SSA just as they are now, and the burden of matching up contributions, balances, and investment choices should fall on the central structure within SSA.

Doing it this way will minimize the total administrative cost. Most of the relevant material is information that SSA is collecting anyway—Social Security numbers, wages, and so forth. We would simply add the additional requirement that the investment funds and specific account contributions and balances be added to the mix.

This does require a few practical concessions. This will not be a system, at least at first, in which individuals can call up today and have their investments shifted to a different fund tomorrow. In the federal employees' Thrift Savings Plan (TSP), employees make their investment choices during a defined open season. These personal investment accounts would establish a similar sort of process. Investors would be given an open season in which to make their choices, and the rest of the year would be used to reconcile the results.

This is critical because a certain amount of lag time will occur between the time that an investor makes a choice and the time when the credits for that appreciation physically appear in the investment account. Under the NCRP approach, a certain amount of guessing will need to be done along the way. The federal government will maintain the total investment of money in the various funds. In many cases, it will be retroactively crediting individuals for their share of the gains from those investments to correspond with the choices made during the year. In order to get the total level of investment right, some sampling will have to be done, a quick culling of the investment choices made by specific individuals. After that is accomplished, the rest of the year can be used to apportion the gains from these investments to each contributor according to the choices made. (Since the NCRP explored these approaches, considerable advances have been made in designing account administration. Pioneering work by Bill Shipman of State Street has likely improved upon these earlier designs, eliminating the need for such "sampling" by holding contributions in one large aggregate fund until they can be properly credited to the individual's investment choice.)

This simplified structure will significantly hold down administrative costs. SSA estimated that it would take approximately 0.105 percent of the funds in each account. Using the centralized structure enables administrative costs to be distributed proportionately among investors, rather than to charge each one a de minimus amount, which would hit low-income investors disproportionately hard.

As the system matures, it may be possible to move to a fancier design, in which more options are offered to the investor. Many have also suggested that when account balances reach a certain size, that they be "rolled over" at the individual's election into accounts much more like IRAs, except with the same withdrawal restrictions placed on individuals who remain in the TSP-style structure. This should indeed be a consideration, but caveats should be raised. Above all, we would need to be sure that this did not begin the process of "leakage" from the Social Security system, that is, withdrawals before retirement age.

Moreover, we should not do this in a way that introduces new employer burdens or new administrative costs. If individuals wish to arrange with the federal government that their sufficiently large balances be rolled over into other accounts, the change should not mandate that employers directly make contributions to these various accounts. Unless we retain the existing relationship between the employer and the system as a whole, we run the risk of making the administrative burdens of reform untenable from the employers' perspective—especially small employers. This and other considerations should be resolved before permitting rollovers out of the TSP structure.

The question also arises of what to do when the employee fails to specify a choice. This qundary can be resolved by simply establishing a "default" or "standard" investment option, essentially a conservative blend of the existing fund choices provided to the employee, mixing some government securities with other instruments so that safety is not achieved at the cost of an unduly poor rate of return.

In sum, administrative questions can be resolved, if we employ a structure that, at first, resembles the TSP system given to federal employees. It will reduce investor options somewhat relative to what ultimately will be possible, but investors would still have far more latitude than they would under alternative types of reforms and would still ultimately have the advantage of individual control and ownership, even if only expressed in limited ways. The gain from such limitations would be a reduction of administrative expenses to the point that they will not significantly impact investment returns. By resolving these administrative questions, we would remove the last significant argument against personal accounts.

WITHDRAWALS

One of the interesting artifacts of the Social Security debate is the great disproportionality between the time spent discussing how to get the money into these accounts and the time spent discussing how the money is to get out.

Creation of personal accounts invariably brings with it the question of how and under what circumstances the individual should be able to get to the money. Clearly, consistency with the basic ethic of the system would require that access be predicated upon the same factors that trigger benefit payments now—that is to say, upon the individual's reaching retirement age or becoming disabled.

But how is reaching retirement age to be determined? There is a philosophical distinction between personal accounts and the money provided through the basic OASDI system. If an individual wants to retire early and take a lower benefit as a result, that's his or her right and no business of ours, providing that this decision does not place a higher tax burden on everyone else. There is no reason to micromanage this decision with regard to the personal account balances.

On the OASDI side, matters are quite different. If an individual wishes to retire early, then everyone else has to pay for that decision. Eligibility ages, unrealistically set, could threaten the whole system's solvency. We must all put our heads together and figure out a balance between what is fair to the individual and what society can afford.

Even within the personal accounts, we can only give carte blanche to a point. We are not likely to shed a semblance of paternalism in the Social Security structure and to say that people can retire at age 25, with benefits that are so small that they amount to nothing, causing them to require public assistance for the rest of their lives. Rather than specify a particular retirement age, NCRP would allow that when individuals have enough to fund a poverty-level benefit (one that is indexed for inflation) they could choose when to access their personal-account balances.

Note that this provision has a couple of critical policy advantages. In the first place, it allows flexibility for different life circumstances. An individual who expects to live only to the age of 60 may wish to make the choice to retire at age 55.

But apart from considerations of personal liberty, there is an ulterior motive in proposing this. Note the incentive to save that it creates. Instead of essentially telling individuals not to save, as we do now, because their Social Security benefits will basically be the same even if they do save, suddenly the prospect of early retirement will rear its head. The more money an individual puts away, the more likely that the total benefit in the personal account can fund a poverty-level benefit by an early retirement age. Individuals would receive the positive consequences of doing the extra saving—as they certainly should. This is a huge improvement over existing incentives, under which individuals have no prospect of earlier access to Social Security benefits no matter how much they put away.

One large question with respect to withdrawals is whether or not an individual should be required to annuitize. It's a temptation, because after all, Social Security has not in the past offered the option of taking a one-time lump-sum benefit. The idea is to provide a steady stream of income for the whole of one's retirement years. Thus, many would say that annuitization of the personal-account balances should be required.

But there are a few problems with this. First, in the case of personal accounts, the annuities market may not provide a good product at that particular time (part of this concern can be alleviated by having the government also offer a basic default annuitization). But timing can be critical. A person who happens to retire in a "down year" for a market and is forced to annuitize will have to live for the rest of his or her life with the consequence of that ill-timed requirement.

Some additional flexibility could be built into the options. One option would be that an individual could only retire when there is enough money into the account either to provide for an inflation-indexed annuity at the poverty level or above or to provide for poverty-level benefit withdrawals of lump sum amounts based on life-expectancy tables. Those who find it to be a bad year to annuitize can just withdraw an amount of cash based on the life expectancy tables. At some point it will become desirable to annuitize, and individuals can do so then.

Markets frequently outperform our expectations, and such a system would allow for the development of some interesting products. Consider the following.

An individual is 60 years old and wishes to retire. He notes that at age 65, his Social Security benefit will be able to fund a benefit that itself is approximately 90 percent of the poverty level. He buys a new kind of annuity with a portion of the personal account balance. It pays him 100 percent of the poverty level, indexed for inflation, from age 60 to age 65, and then 10 percent of the poverty level from that point onward. At age 65, he starts collecting his Social Security benefit, at 90 percent of poverty level. He meets the poverty-level annuitization requirement the whole way and has a significant chunk of the personal account balance left over after the annuity purchase, with the rest of his life to decide how and when to withdraw it and spend it.

Such products will proliferate if millions of Americans are waiting to purchase them, if we allow for this. Individuals would have new flexibility as to when they retire. Further, they will simultaneously be protected against poverty and against overly prescriptive annuity requirements that do not take differing life circumstances into account.

NOTE

1. In a draft of their book *The Real Deal* (New Haven, Conn.: Yale University Press, 1999), Sylvester Schieber and John Shoven conduct a quantitative study of these issues. First, they show that even if one assumes that 15 percent of an individual's retirement income is pegged to the historic fluctuations in the stock market, correcting these charts for current-law contribution rates leaves even those with the poorest returns with retirement income greater than that produced by today's Social Security system. Schieber and Shoven show the proportion of each individual's benefits that would come from personal accounts under a variety of proposals. For the average worker, a 2 percent personal account proposal would leave significantly greater than half of his or her retirement income still provided by the defined benefit system. Given that such a worker, by the time he or she reaches their 60s, is viewed by Schieber and Shoven as unlikely to place more than 30–40 percent of his or her investment in equities, a total investment of 15 percent of one's retirement savings in the stock market is a more reasonable guess than that reflected in charts that show the results of placing all of one's Social Security contributions in the stock market.

16

Putting It All Together: How a Reformed System Can Work

How, then, do we construct a workable plan based on everything we know to this point? The answers can be reached by thinking about it systematically.

The first thing we can do is to see what happens when we attempt a traditional fix that includes no personal accounts. We have already seen in a previous chapter what the effects of this choice would be from the beneficiaries' perspective. Whether it was effected through tax increases or benefit cuts, the treatment of beneficiaries would worsen markedly. How we get from that problem to a solution, however, can be facilitated by looking at the specific ramifications of the "traditional" option upon the operations of the program.

Recall that Social Security reform must meet another fundamental test. Social Security must be sustainable over the long term. In practice, this means that outlay obligations cannot ultimately grow faster than the economy's ability to keep pace. The tax-as-you-must, "paygo" traditional solution fails this test.

Let us, therefore, first examine the route created by benefit growth restraints alone—not because this is ultimately the preferred solution, but because it will help illuminate where we need to go.

Under the trustees' 1997 estimates used by the NCRP to explore this approach, current law would see the Social Security Trust Fund maximize in the year 2018 (since revised to 2021 in 1999 estimates), in nominal dollars. But in terms of how many years' benefits the program could pay based on assets in the Trust Fund, the program's solvency would have been in decline since 2011, when there were enough assets in the Trust Fund to pay 2.65 years worth of benefits (Trust Fund ratio = 265).

Were we simply to balance the Social Security system through benefit cuts, annual surpluses in the short term would get much larger. Under 1997 estimates, the Trust Fund would continue to grow, relative to benefit growth, through the year 2023, in which year there would be enough money in the fund to pay 3.96 years' worth of benefits (ratio=396). From that point, the Trust Fund ratio would gradually shrink over time, to 323 in the year 2059.

This Trust Fund ratio is one key criterion of success, because at the end of the valuation period, it must be rising. We haven't developed a sustainable system if that Trust Fund ratio is still plummeting at the end of the valuation period. If that is the case, then one year after enactment of the plan, it's likely that the program won't be deemed solvent.

Our illustrative benefit-cut example just barely makes the grade. It hits its lowest point in the year 2059 and then starts gradually moving up again. But in order to get to this point, we have had to create a perverse situation. Even when the Trust Fund ratio has dropped, in nominal terms, generally, the Trust Fund has continued to grow.

In order to get to the finish line, we have had to restrict benefit growth enough to make it through the baby boomer retirement period. We have had to create surpluses large enough to survive the worst strains. Those surpluses would need to add up to a huge accumulated trust fund, which means huge annual interest claims. Thus, each year that we have to dip into a bit of that interest in order to meet benefit payments, additional interest is still being accrued by the fund.

In fact, accrual must continue, because if the Trust Fund weren't still growing in absolute terms, it wouldn't have enough in it to make it through the baby boomers. But if the Fund never stops growing, the federal government never really pays it back. Instead of cresting at $4 trillion or $5 trillion, it just keeps swelling. In the package that we're examining here, it approaches $50 trillion by the year 2070.

Forget the policy problem for a moment. Imagine the political problem. Do you think that the United States would stand for that? It's a political issue now, when the federal government has allegedly "raided" the Trust Fund to the tune of hundreds of billions of dollars. Here, in effect, we'd be saying to the United States that we were going to let the Trust Fund build into the tens of trillions—and by the way, folks, the federal government has no intention of ever paying that back. That won't fly.

The following tables make the situation clear. First, look at Table 16.1. Looks fairly ridiculous, doesn't it? But that's what happens if you try to balance the system through traditional means.[1]

We need to come up with something that works a little bit better. At the very least, we need to advance-fund to the tune of approximately 2 percent

Table 16.1
Trust Fund Balances under Current Law versus Benefit Adjustment Option*
(in trillions)

| Year | Current Law: | | W/Benefit Adjustments (1997 Estimates): | |
	TF Balance	TF Ratio[†]	TF Balance	TF Ratio
2000	$0.907	189	$0.907	189
2010	$2.14	264	$2.45	312
2020	$2.83	198	$5.36	394
2030	-$0.812	-4 (Insolvent)	$8.70	368
2040	(Insolvent)		$12.30	331
2050	(Insolvent)		$18.80	327
2060	(Insolvent)		$28.90	324
2070	(Insolvent)		$49.90	372

*Cash flow projections calculated by Social Security actuaries, using 1997 trustees' estimates.

[†]TF ratio is a percentage determining the number of years that the Trust Fund could pay benefits; a TF Ratio of 189 means that the Trust Fund could pay benefits for 1.89 years.

of the payroll tax base. Updated 1998 estimates that were available to the NCRP to examine this option will be cited here.

The point of presenting Table 16.2 is not that 2 percent is necessarily the optimal size for personal accounts. The point is that 2 percent is about the minimum level of advance funding that the system will need to get the cash flow right. One can make the personal accounts bigger if one wishes, by mandating or permitting additional voluntary contributions or by using additional borrowing or general revenues.

The 2 percent personal-account package is a representative package. One could instead design a plan that provided an additional cushion, so that the Trust Fund Ratio would not dip down as low. In any case, there is a fine line to walk. Even under this carve-out proposal, the Trust Fund accumulations become enormously large.

Sometimes it is said that one reason to oppose personal accounts is that they will cut into the size of the Social Security Trust Fund. We should have advance-funded personal accounts not *despite* this fact, but in part *because* of it. Putting the brakes on the accumulation of these enormous multitrillion dollar liabilities is one of the most significant policy reasons to advance-fund. Even with the carve out, we end up with debt to the Trust Fund of more than $11 trillion. Without it, we're pushing $50 trillion. The

Table 16.2
Trust Fund Balances under Current Law versus 2 Percent "Carve-out"*
(in trillions)

| Year | Current Law (1998 estimates): | | With 2% Personal Account Carve-Out: | |
	TF Balance	TF Ratio[†]	TF Balance	TF Ratio
2000	$0.978	209	$0.912	208
2010	$2.49	319	$1.44	204
2020	$3.78	263	$2.19	186
2030	$0.981	61	$2.65	142
2040	(Insolvent)		$2.76	96
2050	(Insolvent)		$3.75	83
2060	(Insolvent)		$5.38	76
2070	(Insolvent)		$11.50	105

*Cash flow projections calculated by Social Security actuaries, using 1998 trustees' estimates.

[†]TF ratio is percentage determining the number of years that the Trust Fund could pay benefits; a TF Ratio of 189 means that the Trust Fund could pay benefits for 1.89 years.

twenty-first century will continue to redefine what we think of as big numbers, but the public won't likely stand for *that* much being owed by the federal government to this program (nor should they).

A 2 percent carve-out account provides about as good a balance as one could hope for in the annual cash flow of the Social Security program. A look at the annual outlay and revenue levels that remain after one does a 2 percent carve-out makes the improvement evident (see Table 16.3).

What a 2 percent personal account does is to bring the revenues and the outlays of the system into closer proximity over time, because over the long run the shift of liabilities off the government ledger holds down outlays in the out-years. Not only are the financing gaps reduced to a manageable size, they eventually disappear altogether before the end of the 75-year valuation window. They never get close to depleting the Trust Fund.

Table 16.3 makes it evident what advance funding is all about. In the year 2000, for example, the federal government would be asked to make good on $9 billion of what it owes to Social Security. That's a small price to pay to knock $539 billion off the $684 billion bill that would otherwise be presented to taxpayers in 2030.

Table 16.3
Revenue and Outlay Projections under Current Law versus NCRP Plan* (in trillions)

| Year | Current Law (1998 Estimates): | | | With 2% Carve-Out in NCRP Plan: | | |
	Revenues	Outlays	Gap	Revenues	Outlays	Gap
2000	$0.468	$0.413	+$0.055	$0.406	$0.415	-$0.009
2005	$0.585	$0.533	+$0.052	$0.506	$0.525	-$0.019
2010	$0.756	$0.724	+$0.032	$0.654	$0.676	-$0.022
2015	$0.965	$1.010	-$0.049	$0.845	$0.882	-$0.037
2020	$1.220	$1.430	-$0.213	$1.080	$1.130	-$0.058
2025	$1.520	$1.960	-$0.433	$1.350	$1.460	-$0.107
2030	$1.920	$2.600	-$0.684	$1.710	$1.850	-$0.145
2035	(Insolvent)			$2.150	$2.320	-$0.166
2040	(Insolvent)			$2.710	$2.850	-$0.146
2045	(Insolvent)			$3.390	$3.490	-$0.095
2050	(Insolvent)			$4.240	$4.330	-$0.091

*Cash flow projections calculated by Social Security actuaries, using 1998 trustees' estimates.

It happens that a 2 percent carve-out results in a very neat and workable cash flow. A greater degree of advance funding would result in a greater amount of savings employed to finance higher benefit levels in the long run. Some will argue for accounts larger than 2 percent, because larger accounts would likely produce higher benefit levels once the transition is fully over. But 2 percent hits the fiscal targets fairly easily.

Now let us return to the basic changes to the traditional benefit formulas that ought to be considered in *any* plan, before proceeding to the trade-offs involved specifically in creating personal accounts.

First of all, the calculation of the Consumer Price Index (CPI) ought to be an accurate one. It is difficult enough to get the system into financial balance without worsening the problem with technical errors. In the particular case of CPI, substantial methodological problems make the problems of Social Security much worse than they need be. In 1996, a commission established by the Senate Finance Committee reported on the methodological problems with CPI, estimating that the degree of overstatement had been approximately 1.3 percent in the past and would likely be 1.1 percent in the future.

This is not the place to debate the precise degree of problems in the Consumer Price Index, except to say that some of the flaws identified by the

Commission receive more broad support among economists than others. The Bureau of Labor Statistics (BLS) has already announced the incorporation of some changes, estimating that these effects would likely reduce future CPI measurements by as much as 0.2 percent. How much further would be accomplished by methodological reforms that enjoy broad support is anyone's guess.

The author of a Social Security reform proposal must decide how much in the way of future CPI reforms to assume. Senator Moynihan assumed a 1.0 percent change in CPI. We at the Retirement Policy Commission assumed 0.5 percent, before the BLS announced subsequent changes. In the legislative implementation of the NCRP proposal, sponsors thus estimated the effects of future reforms to be 0.5 percent minus the effects of changes already accomplished by the BLS.

The Social Security program must also be reformed to give society a fighting chance to slow the decline of the worker-to-collector ratio, which carries the seeds of economic stagnation. The program does not function to reflect the reality that today's 60-year-olds are, more than in any previous time, vital national resources that we should be tapping, not shoving out the door. At one time it may have made policy sense to prod such individuals to leave the labor market. Now we need them more than ever—their experience, their wisdom, and their productivity.

The ratio of normal retirement benefits to early retirement benefits should be made more steep, to reward those who continue to work and to pay payroll taxes between early and normal retirement age. Currently the benefit for an individual who retires three years early is about 80 percent of the normal benefit. It should be closer to 75 percent, to reflect the value of extra payroll taxes contributed. If people keep working past normal retirement age, they should get not an 8 percent increase per year, but a full 10 percent. Only then will an individual's decision to keep working benefit that individual in the way that it benefits the rest of us.

The earnings limit for *all* seniors should also be eliminated as indeed it was in 2000 for those above normal retirement age. Many seniors suffer a loss in their Social Security benefits if they do the productive thing, going out to earn additional income. It is counterproductive to penalize them.

The benefit computation period should be lengthened to reflect the longer working lives that Americans should expect. Currently, only an individual's top 35 earnings years are counted when computing the benefit. This does not adequately reward those who extend their working lives. One highly beneficial provision would be to do away with the practice of simply averaging top earnings years when calculating the benefit formula. Employing an averaging formula decreases benefits whenever the computation period is extended.

For example, the average earnings drop when one's 36th highest earnings year is included in the calculation, or the 37th. If one keeps working part-time, so that the new earnings do not appear in the top earnings years, no new benefits accrue as a result. This is a bad message to those in their mid-60s who may be thinking about working part-time. If we include all years of earnings in the numerator of the AIME formula, then individuals' benefits will continue to go up slightly for every year that they work, no matter how small the amount earned and no matter whether the denominator includes 35, 36, or even 40 years.

It is impractical to attempt to avoid dealing with the question of the eligibility ages for the Social Security program. Consider the following information: In 1940, life expectancy at birth was 61.4 years for American men and 65.7 for women. Life expectancy at age 65 was another 11.9 years for men and 13.4 years for women. Today, life expectancy at birth is 73.5 years for men and 79.6 years for women. At age 65, life expectancy is another 15.8 years for men and 19.3 years for women. In 2020, the trustees project, life expectancy at birth will be 75.7 years for men and 81.1 years for women.

You decide whether current law can work with the age of eligibility never going up. In 1940, the average man didn't even see the age of 65. Bear in mind that current projections include the conservative rate of assumptions of the trustees with respect to how society will age. The Census Bureau believes that life expectancy will continue to rise more sharply.

Our choices are basically whether we will gradually raise the eligibility age or hold it where it is and simply cut everyone's benefits. This is a bit like being in a boat filling up with water. We can come up with various means of shoveling the water out more efficiently—by improving investment returns, raising taxes, or cutting benefits—but as long as the water keeps pouring in faster and faster, all of those measures are only temporary fixes. The crux of the problem is the intake of water, which is reflected in the ratio of those collecting benefits to those paying them. That can't be ameliorated without addressing the age of eligibility.

One important aspect of this particular policy option is that it can be phased in very gradually. No one is talking about raising the eligibility age for your uncle Pete who is looking to retire in the next five years (at least not beyond the level that would occur under current law). This option could be phased in a few months at a time and spread out over the next century, to allow plenty of time for individual preparation.

The eligibility age needs to be evaluated on a number of levels:

1. The age of actual access to retirement benefits, which under a personal-account system could be at whatever age the individual chooses

2. The age of access to early retirement benefits. It should be raised more slowly than the normal retirement age, if at all, to have minimal impact on those who feel the need to retire early to accept a reduced benefit.

3. The normal retirement age, which is an integral part of figuring benefit levels, but which does not necessarily reflect when people retire. Only a small fraction of people actually wait until normal retirement age to collect full Social Security

old-age benefits—fewer than a quarter of them. No one should be misled by the gradual drift upward in the normal retirement age to believe that most individuals will begin to collect benefits at that time. The normal retirement age (NRA) simply determines the degree of actuarial adjustment that will be made in the benefits of the vast majority who retire early.

A point should be made about the normal retirement age. Most individuals retiring under the NCRP plan would get more benefits than under a traditional fix if they retired at age 67, even *with* the increase in the eligibility age that the plan contains. Including the personal accounts increases their benefits more than the actuarial adjustment resulting from raising the eligibility age would reduce it.

This increase is reflected in tables generated by the Social Security actuaries. They say that if the current law system is given a 2.2 percent tax increase, it can provide steady average-wage-earners a replacement rate of 42.1, if they are born in 1963 or later and retire at age 67. If that 2.2 percent is applied to the NCRP plan instead, it would give a replacement rate of 45.1 to individuals born in 1963, 48.2 if born in 1968, 53.7 if born in 1973, and on up from there. If, by contrast, taxes aren't raised, then the plan would provide replacement rates of 36.3, 36.8, and 39.1, but current law could only buy those individuals rates of 35.0, 32.6, and 31.7. Either way, the plan beats current law at the same age.[2] The age of eligibility can go up and people can still get higher benefits at a given age—providing that personal accounts are included.

Some other obvious reforms to Social Security suggest themselves. In 1993, when the tax base of Social Security benefits was increased from 50 percent of received benefits to 85 percent (above the income thresholds), the extra money was not kept within Social Security but was given over to support Medicare. This violates the principle that Social Security and Medicare are supposed to be self-financing programs. Because Medicare is in even more dire fiscal straits, this money should not be restored precipitously or before actions are also taken to restore Medicare to sound fiscal footing. The NCRP advocated gradually restoring this money during the years 2010–2019.

Moreover, procedures should be set in place so that Social Security no longer faces periodic financing crises of the sort that it is now poised to face. If events take a turn for the worse, so that Social Security is again on a course toward insolvency, even after we enact reforms, Congress should no longer have the option of waiting until the crisis and then imposing draconian measures upon taxpayers and beneficiaries. A "fail-safe" mechanism should be added to Social Security law that requires Congress and the president to act whenever there is a projection of long-term insolvency.

Now we come to questions of distributional impact. We have to look at the benefits that result from the preceding proposals for change and evaluate whether they would provide fair treatment of retirees. Two obvious problems leap out of that data. One is the vastly different treatment of one-earner couples and two-earner couples, the latter clearly still subsidizing the benefits of the former to a tremendous degree. Of course, Social Security should remain friendly to the traditional one-earner family. However, the size of the existing transfers of money from two-earner households to one-earner households should be reduced, even though they won't be eliminated. It is simply unfair to require those households in which both spouses must work to subsidize the benefits of those in which one can afford to stay home, to the extent provided for under the current system.

That being said, we should not reduce benefits for those one-earner households who need the money, forcing lower-income people into the decision to send Mom (or Dad) back to work when that person would otherwise choose to remain at home giving their children constant and critical attention.

This principle works hand in glove with another important one, which is that we must review how the changes suggested would affect the benefit levels for low-income individuals, so that the safety net against poverty is not weakened. Both this and the desire to protect low-income one-earner couples specifically argue for establishing new elements in the program to increase its progressivity.

One way to do this is to scale back the benefits paid directly to non-working spouses and then to build those benefits back in for many such couples by creating a new minimum benefit provision that ensures that the benefits of the primary insured individual (the breadwinner) will never go below the poverty line if that individual works a full working life. (The nonworking spouse benefit is calculated as a percentage of the insured individual's benefit. It can remain just as large by decreasing the percentage used to make the calculation, while increasing the benefit on which it is based.)

The NCRP studied various ways of doing this before hitting upon its preferred answer. A flat poverty-protection guarantee was clearly not best, because it would wreak havoc with work incentives. If the individual became eligible for full poverty protection after, say, 20 years of work and if this represented a substantial increase in benefits relative to the traditional computation, then that worker would have great incentives to avoid paying payroll taxes whether by hiding income or simply by not working, over the next several years, because the poverty-protection benefit would not get any bigger as he or she continued to work.

The NCRP proposed to vary the basic poverty protection benefit in proportion to the number of years of covered earnings. In practice, this worked out in a fairly neat way. For steady low-wage individuals who are assumed to work a full 40-year career, a guaranteed benefit of 100 percent of the poverty level would represent an increase in benefits. But many individuals do not work the full 40 years. If individuals worked only 25 years, their poverty protection would be somewhat less—in this case, only 70 percent of the poverty level. But the traditionally computed benefit for a low-wage worker who worked only 25 years would also be lower; and thus, for this individual, too, the new poverty protection would come into effect and increase the promised benefits. The provision successfully builds in additional progressivity and also retains the work incentives created by the other provisions.

When you add all of the preceding provisions together, you get a package that is actuarially sound.

However, it's still a package that doesn't really work. At the beginning of this section we reviewed the cash-flow problems of such a package. It's actuarially solvent, but it requires the buildup of absurd levels of Trust Fund reserves in order to survive the retirement of the baby boomers.

Worse yet, if this is done, the system doesn't treat beneficiaries adequately well. As indicated in previous tables, restricting choices to traditional means of balancing the system does not produce a good deal in the end. The average single male born in 1997 would get an internal rate of return of 0.70 percent out of this system (a single female, 1.16 percent; a one-earner couple, 3.00 percent; an average two-earner couple, 1.38 percent).

In sum, this traditional solution passes some important tests. It achieves actuarial solvency, is affordable without perpetual tax increases, and is thus sustainable. It also fails to achieve a stable and plausible cash flow for the system, and it fails to achieve the best possible rate of return for beneficiaries.

Now we come to why and how to incorporate personal accounts. People often ask why one would "worsen" the actuarial solvency picture by incorporating personal accounts. It is because the alternatives don't work. As we saw, the traditional fix fails to treat beneficiaries adequately or to produce a reasonable cash flow. As government control and ownership of trust fund investment in the private market is a nonstarter within our political system, we must incorporate advance-funded personal accounts.

One clear point should not be missed. Every tough decision taken—on retirement age, on CPI, on everything else—was necessary to balance the system by traditional means. Those decisions are unrelated to the question of whether or not to include personal accounts. They exist to the same degree with or without personal accounts. Creating personal accounts has nothing to do with whether choices on retirement age and CPI are necessary. Those choices are needed to balance the *traditional* OASDI system. Implying that personal accounts cause those tough choices is a disservice to the U.S. public.

With respect to the packages thus far described, we can create the personal accounts simply by making the choice to gradually phase over some of the traditional liabilities, expressed through the bend points in the traditional Social Security formula, to lower levels that reflect their replacement with benefits from the personal accounts. Exactly how this derivation can be made will be explained in the next chapter. Here, suffice it to say that one way the NCRP found was to gradually phase down the upper two Social Security bend points, the 32 percent and 15 percent bend points, by a factor of 2 percent per year, from 2003 through 2022.

This does *not* mean that Social Security beneficiaries see their benefits reduced by 2 percent each year. It means that for each *new* class of Social Security beneficiaries, the top two factors in their benefit formula will be 2 percent lower than for the preceding classes. In the first year of the phase-in, for example, the 90 percent, 32 percent, and 15 percent factors under current law would become 90 percent, 31.36 percent, and 14.7 percent. However, total benefits would still increase because wage-indexing would include more income in the 90 percent factor and because each subsequent class has also had an additional year of buildup in their personal accounts. This gradual and progressive formula turns out to allow the liabilities to phase over from unfunded benefits to personal assets in a workable way that treats beneficiaries comparably.

Some additional points about the formula: Only the top two bend points are affected, so that the impact on the traditional Social Security benefit formula is highly progressive. Any new risk associated with the personal account investments is not visited upon low-income earners, because the lowest bend point remains as it is. It turns out that the minimum benefit-protection provision is so strong that it fully protects low-income people from the impact of the benefit changes, thus making the personal accounts purely bonus income for the steady low-wage earner. Also, this additional progressivity means that another provision, gradually raising the number of benefit computation years from 35 to 40, can be added. It's needed to hit the solvency target, and it won't cause a regressive effect, if combined with the package's other features.

In the end, such a proposal would operate with the stable cash flow that has been outlined and, moreover, would give beneficiaries a much better deal than a traditional fix alone.

Here are some examples. A 30-year-old earning $20,000, under the traditional Social Security system today, would look forward to a monthly Social Security benefit of $3,841. Under this proposal, that would be increased to $5,532.[3]

For a 45-year-old making $40,000, Social Security would currently promise a benefit equal to $2,680. This program would increase that to $3,098.

According to the Social Security actuaries, projections still are similarly improved even if less favorable examples are chosen. Take the average single male born in 1997 who would only get a 70 percent[4] real rate of return if the system were fixed by traditional means. Under this proposal, using the intermediate rates of return assumed by the actuaries, the rate of return would be more than doubled, to 1.45 percent. *That's* why you decrease the traditional OASDI benefit liabilities and put that money into personal accounts. It's because individual beneficiaries get back much more than they give up in the trade-off than if we simply kept trying to make the old system work, which it really can't anyway. For a single female, the increase is from 1.16 percent to 1.72 percent (for a one-earner couple, 3.00 percent to 3.15 percent; a two-earner couple, 1.38 percent to 1.90 percent).

These assume conservative rates of return from the accounts. If we assume a 50/50 blend between bonds and equities, the results, respectively, are 1.84 percent, 2.06 percent, 3.40 percent, and 2.24 percent, extremely significant increases all the way around.

One of the disingenuous things done to reform proposals is to compare them to the benefit promises of current law, even though current law cannot pay those benefits. Basically the attack says: We don't care about rates of return, we care about benefit levels. We care about replacement rates. And we think you should compare benefits not with what current law can buy, but what it would promise to buy if only the money were there.

Even under these circumstances and even looking at a constant age of retirement (which penalizes our new system because of the steeper actuarial adjustment table, decreasing early eligibility benefits relative to normal retirement benefits), the new system is still clearly better. Current law under 1998 estimates would require a 2.2 percent payroll tax increase just to make it solvent, to say nothing of the general taxes required to redeem the trust fund. If we took that 2.2 percent in taxes and added it to our new system, to get an equal comparison of what each system could buy, with an equivalent increase in taxes of 2.2 percent over the 75-year period, we would the results found in Table 15.2. (Figures for birth years not shown in this table favor the NCRP plan by an even greater extent, for example, a 61.0 percent to 42.1 percent advantage in replacement rates for average earners born in 1978.)

We should all "play fair" in comparing plans. If one defends what current law is promising, which includes claiming credit for an additional 2.2 percent of payroll taxes, then let's see what the NCRP plan could do with that 2.2 percent. Of course current law looks better if it gets an extra 2.2 percent in tax revenue, and the reform plan doesn't. But current law doesn't have that 2.2 percent in it. What current law can actually buy would have the replacement rate go down to 28 percent for birth year 1998. This plan beats that, easily.

The plan outlined is not pain free. Because low-income retirees are protected throughout by additional bulwarks against poverty, the lion's share of the transition costs fall on the middle- to high-income baby boomers. On the other hand, these cohorts would best be able to take advantage of the allowance for additional voluntary contributions. If someone is going to foot the bill for transition, it should be those who can best afford it, compensated by the opportunity to build up personal-account income and recoup their rate of return.

The plan is not perfect, nor is it devised so that it cannot be the basis for compromise. In 1999, it became apparent that most politicians would not support the same fiscal standards employed in creating this package, such as avoiding all tax increases. Perhaps, in the end, the United States will be willing to pay a lot more to support benefits for seniors. But this plan works, and it faces up to all the costs of financing benefits. There is as of yet no distinctly better solution on the table.

NOTES

1. Senator Moynihan's proposal did avoid this problem by cutting the payroll tax rate in the near term and raising it in the future, a politically unpopular but substantively viable solution.

2. Memo from Social Security actuaries, April 27, 1998.

3. Financial planner developed by Ernst and Young for NAM.

4. This and subsequent rates of return given in this chapter come from the Social Security actuaries' projections made May 14, 1998. They are being updated to reflect further modifications to plan made upon legislative introduction.

17

Reaching Agreement with the NCRP

On May 19, 1998, the National Commission on Retirement Policy (NCRP) released a package of recommendations to shore up Social Security and private retirement savings, which the commission members had approved the previous week by a unanimous 24-to-0 vote. The unanimity of the Commission was one of willful teamwork rather than internal conviction. Twenty-four commission members retained, to the end, starkly different individual opinions as to the best way to maximize retirement income in the twenty-first century. And yet they voted, unanimously, to forward a report of recommendations. Why was this so?

Credit belongs to no one individual. Staff of the congressional and private-sector cochairs labored into the night in the last several weeks before the final commission vote, negotiating dozens of amendments to the package proposed by the chairmen. Up to the moment of the vote, it was not known with certainty whether the package would receive the two-thirds majority agreed upon, after Congressman Stenholm's suggestion, to be the standard for approval. Rumors of disenchanted commission members circulated. The possibility of a messy and protracted final voting session haunted the staff.

In the markup room, however, a different dynamic entirely played itself out. Gene Steuerle set a helpful tone early on when, during debate over his first amendment, he noted that it lacked a majority of votes and withdrew it. Other commission members began to follow his example. Where amendments could be accepted by consensus, they were. Where they proved divisive or controversial, the sponsors agreed to withdraw them.

The cochairs—Senator Judd Gregg, Senator John Breaux, Congressman Jim Kolbe, Congressman Charles Stenholm, Paine Webber CEO Don Marron, and former Glaxo CEO Charles Sanders—seized the moment. They sensed where consensus was possible and drove the commission quickly in that direction. They sensed when an amendment would fail and nudged sponsors toward withdrawal. Usually, little nudging was necessary, and commission members withdrew of their own accord.

It need not have worked out this way. When the commission was constituted, not only was there no agreement about policy, there was no agreement about the rules—no agreement even on whether or not the commission should seek agreement at all. Some commissioners believed that the NCRP should simply report a list of options to Congress, and not make its policy preferences known.

Worse still, the atmosphere of trust and cooperation in which we operated on that May morning was a long time in developing. More than one commission member had previously threatened to resign, whether because they felt that the commission was being steered too aggressively in a particular direction or because they thought that the commission was rudderless, heading toward no constructive conclusion.

Those who read only of the NCRP product through the distorted prism of press accounts and as mistranslated by various lobbying groups underrate the commission's achievement and underappreciate the thoroughness with which its recommendations were developed. It seems appropriate, therefore, to rewind the tape somewhat, and to show only a bit of how the commission turned from a fractious, confused group, squabbling over procedure, to a unified panel, putting aside disputes over details to carry a concerted and united message to the nation.

The commission was composed of 24 members. Anchoring the commission were the six cochairs—Gregg, Breaux, Kolbe, Stenholm, Marron, and Sanders. CSIS attempted to assemble legislators who were close enough to the political center to work together constructively and also to balance the temperaments of those involved.

My boss has a reputation for being a cerebral legislator, a "workhorse" who understands the specific details of policy. John Breaux has an unerring sense of the art of the possible—and a gift for turning the substantive policy details into a final result that everyone present can live with.

The constitution of the commission was created with considerable care by CSIS. Altogether, the commission included 24 members from a diversity of backgrounds and ideologies, all of them leading experts on retirement income policy.

The commission appeared star-crossed from the beginning. The congressional cochairs were forced by Hill emergencies to miss some early meetings that other commission members had traveled some distance to attend.

Also handicapping the commission was the sheer number of members dealing with a complex and intractable problem. Early in the process, the commission set the limited goal of releasing an interim report that would "define the problem," before proceeding to recommendations.

This proved to be well nigh impossible, given the lack of established procedures. One of the commission's earliest meetings involved drafting a one-page letter to the president. It was a lesson in the perils of "drafting by committee." Several of the commission's members took turns objecting to this or that adjective. Ultimately the text was so watered down that it was judged meaningless by those who had first drafted it.

The congressional cochairs did not wish to spend an exorbitant amount of time "defining the problem," which had been done quite enough already. They saw the commission as the potential antidote to earlier commissions, which had divided irreparably among themselves. My boss Senator Gregg in particular felt that the NCRP would be a public failure if we gave rise to press reports about yet another commission failing to reach agreement. In his view, any long period spent "defining the problem" simply signaled an incapacity to act.

Incapacity to act seemed to be a fair characterization of the Commission's condition during those first few months. Some viewed CSIS's first draft of an interim report as too alarmist and insisted upon adding moderating phrases in several places. Others felt that the text, once edited in this way, had lost all meaning. Only after substantial negotiation of specific wording was an interim report finally issued.

Clearly, the cochairs needed to be more active and involved in steering the commission to agreement. But it was not so simple. Our bosses' time was precious. We could not drag them away from other important meetings and insist that they attend multihour sessions of dubious utility. Only if we provided a framework for fruitful labor could we succeed in bringing their stature to bear in forging a solution.

The cochairs would ultimately be empowered to put together a chairman's mark (an amendable document) of recommendations. Amendments could be offered to the mark by members of the commission, but if we continued to subject the assembly of the mark itself to a deliberative process involving 24 members, we would continue expeditiously on the path to nowhere.

We also needed to break down the tasks that the commission was taking on. The commission had been lurching uncontrollably from legislative policy discussions pertinent to Social Security, to private retirement savings, and then, veering away from policy altogether, into the realm of public education efforts. We proposed to divide the work of the commission into subgroups, one to develop recommendations for Social Security, one for private retirement savings, and one for outreach and education efforts.

Defining the tasks of the commission and of the working groups was not so simple. Medicare was viewed by many seniors essentially as an income security issue. Some members felt that the commission could not make comprehensive recommendations about retirement income policy while remaining silent on the issue of Medicare, the costs of which continue to grow even faster than Social Security and the disposition of which would have enormous repercussions for the adequacy of other retirement income.

A majority of the commission prevailed to have Medicare excluded from the commission's purview. The reason was simple practicality. Commission members were only too aware that several previous commissions had been unable to offer unified recommendations on Social Security alone. Merely by extending the reach of the commission's recommendations into other areas of retirement income, the commission had made its own task more ambitious than that faced by similar groups.

Further, Senator Breaux chaired the President's Commission on the Future of Medicare. It was nonsensical to expect the senator to simultaneously work through another commission, in which his Medicare work could be either duplicated or challenged.

Another troublesome question involved the Disability Insurance (DI) program of Social Security. As was the case with Medicare, the commission did not feel equipped to take on the complex issue of Disability Insurance reform. However, separating the retirement and disability aspects of policy was no easy task. It was the opinion of many experts that a reform program would not be credible if it sought to balance the Old-Age and Survivors' Insurance (OASI) program alone. The year 2034 insolvency date commonly cited for Social Security referred to the combined operation of the Old-Age and Survivors and Disability Insurance programs (OASDI), and the body politic clearly preferred to process information in terms of their combined financial status.

The difficulty arose from the fact that the DI program was in much more serious financial distress than the OASI program. In order to balance OASDI together, we would need to "over-balance" OASI and leave much of DI's solvency problem, when considered apart, in place. If we were to recommend changes that also affected DI, we would be accused of cutting DI benefits. If we specified explicitly that our changes in the OASI benefit structure did not apply to DI, then we would create huge incentive problems, arising from the different benefit formulas for the two programs. There would exist powerful incentives for every able-bodied person to apply for higher DI benefits, and our reforms wouldn't work.

Instead, the commission drafted language noting that it had not chosen to take on DI. Upon legislative introduction, the cochairs proposed a mechanism through which a Disability Council would make recommendations to shore up the program before any other changes could impact it.

Reaching Agreement with the NCRP

The commission's recommendations actually go so far as to essentially subsidize DI through the OASI program. Those who object to our solution and who believe that OASI and DI should be separately considered, could propose a relaxation of some of the changes in OASI, but they would need to propose *additional* austerity measures on the DI side. In other words, if they don't accept the idea of making DI recommendations through the Disability Council, they would need to come up explicitly with far more severe restraints on DI benefits than would occur under the NCRP plan.

Senator Gregg chaired the first meeting of the Social Security working group in his own conference room. He began by stating his determination to hear and to consider the views of each member of the working group, and the first meeting began by allowing members to outline their own highest-priority substantive considerations.

Everyone agreed on certain basic principles that needed to be met in any substantive reform of Social Security—that the program should be made actuarially sound and that this should be done so as to maximize the income received from the program by retirees. A number of the working group expressed the view that reform should be accomplished in a way that did not leave a "cliff effect" (see chapter 14, "The Top Ten Tricks").

More than one commission member expressed the view that the problem should be viewed not narrowly from within Social Security, but from a larger perspective—from the point of view of the federal government as a whole and as Social Security interrelated with other elements of national saving.

Some commission members argued the case that Social Security had simply overpromised. Pointing to the coming departure of millions of baby boomers from the workforce simultaneously, they noted that this was the equivalent of a surge in several percentage points in national unemployment rates, with all of the attendant effects that such a development would have on the future economy.

David Walker came up with the idea to "smoke out" some of the commission members on specific reform questions, to force members to move from general descriptions of the problem toward expressing their views on specific options. He developed a questionnaire that was circulated to the commission, asking members how they felt about various proposals for reform of Social Security.

It was Gene Steuerle who urged the commission to approach the problem by advocating policy first, and only fitting the numbers thereafter. Gene felt that the commission should be asked to debate the merits of each policy option, apart from how it impacted actuarial solvency, and then once the commission agreed on what policies it felt the Social Security system should advance, the staff should be instructed to generate the data and to get the numbers to work out.

Needless to say, David's and Gene's contributions to the process were each indispensable to the outcome. David's questionnaire did more than anything else to get the Commission moving. Likewise, Gene's professional and personal approach to the project helped to keep the discussions elevated and positive at all times.

Of particular delicacy was the question of personal accounts. The working group was acutely aware that the larger commission had not expressed, and would not express, a philosophical preference for or against personal accounts until the very end. It was absolutely imperative that the working group generate the data about various approaches impartially, without taking a position on personal accounts pro or con.

Without violating the confidence of any particular commission members with regard to their thinking on individual policy options, it is possible to provide some meaningful commentary on the commission's early deliberations.

First, the commission committed itself to objective scoring. Commission members disagreed among themselves as to what were realistic economic and demographic assumptions. However, they generally agreed upon the need for a truce on the point, a truce that was effected by an agreement to use the projections of the Social Security actuaries. While each of us may have individually challenged projections made by anyone, including the actuaries, it was felt that the actuaries established an objective standard, and a tough one to meet.

Second, the commission was committed to coming to its solutions without gimmicks. This meant no "cliff effect," as described earlier. There was to be no use of tricks to estimate the problem away, as in some of the "free-lunch" asset-shuffle proposals.

Third, the commission agreed to operate in an atmosphere that was cognizant of fiscal pressures outside the Social Security system—including effects on the overall federal budget, recognizing the reality of Medicare inflation, and interactions with other forms of retirement savings. The Social Security working group could not cut itself off from the parallel group on retirement savings. Repeatedly during these meetings, a point would be made and followed up with, "Of course, this depends on what options are generated by the other working group." These last two considerations almost completely ruled out a Ball-style approach to the problem.

Commission members repeatedly voiced the view that the whole point of the exercise was to create a system that worked well for beneficiaries. It needed to work for them during the time that they were wage-earners and during the time that they were retired. Some objected even to beginning to evaluate the various reform options without first having a context, a sense of how every option worked into a package that could be evaluated for its impact on beneficiaries.

This gave us something of a "chicken and egg" problem. On the one hand, we couldn't know how a package would treat beneficiaries unless we knew what was in it; on the other, commission members were reluctant to select among options for action unless they saw how it all added up for beneficiaries. It was in part this "chicken and egg" problem that David Walker's questionnaire was designed to circumvent, by generating data that could then be used to answer the questions that commission members were posing.

We worked with SSA's Deputy Chief Actuary Steve Goss, to "score" various options that the commission would consider. We prepared for the commission a list of every conceivable option, alongside two estimates: one for how much each option would impact Social Security's 75-year actuarial solvency, and one for how much each option would affect solvency in the 75th year. This latter number was necessary to find whether there would be a "cliff effect" in even an actuarially solvent package.

Commission members were asked for their views on a variety of policy questions pertinent to the traditional Social Security system, before committing to a viewpoint on funded accounts or on other broad conceptual questions. It soon became apparent that the fundamental philosophical viewpoints could be gleaned from the way that commission members responded to the solicitation of their views on specific policy questions.

Consensus developed relatively early on a number of points. The first was the Consumer Price Index. Commission members, as a rule, accepted the view that the traditional Social Security system should continue to provide a defined benefit indexed accurately for inflation. It was clear that commission members accepted a growing consensus among economists that the Consumer Price Index inaccurately modeled inflation in several respects.

On the retirement age, disagreement was more apparent than real. Commission members recognized the relationship between lengthening life expectancy and Social Security's financing difficulties. The commission still displayed ample divisions on what to do about it. Some commission members, familiar with employment trends, had concerns about delaying the onset of full Social Security benefits. Others simply didn't like the philosophy of delaying the age of full eligibility, summoning up images of individuals in their early 60s, perhaps exhausted by manual labor, who feel unable to go on with work. The majority, however, noted that in some way, the government must establish a more realistic policy regarding the fraction of one's expected lifetime that one is entitled to collect benefits.

At this stage the commission members were not prepared to make a final decision about further increases in the normal age of eligibility. The early eligibility age, as we shall see, remained a subject of debate and controversy to the end of the commission's deliberations.

The idea of means-testing benefits did not appeal to the majority of the commission for a number of reasons. While many of them felt that the program could and should be made more progressive, they did not want this to be done in a way that penalized individuals for the extra saving and investment that they did outside of the Social Security system. To do so would run counter to the mission of stimulating savings through private pensions and individual savings, while shoring up Social Security.

David Walker accepted the job of collating and assembling representative packages on the basis of the survey responses given by commission members. Four packages eventually emerged. One was a traditional fix that retained the defined benefit character of the system, and the others all contained personal accounts of one form or another—one with personal accounts "carved out" of the existing payroll tax, one with the personal accounts as a supplemental "add-on" to the current payroll tax rate, and one that was both a "carve-out" and an "add-on" that resulted in a larger personal account.

For the most part, we had felt comfortable with the views expressed by a majority of the experts on the commission, but one item came up that I knew would produce firm opposition from my boss. It involved increasing the taxation of Social Security benefits, so that they would be taxed like other pension income. Two problems with it would provoke my boss's concern. First, it was a straightforward tax increase, and he had hoped to keep the packages free of tax increases. Second, it would affect current beneficiaries. I knew that he felt that we should endeavor wherever possible to limit the burdens of change to those who had the time to plan and adjust, which did not include current retirees.

I approached the staff of the other congressional chairs and found that their members felt the same way that my boss did. It was one of several instances in which the unanimity of the cochairs worked to guide the commission. We had a brief discussion, and each of the congressional staff spoke up as to why it would be a problem. There was some sentiment, very fleeting, at first, that the provision should be retained because it had been one of the provisions that had received the most support among commission members. But the members wasted no time, ego, or emotional energy on defending it once the congressional viewpoint was clear. It was dropped.

Gene Steuerle in particular was an advocate of having Social Security do a bit more of the work currently done by SSI, in keeping the elderly out of poverty. He strongly advocated the inclusion of a minimum benefit provision as an absolute shield against impoverishment.

Designing such a provision was far from trivial. There was the question of what would trigger it. Social Security benefits are earned after an individual has been covered for only 10 years, but many commission members felt that 10 years of work was far too short to qualify for a significant expansion of benefits.

Then there was the problem of work incentives. Suppose that after working 20 years, an individual were entitled to a benefit, through the minimum benefit provision, much higher than what would otherwise have been earned. This would be a powerful incentive to stop paying payroll taxes. Once the individual was entitled to a significant benefit and if additional contributions did not increase the benefit which the individual would receive, why should the individual continue to report wage income? Compliance problems could arise.

Thus, we eventually came up with a minimum benefit provision that gradually increased with the number of years worked, reaching a full 100 percent of poverty if the individual had a full working life of 40 years.

This provision is one of the less understood provisions in our legislation. The only one that confuses people more is the provision that includes all years of earnings in the numerator of the AIME, which increases benefits instead of decreasing them, an assumption that detractors seem to make. But even the minimum benefit provision, which is purely an added benefit, an additional plum, for low-income individuals, has come under attack. Some have apparently understood it to mean that we would reduce people's benefit levels to that amount. Just the opposite is true. It is something that can only send benefit levels up, not down.

Others apparently interpreted the name "minimum benefit" to imply some kind of flat benefit, as in the Schieber-Weaver proposal. Again, wrong. It is just an additional protection, a way of bumping up benefits that would otherwise leave an individual in poverty. Many have also asked, "Where are you going to get the money to pay for that?" as if the cost of the provision hadn't been included in the projections we ran for Social Security outlays.

When I was interviewed by the producer of a Fred Friendly television program on Social Security and was explaining how the minimum benefit provision worked as a function of years of covered earnings, she said, "It sounds very anti-woman." I queried as to what she meant. She said that because it fluctuated according to years worked and since women worked fewer years, it would discriminate against them. Apparently she didn't realize that current law provides benefits in proportion to years worked, too, and to wage histories to boot, which are *both* lower for women. This provision thus created a disproportionate *gain* for women relative to the current system, because the minimum benefit would be guaranteed even for those with lower wages. The Social Security actuaries ultimately provided us with a finding that this provision *alone* would increase the PIA formula amount for 10 percent of men and 50 percent of women.

It inevitably fell on us as staff to work through the details of balancing the packages. In the case of the traditional defined-benefit solution, this was easily enough done. We originally produced a package that "over-shot" the solvency target slightly, and thus we were able to discuss how to amend the package so as to meet the solvency goal in the way that treated beneficiaries the best. Estelle James and Gene Steuerle were most helpful in identifying the provision expanding the denominator in the AIME formula from 35 to 40 years as the one that should be eliminated. This particular provision had a troublesome impact upon low-income beneficiaries and potentially on women specifically.

For the purpose of abbreviating the narrative, I am glossing over the true complexity of this work. Social Security reform packages cannot be thrown together via the oft-styled "Chinese menu" approach, in which provisions are simply selected that the planner hopes will add up to actuarial solvency. Provisions combine with one another in unique ways to affect benefit levels, to have differential impact upon demographic groups and various birth cohorts, and also to have interactive effects that are hard to predict. Two provisions that may in isolation appear to help solve the cash-flow problems considerably might not achieve much more in combination than when considered separately because of a high degree of overlap between their effects.

Getting the formulas to work in a proper way was tough. The basic problem was that most proposals either didn't phase down the liabilities on the traditional side fast enough or reduced traditional benefit growth too much in the long run. The essential problem was getting through the baby boomers' retirement. Suppose, for example, that we simply indexed bend-point growth for inflation instead of for wage growth. At first, this produces little savings. It takes a while for a small change in indexing to compound significantly. If two indexing factors are a half-percent apart, the effects of the change won't be apparent to any large extent until many years later and might be greater than intended at the end of the valuation period.

Various means had been suggested for phasing down the bend-point factors—in the Kerrey-Simpson legislation, in Nick Smith's bill, and in the Gramlich plan. It was the Gramlich plan that provided the answer. The Gramlich plan formula changes seem arbitrary at first. Why simply multiply the existing bend-point factors by a certain amount each year for several years and then ultimately stop? When you first look at it, it appears to be a formula simply hit upon to get to a solvency target, and nothing more.

We didn't use the exact Gramlich formula, but we were eventually convinced that its form was the key to the answer—a steady multiplicative phase-down of the bend-point factors. This was a realistic solution to the reality of an inevitable transition period. We ultimately worked out with the actuaries a formula that would phase down the top two bend points by a factor of 0.98 per year, spread out over 20 years. There are straightforward policy reasons why this works.

Reaching Agreement with the NCRP

From a cash flow perspective, it must be done that fast because that is the only way that the savings on the Defined Benefit (DB) side materialize fast enough to get through the baby-boomer retirement period. After that point, it's not needed, as the system basically stabilizes from that point on.

From the perspective of beneficiaries, what is happening is as follows. Each subsequent birth cohort gets an additional year of accumulations from their personal accounts, and thus a portion of their traditional benefit is scaled back to reflect that extra year's accumulations—not scaled back in actual terms, but only relative to the growth that would otherwise happen. The bend points are still indexed upward for wage growth, and the 90 percent bend-point factor is not reduced at all. In nominal dollars the basic benefit has continued to grow, but in real terms it has been reduced a little, though offset by the extra year's growth in the personal account through additional contributions and appreciation.

What happens because of this temporary 20-year transition period is that benefit levels stay flatter from year to year for those birth cohorts in the transition and then, at the end of the game, when transition is complete, future benefit levels begin to rise again markedly. That is basically what should be expected in creating a reformed system. Once the reforms are fully implemented, future generations will fare much better.

Interestingly, the 2030 Center, a group trying to position itself as the statist counterweight to the bipartisan youth advocacy group Third Millennium, alleged afterwards that the NCRP plan would hurt Gen-Xers. This could not be more wrong. Generation-Xers, and those coming after them, are precisely the ones who fare best. In fact, one would have a difficult time constructing a 2 percent personal account plan in which Generation-Xers *didn't* do better.

The actuaries' data refute the charge. What's a typical Gen-Xer? Let's take someone born in 1973. Under our plan, the Social Security actuaries told us,[1] the average single male's internal rate of return would increase from 0.68 percent under a traditional fix to 1.17 percent (let alone eliminate more than two-thirds of the cost of the general taxes that individual would face in buying down a Trust Fund). For single females, the change would be from 1.18 percent to 1.52 percent; for two-earner couples, from 1.35 percent to 1.69 percent. All the figures are low because they are dragged down by the low rates of return in the traditional system. Even a 2 percent account bumps them up considerably, without considering either the savings in general taxes or the opportunity to make voluntary contributions.

One could write down everything that the 2030 Center has correctly said about Social Security on a piece of letter-sized paper, in large capital letters, and still have enough room left over to make a functional paper airplane. But when the Fred Friendly Seminar wanted to construct a panel to discuss Social Security issues on public television, they glossed over many centrist experts to invite the 2030 Center to send a representative. This is somewhat akin to inviting Lyndon LaRouche to the presidential candidates' debates, in the interest of giving equal time.

But back to the bend-point formula. It had to be constructed properly, to conclude the transition period before the baby-boomer retirements reached their worst extremity, and to phase in the changes gradually, to offset the appreciation in the personal accounts.

When it finally worked out, it was almost a thing of aesthetic beauty. The formula that we developed worked smoothly, achieving exactly the desired relationship between revenues and outlays, and preserved an equitable distribution of benefits from the Social Security system. With this last piece of the puzzle in place, we were ready to present the packages to the commission and to determine the philosophical direction in which it wished to go.

The question of administration of personal accounts now became very important. A number of commission members felt that a higher burden of proof should be placed on a personal-account plan. It was not sufficient, in their view, to simply put a plan out there that included personal accounts, that advertised great results for beneficiaries and taxpayers alike, but that had not answered the fundamental questions of administrative feasibility. Dallas Salisbury of the Employee Benefits Research Institute (EBRI) was particularly concerned about this.

The commission devoted several hearings and meetings to administrative questions. As a consequence of these meetings, it ultimately came around to the view that a structure should be created that resembled the Thrift Savings Plan (TSP) provided to federal employees. There were several reasons. One was a desire to work within what was already taking place and not to fundamentally change the relationship between employers and the Social Security system. We did not want a structure in which employers would be required to track and to forward investment contributions by employees to any number of places. The administration and record-keeping should be done by the federal government, and we worked with the Social Security actuaries to receive estimates as to the administrative expenses that would be required to run a TSP-style system.

These administrative expenses were pivotal considerations in the end. We were dealing with small personal accounts at this point, and we were receiving estimates of administrative costs for privately administered personal accounts on the order of $30 a head. That would have swallowed up the appreciation received by low-income individuals. We still had a distributional analysis to run, and we were doing back-of-the-envelope calculations to try to anticipate its results. It became very apparent that we needed a structure that minimized administrative costs and allowed them to be distributed throughout the system proportionately.

Rate of return was another area in which we made it hard on ourselves. We had substantial disagreements within the commission as to what rates of return to assume from the personal accounts. Many felt that it was plausible to assume a 50:50 blend of equities and bonds. But others felt just as strongly that low-income people would be unlikely to receive more than the bond rate of return. In the end, we agreed to use the conservative assumptions that the actuaries employed for the Advisory Council and to subtract administrative costs from that. Our "high" return would be the 50:50 blend, the low return would be the bond rate, and the intermediate return would be a blended portfolio that compromised between the two. Analysts could consult whichever numbers they chose, but the commission would not make any representations about gaudy rates of return from the accounts. As a consequence, all of our projections likely undercount the amount of money that beneficiaries would get from our proposed system.

Once the commission started to settle in the direction of a TSP-style system, many fears were allayed. Commission members who had been skeptical of personal accounts on administrative grounds now began to consider them realistic, and thus they moved to a position from which they would ultimately have to select the personal-account plan, based on the superior income that it would provide to retirees.

The final numbers clearly showed that there was only one best choice, the personal-account 2 percent "carve-out" plan. Clearly it was superior to a traditional fix, both in terms of the treatment of beneficiaries and the improved cash flow for the system as a whole. And this was the case even before taking into account the opportunity that it provided for increased savings contributions and the characteristic feature that it added, of personal ownership of some Social Security benefits.

What further clinched it was comparison with the results of the "add-on" plans. Particularly in the case of low-income people, the "add-on" plan, requiring the additional 2 percent increase, did not treat beneficiaries better than our 2 percent "carve-out." In fact, replacement rates for the two plans were in many cases absolutely identical.

Why was this? It was because we had succeeded beyond expectations in building poverty protections into the plans. Thus, the personal account contributions "carved out" in our preferred plan did not decrease the benefit levels paid to low-income recipients, who were held completely harmless from the effects of the bend-point changes. Low-income people would get the same benefit from the "carve-out" as from the "add-on" plan. Given that reality, there was absolutely no point in advocating an effective tax increase.

We had done it. We had created a plan that not only avoided tax increases and achieved solvency but also fully maintained the safety net within Social Security. Now the chairs had to sell their conclusion to the rest of the commission. This would not be easy.

We began the time-honored process of vote-counting. The staff of the cochairs met more frequently than ever, talking to various members of the commission, trying to sort out what their views were, what in the end they would support. There were a few whom we counted at every stage as being "no" votes. But there did seem to be developing a core of supporters for our favored approach. It seemed quite likely that we could get to a majority, simply by convincing 7 of the remaining 18 commission members. But two-thirds would be tough.

We scheduled a "walk-through" of the chairs' recommendations that proved to be a pleasant surprise. Praise for the package came from unexpected quarters on the commission, after we had prepared our bosses to deal with every conceivable complaint.

We had agreed upon a procedure by which commission members could offer amendments to the chairman's mark and agreed also that we would work through these amendments beforehand to the extent possible, incorporate the uncontroversial, and vote on the remaining contentious amendments at the final markup. Despite the goodwill that prevailed at the previous meeting, amendments poured in, literally by the dozens. Staff spent many a day and many a late night poring through the amendments, categorizing them, discussing which the chairs could support, letting commission members know which would likely be the subject of contested votes, and negotiating frantically.

Nothing would have been achievable at this stage were it not for the helpful attitude displayed by each commission member—*every* one. We were placing panicked phone calls to member after member to discuss disposal of amendments; each time, the commission member reacted in a way that was helpful to the process.

The following is a sampling of the process to which the package was subjected.

One subject of early contention was the early eligibility age. The commission was starkly divided on this point. Some felt that the normal retirement age should be gradually phased up, but that the early retirement age should be left permanently at 62. The feeling on the part of those who wanted it to stay at age 62 was that it should be individuals' prerogative to retire early if they wished, providing a true actuarial adjustment was made to their benefit levels, which would simply be made as low as was necessary to deal with the growing gap between 62 and the normal retirement age.

The arguments on the other side were cogent and varied. Some felt that a philosophical distinction was to be drawn between choosing to retire early on one's personal account and having the right to gain early access to tax-payer-financed retirement benefits and that the early retirement opportunity should be provided through the personal account option, not by requiring taxpayers to pay more. Others felt that allowing very early retirement at a vastly reduced benefit could not be made a truly actuarially neutral choice, because if given the opportunity, many individuals would retire too early, outlive their savings, and be left in poverty, which would require additional SSI payments, so the taxpayers would wind up paying for those decisions anyway. Still others felt that it was important that the overall package send a signal that the nation needed to rethink its attitude towards aging and not hold out the unrealistic prospect that individuals could expect to retire at 62 on public support.

Underlying all of these philosophical arguments were some complex mathematics. One argument advanced for leaving the early retirement age where it was, was that this ought to be doable as an actuarially neutral proposition that did not harm the overall package. The idea of an actuarial adjustment was that individuals who retired early would still get the same amount of benefits as if they had lived a full life and thus, in sum, it should be a matter of indifference to the system whether individuals retired early or not.

In practice, however, it made a big difference. Suppose individuals retire early and collect a lower benefit. For a period of time those individuals are collecting benefits when they otherwise would not, had they waited until normal retirement age. When does it even out from the system's perspective? Only when that individual gets to his projected life expectancy. By the time that matters have evened out in the case of that particular individual, several others have already taken early retirement; as a whole, the system is still losing money.

It never really evens out. In theory, it should even out if you look out toward an infinity of time, but we didn't have an infinity of time. The solvency of the whole system depended not so much on how things looked by the end of 75 years—which was more easily achieved—but whether the system could make it through the baby boomers' retirement. The early retirement option would need to pay for itself, not by the end of 75 years, but really within the first 25 or 30.

Once the benefit adjustments required to achieve this were fully understood, support for the early eligibility age option collapsed, and commission members began to recognize the funded personal accounts as the place to provide for early retirement.

Equally vexatious was the question of the implementation of the personal-account system. It would be wrong to say that each commissioner had fully abandoned concerns about the administration of personal accounts, and some advocated a slow phase-in of their implementation in order to provide time to work out any bugs. One idea was simply to establish the accounts themselves, but not to create the different investment options until one year had passed. The cochairs opposed this, feeling that it was important to allow at least three investment options from the get-go. Other proposals were put forward to delay the implementation of the personal accounts until a few years after the enactment of the plan into law, to defuse expectations that the accounts would be instantly working and able to accept contributions immediately upon being legislated.

Though these were valid concerns, there were tremendous problems with these amendments. The basic problem was that the whole plan was quite intricate and balanced. One can't simply, as Judd Gregg said at one meeting, "pull on one string and expect the whole structure to hold together." The calculations as to what would work and what wouldn't, from the beneficiaries' perspective, all depended on the enactment dates included in the plan.

Ultimately we passed language specifying that the accounts should not be started up until it was practicable to do so, which would involve a gap of at least one year after enactment. This was a good solution, not only because it bowed to reality, but also because it did not undo the good things in the plan. If 1999 was truly to be the year of legislation, then the accounts would start in the year 2000 at the earliest, which was our projection date.

Estelle James was one of the commission's best analysts, and she retained many concerns about the plan. Her main critique of the proposal was that it was too lean fiscally. We had made the choices that we made in order to create a better system without raising taxes along the way. She felt that this put too much of a squeeze on the benefit levels paid to the baby boomers. To the explanation that this was an inevitable consequence of effecting the transition without a tax increase, her reply was that this was why she was willing, at least in the short term, to effect a contribution increase, to be able to offer higher benefits to the baby boomers than what we were planning.

Note the difference between this mode of argument and what one usually hears. She felt that society should pay for higher additional costs in the transition period (commission member Beth Kobliner agreed with her), and she recognized that additional taxes or contributions, beyond current law, would be required to get us there. This is a far cry from what is peddled by many others, who assert that desired benefit levels can be attained without paying a cost. James would likely have been happier with a larger personal account, one that had a bit of an additional required contribution on top of the amount "carved out" from the existing payroll tax. As will be seen, subsequent work by the cochairs made use of many of her insights.

The skills of the cochairs in presiding and the goodwill of the commission members in pulling together were what made the final markup work, not any special acumen on the part of the staff. The morning was long and tedious, but the commission never bogged down.

After a few hours disposing of amendments, the chairs of the National Commission of Retirement Policy asked for a show of hands as to whether commission members would vote for a package that, unlike so many other attempts, represented a united series of recommendations as to how this greatest of all public policy challenges would be met.

All 24 hands went up.

The legislative package approved unanimously by the National Commission on Retirement Policy was quickly perceived as the nation's best bipartisan chance at a Social Security solution. By the end of the summer, it had attracted more cosponsors than any other Social Security solvency plan introduced in the Senate.

NOTE

1. Memo from Social Security actuaries, April 27, 1998.

18

Slings and Arrows

A few weeks after the NCRP completed its proposal, I was surprised to receive a heads-up from our press secretary, who said that a story was running in *USA Today* suggesting that our plan would cut benefits by more than 20 percent. I knew that this couldn't be right, for our numbers from the Social Security actuaries showed that our plan would increase benefits for most beneficiaries relative to a traditional solution. After placing a few frantic phone calls, I learned what had happened.

What had happened was that the Congressional Research Service (CRS), a nonpartisan research and analysis arm of the Congress, had been approached by the staff of a member of Congress who opposed personal accounts. What was requested was that CRS do a study that only looked at part of our proposal and ignored the other pieces. CRS, conscious of the importance of maintaining its position of neutrality in policy studies, balked. It did not seem proper to score only half of a bill. The staff persisted, indicating that whether CRS felt that the analysis was objective or complete or not, Congress was the employer of CRS and it was simply to do as it was told.

CRS completed the analysis as instructed, but it was conscious of the potential impropriety of what it had been asked to do. Accordingly, it took the unusual step of highlighting, in italics, a caveat on the front page of the report, which read as follows:

As specified by the requester, the analysis is confined to the potential reductions in Social Security benefits prescribed by various provisions of the three reform packages (the NCRP plan, the Moynihan plan, and the Ball plan). Accordingly, the memorandum does not examine the impact of the changes in payroll taxes included in the packages, the benefits or annuities that may result from the "personal savings" components of the packages, nor in the case of S. 1792 and the NCRP plan, the elimination of the Social Security earnings test. Analysis of all of these would be necessary to gauge the full effects of the three plans on the national economy and individual retirement income.[1]

In other words, the report was not a gauge of the level of retirement income benefits that each of the plans would provide, nor did it take into account the tax levels required in each case to finance those benefits. Aside from bearing no relevance to benefits received and to revenues paid, the report accurately delivered what was asked for.

CRS knew the problems with the request that had been made and responded favorably to our call for a report on the *entirety* of our plan. Any sponsor of legislation can call up CRS and ask for an objective analysis of its effects. CRS worked extremely hard to get it done and ultimately released a comprehensive, detailed report on December 3, 1998. Subsequent to the corrected report's release, I received calls from some congressional staff wanting to know why CRS had invested the more than 100-page report with such detail. The answer was that CRS was determined to do a complete job and to be absolutely certain that this time around, there would be no selective withholding of information.

It was disillusioning in the extreme that the press—in this case, *USA Today*—would be so easily hoodwinked by the attempt to cook the books with the first report. The newspaper had no axe to grind against personal-account proposals. They simply trusted the information they were given. The staff who asked for the analysis immediately fed it to the press for the purpose of generating unfavorable publicity against reform proposals. CRS had been led to believe that the information was being developed for a congressional hearing, and instead it was blindsided by being brought into a partisan PR blitz.

Just for the sake of thoroughness, let's cover a few of the elements that undermined the validity of that first CRS study—again, through no fault of CRS. The details of the plan given to CRS were not correct or up to date. It was asked to work from data provided by the Social Security actuaries that corresponded to an interim version of the plan developed by the retirement policy commission. Since those tables were generated, substantial revisions had been made to the plan that would affect every number in the CRS report.

CRS was instructed to score a personal-account reform plan without the income from the personal accounts. It is difficult to adequately express the reasons that such an instruction is nonsensical. If no benefits were to come to individuals through the personal accounts, there would have been no reason to phase in the plan's restructuring of defined benefits into other benefit forms.

To illustrate: if I told you that, instead of promising to pay you $20 in 30 years from now, I was going to put $10 in an account for you today, you wouldn't consider that to be a cut in my promise to you. Not only would you wind up with more money in the end simply by putting it in the bank, but you would have something, now, that you own. No suggestion was made to eliminate the $20 promise except in combination with a more reliable method of financing the same or larger benefit through the immediate account deposit (apart from the benefit changes already deemed necessary to balance the system without personal accounts).

Not only did the requesters insist that CRS eliminate the income from the personal accounts, they also instructed CRS to assume a generous rate of return if *government* invested the money in exactly the same way. In other words, exactly the same investments could be made by two different approaches, but CRS was told to count the return if government controlled the investment, but to assume that the money disappeared if individuals did.

CRS was also not to consider the fact that the benefit levels for each scenario would require vastly different levels of taxation. For example, it was instructed to compare benefit levels under the Moynihan-Kerrey and NCRP plans to "current law," even though there existed no financing mechanism under current law to provide those benefits, and to each other even though the tax levels under each plan would be vastly different.

Moreover, CRS was also told to assume that something could be had for nothing, that the Ball plan could magically produce higher returns without changing revenues or outlays and with no costs to the economy.

But of course, there was no intention here to study the realities of the subject. CRS knew it, which is why it hesitated and issued their unusual caveat. The staff who requested the study knew that, too—which is why they immediately ran to the press with the story:

When the CRS study was released, demagogues around the capital had a field day. The 2030 Center did a press release that gleefully claimed that the CRS study had shown the shortcomings of personal accounts. Shortly thereafter, the member of Congress whose staff was behind the study circulated a breathtaking letter. Its title was "CRS Study Finds that Social Security Privatization Plans Would Lead to Massive Cuts in Social Security Benefits." The letter stated:

Such steep cuts are inevitable under partial or full privatization proposals. The more payroll dollars that are diverted into private retirement accounts, the steeper the benefit cuts retirees will face. The reason for this is simple: privatization requires huge transition and administrative costs:

This is not correct; in fact, such claims were not even alluded to in the CRS study. Transition costs were not an issue that CRS took up. Personal-account proposals *do* have transition issues, but the CRS study had absolutely nothing to do with this. The analysis assumed no transition problems whatsoever.

It also presumed *nothing* in the way of administrative costs. In fact, it couldn't begin to estimate the effects of administrative costs upon benefits, as it wasn't allowed to count those benefits to begin with. What CRS thinks about the administrative costs of personal accounts we don't yet know, since they weren't even asked the question.

The "Dear Colleague" letter was particularly absurd in claiming that "cuts in Social Security benefits" were caused by any "privatization" in Senator Moynihan's plan. Senator Moynihan had developed a proposal to balance the traditional Social Security system and created a system of personal accounts as a voluntary addition to the system.

What was particularly painful was to see the CRS study picked up and given credibility, not by journalists who didn't know better, but by the Center for Budget and Policy Priorities. The center, with its outstanding director Robert Greenstein, is an important voice not only in the Social Security debate but also in all aspects of budgetary policy. Though we often disagree on policy choices (the center being a liberal-leaning think tank), it is known to us for the intellectual integrity of its work.

It was thus especially unfortunate that the Center on Budget and Policy Priorities chose to release a paper in which it essentially echoed the CRS conclusions—at the very time that CRS was working on the corrected study. It alerted us to the fact that the paper was coming out, and we informed it that CRS was about to complete work on the complete analysis. We let it know that the numbers in the CRS report did not even reflect the fully updated plan. Determined to press on with the paper, the center published it on September 8. It was a great disappointment that the center rushed to press rather than waiting on CRS's corrections.

The Center on Budget and Policy Priorities is clearly committed to playing a constructive and truthful role in the Social Security debate, albeit from a perspective different from ours. Subsequent reports from the Center, despite voicing opposition to our proposal, accepted the responsibility of understanding and reporting what tried to do.

But this first report repeated a familiar litany of dubious allegations, that our proposal would "cut benefits" in a way that the Ball plan would not. It asked, "What accounts for the CRS finding that the Ball plan would reduce the defined Social Security benefits much less than the other two plans while doing as well in closing the 75-year balance?" They then answer their own question by saying that the individual accounts "reduce" the trust fund, whereas the Ball plan does not. But as we have noted, the ability to finance benefits has absolutely nothing to do with whether we inflate the Trust Fund to its projected maximum worth of $4.46 trillion. Contributions of trillions in new benefit financing would at least as effectively generate savings through funded accounts.

The first CRS study found higher benefits through Ball because they couldn't count the money from our personal accounts and because they were forced to assume that the Ball plan provided a higher investment return cost-free. Had CRS done for Ball what was done to us—assume that money invested in the private market simply vanished and then measured the remaining benefits provided under Ball—then Ball would have been tagged with benefit cuts, too.

The center's paper contains the sort of graph and the sort of argument that drive one to distraction. The paper notes that the actuarial deficit of Social Security is 2.19 percent. It then notes that by putting an additional two percentage points in personal accounts, the actuarial deficit is increased to 4.01 percent. Thus, they imply, personal accounts are counterproductive because they make the job that much harder to accomplish.

As reviewed in a previous chapter, NCRP chose a personal account plan not out of a pointless desire to make the job harder, but because of the income it would restore to beneficiaries relative to the benefit cuts required to balance the traditional system within existing tax rates.

CRS's data revealed the same conclusion. On December 3, it released its full and comprehensive study. What it found was that under conservative rate-of-return assumptions, the Ball plan led to insolvency, whereas the NCRP plan and the Moynihan/Kerrey plan were actuarially sound. They also found that if aggressive rates of return were assumed, the Ball plan would balance, but our plan would provide higher benefits for most beneficiaries in the long run.

Another aspect of the center's analysis was troubling. Essentially, the Ball plan's aim is to spare individuals the changes from current-law benefits that would be necessary if we simply balanced the system without having the government change its investment practices. This can be accomplished more straightforwardly by raising taxes; economically, the effect is essentially the same. If government is going to guarantee the same benefit, it will collect the money from the private economy one way or the other. The center should not have accepted the notion that the Ball plan solves Social Security's financing problems essentially out of thin air, without recognizing that, to the extent that it ducks the choices on the benefit side, it extracts that revenue from private savings income through a sort of indirect taxation. There is no mention in the center's paper of the costs placed on the private economy in doing so.

If one accepts this logic, why stop with what Ball proposed? Why not take the *entire* trust fund, put it in an even more aggressive growth fund, see how much additional money it generates, and then endorse that plan as allowing us to raise Social Security benefits maybe 20 percent, 30 percent, or 40 percent? That's essentially the type of analysis that this logic endorses. If we're going to accept such arguments as meaningful, then let's do it right—let's get the trust fund into a hedge fund somewhere and legislate a *doubling* of Social Security benefits. Of course, we know better than to think that would work.

Subsequent to the release of our plan, an episode occurred that was all too symptomatic of the tactics employed in a spirit of public opportunism. The National Committee to Preserve Social Security and Medicare and the 2030 Center commissioned Peter Hart Associates to conduct a "push poll." Respondents were essentially told that personal-account plans would mean all sorts of horrors and that a plan without personal accounts would mean none of them, and then were asked which plan they favored. You can probably guess the result.

This is how Peter Hart described our plan to poll respondents.[2]

The plan's four main features were described as follows:

1. Place about one-sixth of employed people's Social Security taxes in private investment accounts to be used for income at retirement.
2. Reduce by thirty percent the average guaranteed monthly benefit for future retirees, who will also have the income from the private accounts.
3. Raise the eligibility age for receiving Social Security benefits to 70.
4. Reduce the annual cost-of-living increase for all retirees below the rate of inflation, a reduction of about one-fourth in the current cost-of-living adjustment.

Then they proudly announce the finding, that "By a 10-point margin, 52 percent to 42 percent, the young people reject the NCRP plan." Poll respondents were asked to compare it to one in which the wage cap was lifted, the full cost-of-living allowance (COLA) given, and the Social Security Trust Fund was invested by the government in the equities market.

Do you notice a few inaccuracies in here? And a few key omissions? Let's begin with the description of the NCRP plan itself. The description of the personal accounts is not so bad, but what about "reducing benefits by 30 percent?" The plan actually increased the benefits paid to low-income retirees, even *without* counting the benefits from the personal accounts. Neatly missing from this little description is the fact that the total benefit amount under the proposal would in general be higher, not lower, than under a traditional plan.

Now let's review their description of the retirement age provision. If you were given that question, stating that we were raising "the eligibility age to 70," would you suspect that you could still retire up to five years early? Would you know, on the basis of that question, that you could retire at any age you chose, depending on your personal-account balance? Would you have any idea *when* the normal retirement age—which fewer than one-quarter of retirees wait for anyway—would reach 70? The answer, under the plan, is 2037, by the way. The question makes it sound as though people immediately couldn't get Social Security benefits until they were 70 years old.

Slings and Arrows

The silliest statement is the last: "Reduce the cost-of-living increase for all retirees, below the rate of inflation, a reduction of about one-fourth in the current cost-of-living adjustment." There is no way to twist this statement into anything resembling the truth. No one advocated reducing the cost-of-living allowance (COLA) "below the rate of inflation." NCRP made an estimate of how much future reforms in CPI would affect the COLA and wrote that assumption into the proposal. It should be noted that the plan that Peter Hart's poll compared it to would do the same thing, although it made a different estimate of the total effect of these changes (0.21 percent as opposed to 0.5 percent). No one said anything, ever, in the construction of the plan to suggest that the COLA be reduced below inflation.

Further, where did they come up with the phase "a reduction of about one-fourth in the cost-of-living adjustment?" Let's see. The plan was written to take into account recently announced changes by BLS in the CPI, on the order of 0.2 percent of CPI. That means that, at most, further changes in CPI as a consequence of the proposal would be on the order of 0.3 percent. One-quarter of the current cost-of-living adjustment? That's one-quarter only if we assume current projections of inflation are about 1.2 percent. What economist believes that?

Note, also, that anything in the plan that increases benefits is neatly omitted. Repeal of the earnings limit? Not mentioned. A new poverty-protection benefit guarantee for low-income earners? No. An increase in the delayed retirement credit? Not here. Crediting an individual for all years worked? Missed it.

The real intellectual pickpocketing, however, comes in the implication that the choices pertaining to retirement age or CPI were somehow related to the creation of personal accounts. The Hart poll's materials play this up: "The results suggest that it is not the private accounts per se that trouble young Americans about the NCRP plan, but rather the changes that it would make in benefits." The problem is that the changes that the poll identifies as the "poison pill" for personal accounts—such as raising the eligibility ages—are not caused by the creation of personal accounts.

If Peter Hart Associates had read the NCRP report, they would know this. The NCRP report spells out four different packages to reform Social Security, some with personal accounts and some without them. Each has exactly the same retirement age provisions, and it is spelled out explicitly that the only choices on the benefit side made to carve out room for the personal accounts are the change in bend-point factors and a change to the AIME formula.

What's truly deceptive about the Hart analysis is that it contrasts the NCRP proposal with a Ball-style plan, the inadequacies of which we have already seen. Although the Ball plan also recognizes that CPI changes must be included, the Hart poll editorializes that it "maintains the COLA at the inflation rate." If a pollster is telling you that one plan gets inflation right and the other gets it wrong, how are you to know the difference?

Of course, the Hart poll displays no recognition of any of the considerations that this book is spelling out. The Ball plan is touted as "working" even though many things it includes don't accomplish anything. Lifting the wage cap, for example, helps with the measure of actuarial solvency, but essentially displaces the problem onto tomorrow's workers by simply allowing additional assets to be credited to the Trust Fund, which it will have to pay off. Nor, in the Hart descriptions is it recognized that the distribution of benefits under the Ball plan is *also* distributed between benefits funded by equity investment and those financed in the traditional way, through T-bills. They simply choose, when discussing the NCRP plan, to refer to the reductions in the proportion that is financed by T-bills as "benefit cuts," whereas in discussing the Ball plan, they simply add the two forms of benefit financing together.

One has to wonder: How did our plan get even 42 percent support with this description? Personal accounts must be more popular than ever realized.

It's all in how you ask the questions. In 1999, pollster Linda DiVall surveyed Americans as to whether they favored a provision characterized in a manner similar to the updated Senate version of our plan, introduced in the 106th Congress. It correctly described the funding placed in personal accounts as a advance payment on future retirement benefit promises. Respondents, when asked this way, overwhelmingly favored receiving a portion of those benefits now, in a form that they could save and invest, as opposed to receiving all of them later (the latter being the only way, under the Peter Hart definition, to avoid a "benefit cut").

Finally, the plan Peter Hart compared ours to doesn't work. Remember, CRS found that if you assume a moderate rate of return, the plan doesn't balance, and the Trust Fund goes bankrupt.[3]

We wrote to Peter Hart to complain about the push poll, and to ask that, at the very least, they refrain from referring to the fictitious plan that they described as the NCRP plan. But they continued to circulate this poll as though it were meaningful. No wonder people do not trust pollsters.

Of course, the left isn't the only direction from which we were attacked. Shortly after the NCRP plan was released, an editorial from Dan Greenberg of the Cato Institute appeared in the *Washington Times*, blasting us for not going further than we did to advocate total privatization. (Among the provisions for which we were criticized were increasing the retirement age and enacting reforms in CPI. Greenberg wrote that we compromised "for no reason besides raw politics," perhaps the first time that anyone has been accused of proposing to increase the retirement age for political reasons.)

The *political* argument holds that Social Security reforms will founder if combined with tough choices on the benefit side. Consequently, the Cato Social Security framework embraces a much greater devotion of government resources to retirement income over the next 40–50 years than almost any other contender, because of the sum of maximizing the size of funding in the new accounts and the large size of the remaining pay-as-you-go benefits. This adherence to political judgment over the goal of limiting the size of government sometimes makes the lectures on political expediency not terribly well received, even if they are only disagreements among individuals committed to reform.

But Cato's criticism of "halfway" measures, just like the criticism from the left, is not all that hurtful, because it fuels the perception that the NCRP plan is closer to the political center. In any case, its commitment to actual substantive reform and true individual ownership over personal accounts continues to set an important benchmark for the debate.

Just one brief final example of the sorts of fun that detractors have with Social Security reform plans: The Institute for America's Future also published a paper that "showed" that our plan provided an inferior deal for beneficiaries relative to current law. It would take too long to review all the factual errors in this document, so let us mention just a couple.

First of all, the institute paper juxtaposed two sets of numbers from the Social Security actuaries' rates-of-return tables that have nothing to do with each other. One is given as "current law," the other as the "NCRP plan." In fact, these rates-of-return tables were generated for an interim version of the plan and do not incorporate the latest modifications made for the 1998 trustees' estimates.

Still, the institute's authors might be embarrassed to realize that they have no idea what the actuaries' tables and labels mean. They compared a "current law" rate of return, which assumes insolvency, with rates for a working plan. These numbers are rates of return that would be received only if the benefits materialized magically, with no one paying for them. In other words, that line is essentially meaningless. That's why, right underneath it, the Social Security actuaries included "current law paygo," which shows the rate of return that the Social Security system can provide if it is *kept running* to provide current benefit promises (though these figures don't include the effects of general tax increases).

Not only the numbers, but their descriptions of them, are wrong. Underneath these tables, the authors assert that "the present Social Security system, fully funded, actually performs better than the commission plan." One cannot produce an interpretation of this statement that is true. Are they saying that the current system is fully funded? It isn't. Are they saying that the current system would do better if it were fully funded? If so, they're using the wrong table.

Some of their mistakes must have been difficult to produce. For example, on the first page, they say that "the NCRP plan would consume all budget surpluses between now and the year 2000." However, the provisions of the plan don't even become effective until the year 2000. Moreover, how they could justify saying that a plan that improves the government's fiscal position by hundreds of billions per year by the 2020s "worsens deficits" is beyond comprehension.

We actually received a call from a reporter in which he suggested that the institute study would provide some interesting information for a story. If the press can't do its homework well enough to determine that the institute can't read a numerical table or an effective date, we're all in trouble.

NOTES

1. Congressional Research Service, Memorandum, "Benefit Analysis of Three Social Security Reform Plans," June 17, 1998.

2. Peter D. Hart Research Associates, Inc., "Young Americans View the Social Security Reform Debate," July 1999.

3. Congressional Research Service, *Social Security Reform: Projected Contributions and Benefits Under Three Proposals,* Report for the U.S. Congress, December 3, 1998, page 24.

19

1998–1999: The President's Year of Discussion–Then More Discussion

At the start of 1998, hope reigned that policy might triumph over politics and that parties on opposite sides of the political spectrum might work together successfully to place Social Security on a sound long-term footing. By the end of 1999, Republicans and Democrats had essentially written off any prospect of meaningful Social Security reform and were casting about for the best way to blame each other for that unwillingness to act.

How did we descend so rapidly from the heights of optimism to the depth of cynicism, in the span of a few short months? The answers lay partly in political cowardice, partly in ideological zeal, partly in ignorance, and partly in opportunism. Many who adopted destructive positions in 1999 knew not what they were doing. Many did.

Every segment of the body politic deserves censure. A Democratic administration willfully decided to duck the issue and to paper it over with accounting gimmicks. Republican leaders opted for self-protection over principle and refused to spell out the cost to taxpayers of buying into free-lunch solutions. Some interest groups on the left circulated fictions about the costs of the current-law path, in order to make the choices involved in reform seem gratuitous. Some interest groups on the right made the political decision that conservatives should out-bid the left in terms of benefit promises and costs. Seniors' groups fell back to stances in favor of ever higher spending and taxes, after giving polite but unresponsive audience to fiscally responsible proposals. Youth advocacy groups failed to generate counterpressure on legislators to consider their interests. Many of the most influential news publications refused to do their homework, prattling occasionally about the need for reforms, then mindlessly parroting whatever was thrown their way.

At the end of 1999, not only has there been no substantive progress on Social Security reform, there has actually been retrograde motion. Legislators in both parties who began the year with an open mind have dug into positions from which it will be very difficult to dislodge them, positions that would preclude responsible reform.

The president did, as was so earnestly hoped, place saving Social Security at the center of the national agenda in both his 1998 and 1999 State of the Union addresses. Doing so made political as well as policy sense. There is no better place for a politician to be placed than defending the gates of Social Security. He performed an important service by lending the issue a prominence that only presidential leadership can provide.

The president was canny, moreover, in the way that he went about it. He declared that the projected budget surpluses should be used to "save Social Security first." The statement provoked cynical outbursts privately by many Republicans who had been on the receiving end of partisan attacks. Why this sudden conversion to the cause of taking decisive action on Social Security, after making it so difficult for Republicans to go anywhere near the program in the past?

But sometimes good politics is good policy. The "save Social Security first" mantra proved to be a potent political weapon. And it did—at least until late in the 1998 session, when a spending fever gripped the Capitol—provide a check against other actions that would diminish the size of the projected surpluses and thus diminish the resources available to finance a transition to a partially funded Social Security system.

There was another aspect of the president's tactic that was more clever than first appeared. The president announced that 1998 would be a year of national discussion on Social Security and that forums would be conducted around the country, sponsored by the AARP and the Concord Coalition. As you might imagine, it was hard for Republicans to have much confidence in such a process. In the first place, there was never a shortage of views offered by the public about Social Security. Second, the substantive groundwork had already been plowed, ad nauseum. Further, many feared that political operators would take advantage of the statements made at these forums.

But all this underrated the president's planning. In the first place, his co-opting of the AARP into the process was deft and artful. The AARP had suddenly been transformed from a partisan advocacy group into appearing as an honest broker, compelled not to take an unyielding stand against any particular proposal. Of course, one should not naively believe that AARP will suddenly abandon its advocacy position. At the end of the game, the AARP will make its views known, and it needs to be reckoned with. But it tried especially hard last year to appear to be more objective brokers of a discussion.

The President's Year of Discussion

Within Congress, Social Security proposals proliferated. Congressman Nick Smith reintroduced his Social Security proposal. Congressman Mark Sanford put forth an even bolder plan than any that had yet been offered, proposing to completely overhaul the old Social Security structure and to replace it essentially with a defined contribution system. To advance the debate on the House side, Sanford also introduced companion pieces to various Senate proposals to reform Social Security, including Senator Gregg's bill S. 321.

Early in 1998, Senator Moynihan—with Al Simpson performing the introductions—announced his plan to restore actuarial solvency to Social Security. The Moynihan plan essentially would place Social Security's OASDI system on a pay-as-you-go basis, reducing the payroll tax in the short term and raising it in the long run, to do away with the need to redeem a large Trust Fund. The Moynihan proposal also included supplementary, voluntary personal investment accounts.

Moynihan's entry into the discussion was equally important for political as for policy reasons. Simply put, the senator had the most impeccable Social Security credentials of anyone involved. He was a member of the 1983 Greenspan Commission that oversaw the last major overhaul of the program, and he was currently the ranking member of the Senate Finance Committee, which had jurisdiction. He had been at the center of debates about Social Security literally for decades and knew more about the institutional history of the program than anyone else in Washington.

Also in 1998, Senators Gramm and Domenici waded into the debate with a proposal of their own. They had consulted with renowned economist Martin Feldstein to develop the ideas behind it. The participation of both of these senators in the development of original proposals was significant. Gramm is one of the best quotes in Washington and a marketer of bold ideas. Domenici is chairman of the Budget Committee, with a long and distinguished record in budget policy. Both senators bring intellectual credentials and jurisdictional responsibilities that ensure that they will continue to play a major role in the future course of Social Security.

Senate Majority Leader Trent Lott had been prevailed upon by several senators, including Senators Gregg, Santorum, and Gramm, to move Social Security to the forefront of the Senate Republican agenda. These senators saw an opportunity to relate the issues of tax relief, personal control over government control, budgetary soundness, care for the elderly, and responsibility to future generations. Lott felt that the party as a whole was not yet ready to go where Gregg and Gramm had already gone, and he convened a task force aimed at educating a small coterie of Republican senators, who would then share their knowledge and findings with the others. Senators Gregg and Santorum were named to lead it. Another similar task force of Senate Democrats was subsequently convened, in late 1998, by minority leader Tom Daschle.

Reforming Social Security

One of the successes of 1998 was the avoidance of rash mistakes by all sides in the Social Security debate. But the avoidance of such mistakes was also the avoidance of bold leadership. Republicans needed to find a way to act on the president's giving highest priority to Social Security. Later in 1998, Ways and Means Committee Chairman Bill Archer and Speaker Newt Gingrich steered through the House a proposal to create a Social Security commission that would make recommendations to shore up the program.

House and Senate dynamics were very different. On the Senate side, senators were jumping into the deep end. Republican senators who cosponsored or were developing substantive proposals included Gregg, Thompson, Thomas, Coats, Gramm, Domenici, Roth, Santorum, and Grams; the Democrats included Moynihan, Breaux, Kerrey, and Robb. The fights in the Senate were not over how to deal the issue without being held personally liable, but over who was going to get a piece of the action.

The House Republicans then felt very strongly that the commission was the way to go. Speaker Gingrich felt passionately—not unlike the president—that important public-education groundwork had to be paved before anyone could make tough political calls. Chairman Archer recalled the experiences of the 1980s when he felt that Republicans had leapt without looking. They felt that the senators were well intended but did not appreciate, as could House Republicans, the political dangers inherent in venturing too close to the flame. After all, the political margins in the House were very slim and could easily be manipulated by issues much less explosive than Social Security.

An effort was made by the Senate to turn the House commission proposal into something that did not threaten the pride of authorship of various senators—to delete the portions of the proposal that dealt with making legislative recommendations and to preserve instead the forums for public discussion and deliberation. In the end, the chambers could not come to agreement, and time simply overtook the idea.

In the meantime, the Senate continued to press ahead to create a bipartisan atmosphere for reform. On September 24, a bipartisan coalition of eight senators, led by Senators Gregg and Moynihan, circulated a "Dear Colleague" letter in which they announced their criteria for reform. These included a payroll tax cut, personal savings accounts, a progressive benefit formula, accurate cost-of-living adjustments, permanent actuarial solvency, and a rough annual balance between revenues and outlays.

In mid-October, as partisans began to step up election-season attacks on those who had advocated rescue plans, a larger group of 18 senators—nine Republicans and nine Democrats—wrote to the president, urging him to use his position of leadership to discourage the politicization of the Social Security issue.

In many ways, the political stars at the end of 1998 were in perfect alignment to enact major and lasting reform. Consider the following:

The President's Year of Discussion

1. The president and a Republican Congress proved that they could work together in 1997 on a major balanced-budget agreement.
2. The president and several leading members of Congress publicly committed themselves to working in a cooperative way to shore up Social Security.
3. The president succeeded in focusing the attentions of the nation on the need for Social Security reform in his State of the Union address and subsequent forums.
4. Neither the president, the AARP, nor any other influential group at those forums acted to take certain provisions permanently off the negotiating table, leaving major policy options still open.
5. The proponents of various Social Security reform proposals managed to survive the year without major political fallout.
6. The projections for federal budget balances were vastly improved, creating for the first time in decades the opportunity for the removal of surplus Social Security taxes from investment in Treasury securities and their use to advance-fund some future Social Security liabilities without necessitating an immediate return to unified federal deficits.

But there were problems, too. There was a 1998 election campaign. The cause of Social Security reform came under direct assault from political operatives. Although some of the attacks stung, for the most part both ideas and reformers survived 1998's election unscathed.

On December 8 and 9, 1998, the White House held a conference that brought hundreds together to discuss Social Security. The last days before the summit were tough ones for a few would-be reformers. On the morning of December 3, CRS issued its report finding that the Ball plan would lead to insolvency unless a lofty rate of return were assumed. In the afternoon, the Social Security actuaries issued a finding that the Feldstein proposal would postpone insolvency by only four years, from 2032 to 2036, and also add to the system's net cost. Under current law, the net cost of Social Security is scheduled to rise from 12.19 percent of the national payroll tax base in 2010 to 18.17 percent in 2035. The actuaries projected that the plan would cost 18.57 percent in 2035 and add trillions in new federal debt.

These findings were consistent with many of the arguments in this book concerning the consequences of attempting to find a "painless" solution to Social Security. But interestingly, though only a few reform proposals were left standing as fiscally sound at the time of the summit, the audience at the summit seemed to gravitate toward the "free lunch" options that were not fiscally sound. Staff who were present at the White House discussion on the second day reported that members of Congress seemed tempted by such solutions and failed to ask enough questions about the net costs of these approaches. Leading Democrats and Republicans alike were quoted during the week as saying that if personal accounts were included, they should supplement Social Security, not replace it. This meant that both parties were being tempted by solutions that might increase net liabilities, rather than funding them.

The real downward spiral began in earnest with the president's 1999 State of the Union address. Given against the backdrop of an impeachment trial in the U.S. Senate, political analysts were divided on whether the president's scandal troubles would cause him to tack left to shore up the political base that he hoped would save him or whether he would move for a bold bipartisan stroke, to prove that he had vision too great to be sacrificed on the altar of scandal politics. He chose the former.

Many in the administration have defended the president's address by stating that he could not afford to make a bold and specific proposal for Social Security reform, because in so doing he would have placed such reform on a target that Republicans, in their partisan zeal, would attack. But to advance the cause of reform, it was not necessary for the president to be so detailed. Any one of a number of lesser gestures would have been helpful. Among them:

- The president could have leveled with the American people about the nature of the Social Security Trust Fund, and to explain that the existence of large Trust Fund balances had no actual relationship to the government's ability to pay Social Security benefits.

- The president could have leveled with the public about the fact that surplus Social Security taxes currently do nothing to fund future benefits, and thus saving those taxes in personal accounts would not "weaken" Social Security relative to using that money to underwrite current consumption.

- The president could have refrained from endorsing new entitlement programs, such as USA Accounts, that would add to our financing challenges instead of solving them.

- The president could simply have pointed to any of a number of Social Security plans that met his stated criteria for reform, without necessarily endorsing them, and invited Congress to review those proposals.

Instead, the president did precisely the opposite, proposing that the projected Social Security surpluses be credited to Social Security a second time, to extend the stated life of the Trust Fund. In addition, a portion of the Trust Fund would be invested in the equities market, to improve the rate of return. These two actions, taken together, were advertised as extending the solvency of Social Security.

Neither measure would add one penny to national saving. Neither measure would reduce Social Security's liabilities by one penny. Essentially, the administration told the public that we didn't have to do anything. No benefits would have to be adjusted, for either present or future retirees, and none of the tax costs of redeeming this now larger Trust Fund were our concern.

Moreover, the president used unfortunate and misleading terminology to promote his proposal. He spoke of "saving the surplus for Social Security." The president's proposal to transfer general revenue credits to Social Security would in fact bear no relationship to overall federal saving. Near-term public debt would not be reduced one bit by any such intragovernmental transfers. The transfers would have one effect, and one effect only: to create new explicit general revenue liabilities as a means of financing future Social Security benefits.

The president also took the cue from his left that personal accounts could only be a "supplement" to Social Security. In other words, we still would have no plan as to how to redeem the Social Security Trust Fund and to pay future benefits from the Social Security system. Rather than to create some advance funding with surplus payroll taxes, we would create a *new* entitlement to establish personal savings accounts and add the cost of that entitlement to the cost of financing Social Security.

Reformers were dumbfounded by the president's proposal. Had he done something constructive, the reform community was poised to find something good to say about it. When the president made his proposal, he left it literally with nothing positive to say other than to praise the program's being mentioned in the State of the Union address.

On February 12, the Social Security actuaries analyzed the cash-flow implications of the president's plan, on the basis of the assumptions in the 1998 Trustees' report. Afterwards the administration cited only the finding from the Social Security actuaries that the president's plan would extend Social Security solvency. The most important findings went unremarked upon.

The president proposed to transfer credits from the general Treasury to the Social Security Trust Fund.[1] Again, it bears repeating that these transfers bore no relationship to total public debt and would simply be an issuance of new gross debt. In a period of cash surplus, such as the present, the taxpayer would feel no difference. One could make a transfer of $1 or $1 trillion, and there would be no immediate effect. The effect of such transfers would be to provide Social Security an increased claim on *future* tax dollars.

Billed as "saving the surplus for Social Security," the proposal had nothing to do with saving anything. The transfers could just as easily take place whether we enacted a $2 trillion tax cut or a $2 trillion tax increase.

The newly installed Comptroller General of the United States, David Walker, was the first to effectively and publicly describe "What the President's Proposal Does and Does Not Do." In televised testimony before the Senate Finance Committee, Walker noted that the spresident's proposal would not change, by so much as a "nickel" or an hour, the date and size of the cash-flow deficits that the Trust Fund would begin to face in 2014.

Transferring this additional principal would cause more interest to be credited to the Social Security Trust Fund. Taxpayers would be liable for paying off that interest, and the program would thus be entitled to claim additional tax revenues from 2014 through the new projected insolvency date of 2055. The actual funding shortfalls of Social Security would not be changed.

According to the actuaries' analysis, the assets held by the Trust Fund under the proposal would rise from $864 billion in year 2000 to $6.680 trillion in 2014. (Under current law, it would increase to $3.032 trillion.)[2]

The proposal was given in the context of distributing a projected $4.5 trillion federal surplus over 15 years. Giving Social Security's surplus to it a second time meant a claim that somehow the projected $4.5 trillion surplus could swell the Trust Fund by $5.8 trillion—and also fund USA accounts, Medicare spending increases, defense increases, and other of the president's spending priorities.

Under the proposal, the Social Security program would still face an excess of outlay pressures over actual cash revenues from payroll taxes and benefit taxation within a few years. The gaps would be met as shown in Table 19.1.[3] What these figures mean, essentially, is that the president had proposed that, instead of being entitled to claim general revenues on the order of more than approximately $900 billion a year by 2034, in addition to payroll tax and benefit tax revenues, the Social Security program would now be entitled to claim more than $1 trillion a year in new tax revenues by the year 2043, with an additional set of costs imposed upon the private retirement

Table 19.1
Sources of Revenues Required to Meet Cash-Flow Deficit under Clinton Plan

Year	General Revenues Required (Current Dollars, Billions)	Stock Sales	General Revenues Required (1999 Dollars, Billions)	Stock Sales
2020	$135	$79	$67	$40
2025	$312	$121	$132	$51
2030	$519	$166	$176	$58
2035	$720	$205	$215	$61
2040	$911	$237	$229	$60
2045	$1,159	$270	$246	$57
2050	$1,439	$300	$272	$55

savings system through the reshuffling of the government's investment portfolio. Nothing was said by the president about the difficulty of generating that level of new income taxation; indeed, he allowed the implication to stand that the problem would not exist at all through 2055.

The president's plan emboldened those who had argued that nothing need truly be done to address Social Security's long-term fiscal health. Some on the left end of the spectrum who understood Social Security's difficulties labored to find something good in the president's proposal. Bob Greenstein cautioned Congress that the president's proposal did not solve all of Social Security's problems and suggested that every $1 dollar in transfers per the president's plan be contingent upon $1 dollar of actual liability reductions. Were this done, then the president's proposal would have only the virtues of Greenstein's recommendations, but no others.

Nothing is achieved by making any such transfers à la the president's recommendations, other than to obscure the realities of the problem. At a time when the president could have educated the public about the debt they face to redeem the Trust Fund, he chose instead to give false assurances that what was needed was more of that same debt.

NOTES

1. February 12, 1999, Memorandum of Social Security actuaries analyzing the president's proposal. The transfers would take place from 2000 to 2014, starting with $81.5 billion in fiscal year 2000, dropping to $67.5 billion in 2001, and thereafter increasing gradually until a transfer of $324.5 billion in 2014.

2. Stephen Goss, deputy chief actuary, and Alice Wade, memorandum to Harry Ballantyne, chief actuary, Social Security Administration, February 12, 1999.

3. Ibid.

20

Congress Reacts to the President's Proposals

When the Social Security actuaries issued their 1999 report, they confirmed the previous year's projections of out-of-control cost growth in the upcoming decades. Many in the press and public missed the story and wrongly interpreted the document as implying that the outlook had significantly improved.

The actuaries in the previous year had projected that the OASDI system would have a cash-flow deficit of $7 billion in the year 2013. In the updated projections, they projected a surplus of $7 billion—a mere $14 billion swing, nearly 15 years away. That's less of a change than the Congressional Budget Office must typically make for the federal budget projections every year, let alone fifteen years hence. The trustees' projections were essentially unchanged, although they had updated them to assume improved economic conditions. Some alleged that the report indicated that the problem was receding into the distance, that Social Security's insolvency date might continue to be postponed indefinitely, if only economic growth continued apace.

Let's revisit reality. Again, the Social Security trustees projected the cash-flow situation for Social Security each year, as a percentage of national taxable payroll. The new projections have already been summarized in Table 6.1. Reviewing that table, it can be seen that the trustees were projecting that by the year 2035, the equivalent of a 5.05 percent increase in the payroll tax would be required from general (income tax) revenues. The unfunded liability gaps were larger in the 1999 report than in the 1998 report, although the qualitative picture had not changed—despite the fact that the trustees employed improved economic assumptions in 1999, relative to the previous year. On page 13, they indicated

Compared to the 1998 report, this year's report generally reflects assumptions of lower CPI increases, lower unemployment rates, higher productivity gains, faster labor force growth and a higher ratio of wages to total compensation throughout the first 10 years of the projection period. In combination, these changes produce somewhat higher levels of employment, productivity, real wages, and real GDP throughout the balance of the 75-year projection period.

The 1999 trustees' report was a case study in how tweaking the assumptions in a favorable way doesn't make the problem disappear.

The president's proposal and the new political dynamics resulting from it had a chilling effect upon the persuasive stature of Social Security reformers. Republicans divided among themselves as to how to react. Senator Judd Gregg, Congressman Jim Kolbe, and others had put forth fiscally conservative proposals that sought to avoid projected acceleration of costs in the coming decades. Other Republicans felt that the flaws in the president's proposal should be made known, but that no concrete proposal should come forth labeled as the "Republican plan." Others argued that Republicans should offer a plan, but not one that used a portion the payroll tax to fund personal accounts in combination with reforms to scale back the liabilities of current law. Instead, these Republicans argued, personal accounts should only be employed as a means of funding, from additional commitments of general revenues, the system's current defined benefit promises.

Senator Gramm had in the previous year joined with Senator Domenici in offering a proposal that would fund personal accounts from general revenues, with an 80 percent clawback. In 1999, Senator Gramm, working now on his own and with more optimistic updated budget projections, came forward with a new and more ambitious proposal to create larger personal accounts.

The Gramm plan, for no reason inherent in the plan itself, rivaled the Clinton plan in the share of misunderstanding that it generated. The character of this misunderstanding, however, was very different. The Clinton plan was more of an ideological statement, and those who misdescribed its effects were typically those who favored doing nothing. The Gramm plan seems to have been inadvertently misunderstood by supporters, neutral parties, and detractors alike. The Concord Coalition, the National Center for Policy Analysis, and Charles Schwab all at times published papers describing the Gramm plan as a "carve-out" of the payroll tax. Each repeated numerous errors in describing the Gramm plan and its effects, misperceptions that were shared by legislators and media.

The distinction between "carve-out" and "add-on" accounts is arcane but critical. As previously discussed, one essential choice facing policymakers is whether to attempt to fix Social Security within something close to its current tax rate or to accept the necessity of bringing new tax revenue into the system in order to fund future benefits. There are a variety of ways to pursue the latter approach. One can simply raise taxes outright to fund the traditional system, or one can use other revenue, outside the 12.4 percent payroll tax already devoted to Social Security, to establish personal accounts. The "add-on" approaches make it easier to meet or to exceed promised benefit levels, but in the long run they mean higher tax liabilities as well. The "carve-out" approach seeks to avoid increased tax liabilities, but some restraints in outlay growth are therefore necessitated.

There are different ways to fund an "add-on" personal account. One way is simply to fund personal accounts directly out of income tax revenues. Revenues flowing to the Social Security Trust Fund from the payroll tax are not affected, and the cost of redeeming Trust Fund surpluses down the road is also left essentially the same. Another way to fund an "add-on" account is to fund the personal accounts from the payroll tax, but then to use general (income tax) revenues to reimburse the Trust Fund for the revenues lost. Either way is economically equivalent. Each preserves the entire 12.4 percent for the Trust Fund and commits additional money to personal accounts, and neither resembles a carve-out in its long-term economic effects.

Many who discussed the Gramm plan simply missed the fact that the Treasury would be required to reimburse the Trust Fund for any money taken to fund personal accounts. Had the Gramm plan carved out 3 percent of the payroll tax in order to fund personal accounts, leaving only 9.4 percent to fund defined benefit promises, these promises would need to be scaled back more than was the case for a plan that left 10.4 percent in that system, such as the NCRP plan. By contrast, the Gramm plan boasted none of those outlay restraints, something made possible only by maintaining the current-law flow of revenues to the Trust Fund in the short term, in addition to the money flowing into personal accounts.

Whatever confusion there was over Gramm's plan was not in any way the fault of Senator Gramm himself. He printed a "prospectus" describing his proposal that clearly spelled out the sources of his funding and also freely circulated the Social Security actuaries' analysis that showed the total amount of money that his plan would employ.

This confusion over the nature of Senator Gramm's plan obscured the most interesting innovation that he made in the 1999 version of his proposal. The essence of the Gramm plan was to establish personal accounts and then to use the buildup in those accounts to fund a benefit based on the promise already made to the retiree. The retiree would receive the current-law benefit plus 20 percent of the annuitized value of the personal account. In other words, the retiree couldn't lose and could only do better than under the current system.

The Gramm proposal therefore banked strictly on two things in order to achieve budget savings in the long run: (1) The improved rate of return coming from personal accounts as opposed to Trust Fund investment in federal securities and (2) The benefits of advance funding, of using surplus revenues in the years 2000–2010 to offset the size of liabilities shouldered in years such as 2025 and beyond. He did not propose to reduce outlays directly or to raise the payroll tax (though the plan would require significant increases in income tax revenues).

Outlays from the federal treasury would be reduced as assets in the personal accounts built up. The more money that beneficiaries had in their personal accounts, the less the federal government would need to tax in order to make them whole again relative to benefit promises. But when would these savings be larger than the extra cost of the new investment itself? Under the previous Gramm proposal, not until after 2030. In his new proposal, Gramm accepted the challenge of getting the largest immediate return that he could for the advance funding that he proposed.

The means that Gramm found was to weight his personal accounts to be larger for older workers, specifically those aged 35–55. These workers would hit retirement first. The larger the balance in their accounts, the more that federal outlays on their behalf would be reduced. Putting the same amount of money in the accounts of those 25 and younger would delay the "payoff" of advance funding until after those younger workers finally retired at a distant date. By front-loading the accounts to be larger for older workers, Gramm sought to accelerate the return from the advance funding.

On April 16, the Social Security actuaries issued their analysis of the Gramm proposal. Table 20.1 shows the net tax burden costs of the Gramm approach relative to current law, subject to SSA's assumptions.

As with any advance-funded plan, the costs are "higher" under Gramm in the early years, relative to current law. The full cost of making benefit payments to current beneficiaries must be met in either case, whereas with a personal-account plan, additional investment must be directed to the new accounts. Later, the cost of the personal account plan becomes lower, as less of the cost of maintaining benefits is met by collecting and redistributing tax revenues.

The largest and most important correction required to this table, however, is the effect of any advance-funded proposal upon public debt. The figures here assume that all costs of the system are met by current taxation and none by additional borrowing. In other words, in 2020, under the Gramm plan, we assume that the nation has decided to tax itself at an effective rate of 17.3 percent for Social Security, more than the 15.0 percent scheduled under current law. But if the nation does not decide to do this and instead meets the cost of transition by engaging in additional borrowing or, under some current projections, reducing the planned schedule of federal debt reduction, then the cost of the additional debt service must be added to this or any other advance-funded plan relative to current law.

Congress Reacts to the President's Proposals

Table 20.1
Projected Cost Rates, Gramm, Archer-Shaw, Kolbe-Stenholm, Senate
Bipartisan, and Kasich Proposals*

Year	Current Law	Gramm	Archer-Shaw	Kolbe-Stenholm	Senate Bipartisan	Kasich
2000	10.8	15.0	12.8	12.9	12.7	12.8
2010	11.9	15.6	13.4	13.2	13.4	13.8
2020	15.0	17.3	16.4	14.8	14.7	15.6
2030	17.7	17.1	17.8	15.7	15.7	16.4
2040	18.2	15.2	16.2	14.5	14.8	15.3
2050	18.3	13.3	13.8	13.3	13.9	14.0
2060	19.1	12.8	12.6	13.1	13.7	13.3

*As a percentage of taxable payroll.

Source: Analysis of Gramm plan by Social Security actuaries, memo of April 16, 1999. Analysis of Archer-Shaw by Social Security actuaries in memo of April 29, 1999. Analysis of Kolbe-Stenholm by Social Security actuaries in memo of May 12, 1999. Senate Bipartisan plan in memo of June 3, 1999. Kasich plan in memo of June 14, 1999. Figures include net cost to wage-earners of paying OASDI benefits plus contributions to personal accounts.

This is a critical issue to raise for two reasons: (1) The total tax cost of the plan relative to current law cannot be adequately estimated without including the effects of transition upon federal debt service costs, and (2) proponents of such plans argue that they will create new saving relative to current projections, and thus faster economic growth can be assumed. However, if increasing saving in personal accounts is paid for directly by increasing public debt, then there's no net gain in national saving, and thus no basis for assuming higher economic growth.

To maintain self-consistency in our projections, we must either

(1) assume that transition has an impact upon public debt and thus that we cannot posit greatly improved projections of economic growth, or (2) assume that all costs of transition are met when imposed or, in other words, agree that the plans will have higher tax costs than current law for several years. Some combination of the two is the most likely result. In reality, advance-funded plans will have higher costs than current law in the short term and will also result in some additional debt relative to the baseline. Some of the saving in the personal accounts is likely to be new saving, net, although the percentage cannot be estimated.

This aside should not distract from the essential point about the Gramm plan. Gramm essentially proposed that the whole of the budget surplus—Social Security and on-budget surpluses alike—be devoted to Social Security reform, as opposed to Medicare, tax relief, or other appropriations. In this sense, Gramm was the one who was proposing that the largest

225

amount of the surplus be "saved for Social Security," both now and for the next few decades.

Another feature of the Gramm plan should be highlighted before moving on to the similar plan offered by Congressman Bill Archer, chairman of the Ways and Means Committee. A critical choice made in devising the Gramm plan was to maintain the current set of defined benefit promises, plus a "bonus" amount awarded as a function of the accumulations in the personal accounts. In other words, the government would continue to insure individuals against the variance in their investment performance. The beneficiary cannot lose; if investments do not turn out as hoped, the taxpayer makes up the difference.

Consequently, investment through such plans must be constrained to reduce the variance in projected rates of return. If such investment results did not reach their desired levels, then costs to the general taxpayer would rise, and long-term cost-reduction projections would fall apart. The Gramm plan was scored on the assumption that a 50:50 blend of stocks and bonds would result in a higher rate of return than the Trust Fund currently receives. Under the assumption that the personal accounts only received a rate of return equal to that currently received on the Social Security Trust Fund, the Gramm plan would not result in a reduction of overall tax rates in the long run relative to current law, though it would attain program solvency.[2]

After the president's State of the Union address, Ways and Means Chairman Bill Archer found himself in a political box. President Clinton had implied that the Social Security system could be made permanently solvent without tax increases or defined benefit reductions of any kind. Moreover, though the president had not actually offered a workable Social Security plan, the president had convinced a sufficient number of the press and public that he had a framework for Social Security to which Republicans must respond. But at the same time, a responsible Republican proposal to reform Social Security for the long haul would be subject to the claim that any tough choices were unnecessary and gratuitous. After all, the president had proposed none.

Chairman Archer responded with a plan that was similar in many respects to the president's. It left the existing defined benefit system intact, it attempted to meet funding shortfalls by devoting new general revenues to shore up the program, and it would permit new investment in the equities market. Personal accounts would be established, but in name only, as a means of funding the current Social Security system.

The Archer Shaw (cosponsored by Social Security Subcommittee Chairman Representative Clay Shaw) plan would establish personal accounts with 2 percent of taxable payroll, funded directly from general revenues. The accumulations in the personal accounts would be converted into an annuity at retirement age, which would be exactly equal in size to the Social

Security benefit reductions, so total benefits would not change. Essentially, the personal accounts would have no ultimate bearing on benefits at all. Individuals would be required to invest in a 60:40 blend of stocks and bonds.

The chairman faced opposition from the reform community, which noticed that the extra tax cost of funding the personal accounts meant that individuals would be additionally taxed in order to give them benefits that they were already promised. The actuaries' projections for the cost of the plan revealed the picture shown in Table 20.1.

Through at least 2030, according to SSA, the total cost of the Archer-Shaw plan, including the 2 percent account contribution, would be higher than under current law, though providing the same benefits. (This is a critical point; materials citing the "cost" of the Archer-Shaw plan defined this "cost" as the cost relative to current law, meaning not costs relative to today's levels, but higher costs relative to projected current-law increases.) In the long run, however, the advance funding would reduce tax costs, and an increasing share of benefits would be paid for from personal accounts and less from taxing workers.

Again, the caveat must be made that this would be true only if taxes were contemporaneously raised in order to fund the plan in the transition period. If any of the cost of the advance funding resulted in increased federal borrowing, then the cost of Archer-Shaw would not become less than under current law until much later. SSA and GAO estimated that this would not occur until the 2060s.

The Social Security actuaries' projections given in Table 20.2 show the budgetary effect of Archer-Shaw relative to current law, taking these increased debt service costs into account.[3] This is a case study in the perils of long-range forecasting. Ultimately, it is hoped, there would be a point past 2060 at which the net effect of Archer-Shaw upon federal budgets would be positive. That year would be 2069 under the actuaries' projections. But if the projections for the rate of return on the personal accounts are exaggerated even a little bit, less than 1 percent, then there is no point within the valuation window that net federal indebtedness as a result of adopting the plan would not increase.

Beyond the figures shown in Table 20.2, the plan peaks at more than $16 trillion of new debt created some time around 2050, after which it provides a net improvement in annual cash flows; by the late 2060s, it has paid for itself.

This analysis is unfair to Archer-Shaw for a variety of reasons. First, and most important, it compares the plan to a baseline scenario in which all money not used for Archer-Shaw accounts is simply saved by the federal government or used to reduce other debt. There is no historical basis for the presumption that we would otherwise save the money required to fund the accounts under Archer-Shaw. Even now, Congress and the president are finding myriad ways to project federal surpluses before they have even

Table 20.2
Projected Impact of Archer-Shaw and Kolbe-Stenholm Proposals upon Federal
Budget Balance

Year	Change in Annual Cash Flow, Archer-Shaw (in billions)	Cumulative Effect on Total Savings, Archer-Shaw (in trillons)	Cumulative Effect on Total Savings, Kolbe-Stenholm (in trillions)
2010	-$115.6	-$1.452	-$0.982
2020	-$126.0	-$4.430	-$1.820
2030	-$8.2	-$9.402	-$0.387
2040	+$443.2	-$15.072	+$8.410

Source: Social Security actuaries memos of April 29, 1999 and May 12, 1999. Kolbe-Stenholm
figures from author's calculations based on data in actuaries' May 12 memo. Positive
figures indicate additions to net federal savings, negative figures additions to net federal
debt.

been generated. To hold Archer-Shaw up against a standard in which all of
this money is saved is to hold it up in comparison with an implausible fantasy.

Second, Archer-Shaw would begin to show a positive effect on federal
budget balances earlier if the plan did not envision cutting the payroll tax in
the year 2050. The plan has generated enough savings at that point to begin
to exert a positive effect on overall federal balances, if Congress were to
make a different choice than lowering the payroll tax.

Reformers had great concerns about the Clinton, Gramm, and Archer
proposals. Essentially the Gramm and Archer plans would establish a new
entitlement from general revenues, with the value of the entitlement taxed
at 80 percent and 100 percent rates, respectively. Each promised as much or
more than the government currently did, while hoping that it would ultimately pay less. With the president and key Republicans each staking out
positions upholding the entirety of current outlay liabilities and opposing
the introduction of a Social Security component tying benefit levels to differences in individual contributions, a new burden lay on fiscal conservatives and Social Security reformers to steer the debate to a different course.

Moynihan reintroduced his Social Security proposal on the first day of
the new Congress. It was identical to his previous proposal except in one respect. Whereas the previous proposal had contained a provision increasing
the "Normal Retirement Age," the new one left the retirement age alone
and instead applied a "life expectancy factor" to the basic (PIA) benefit formula.

Senator Moynihan had long been disturbed by what was said about proposals that contained a change in the "normal retirement age." The "nor-

mal retirement age" did not in any way determine when one was eligible to receive Social Security benefits. That was determined by the "early eligibility age." Moynihan's proposal did not change the "early eligibility age" by so much as an hour, and consequently his proposal in no way affected when people could choose to retire.

Thus, in the new version of his legislation, Moynihan abandoned any references to raising the normal retirement age and instead applied an idea that he borrowed from Sweden's public pension reform. An individual's total retirement benefits were the promise to be maintained. If individuals were expected to live longer, then they should expect to receive a smaller benefit as a consequence of their benefit being spread over more years. Moynihan thus indexed his benefit formula to projections of life expectancy.

While Moynihan had moved forward, other backers of bipartisan plans held back, waiting to see what the president would propose. After the State of the Union address, it became clear that the president and congressional leadership would not only refuse to meet reformers halfway, but would propose *no* amelioration of projected cost growth. Thus, reformers thus had very little to work with.

Senator Kerrey's instinct from the beginning was to reach out to anyone who was willing to show any willingness to act on Social Security. He engaged in private overtures with Chairman Archer until it became clear that Archer would not accept any cost restraints without presidential leadership.

In the House, Congressmen Kolbe and Stenholm were each impatient for action. Congressman Kolbe was particularly concerned that leadership on the question was in effect being ceded to the "free lunch" position.

My boss, Senator Judd Gregg, and Senator Kerrey felt that the best way to reenergize the debate was to broker a solution that brought together the largest number of reformers to date. These talks brought together Senators Gregg, Moynihan, Breaux, Kerrey, and Santorum and other senators who cannot be named here.

Kolbe and Stenholm meanwhile developed a new version of their own proposal, loosely based on the previous year's plan, but in some ways influenced by the ideas airing in the Senate discussions. The House sponsors made their own policy statement, while time signaling their fundamental sympathy with the Senate effort.

The question of general revenues remained a stubborn problem. Refusal to commit new general revenues to the system had long been one of the rules that fiscal conservatives forced themselves to work within, finding that such commitment of income tax money to Social Security was little more than a disguised tax increase. The Social Security Advisory Council had included among their few unanimous recommendations the principle that Social Security should continue to be a self-sustaining system. The

AARP had included among its principles for reform the guideline that Social Security should remain self-financing.

The president's plan changed all that, in combination with the Archer and Gramm plans. Each plan assumed that sufficient general revenues would be available to fund currently promised benefits or more.

The bipartisan negotiators wished to avoid open-ended commitments of general tax dollars in the manner of these other plans. But to reintroduce a new version of NCRP plan would risk irrelevance in light of political developments. What the bipartisan negotiators needed was a way to move in the direction of the rest of the political spectrum, without wholly sacrificing the fiscal imperatives that remained uppermost in their minds.

It was Senator Moynihan who provided the solution. Moynihan pointed out the untenability of suggestions that corrections in the Consumer Price Index should apply to Social Security benefits alone. If the CPI was wrong, then it was wrong for all federal indexation, not just indexation of Social Security benefits. CPI corrections to the income tax indexing would have the effect of increasing income tax collections relative to current law. It was suggested that these collections should be transferred to the Social Security Trust Fund.

This suggestion dovetailed nicely with the concerns of Republicans. Senator Gregg knew for example that he had the most fiscally conservative plan on the table, one that avoided tax increases of all kinds—payroll taxes, benefit taxation, and "hidden" general revenue costs alike. There was no way that he would accept changes in CPI that would create a new revenue source for other federal spending. But Moynihan's point was unassailable—if CPI was wrong, then it was wrong, and applying the proper CPI would not mean a tax increase for anyone whose income stayed constant in real terms. Negotiators therefore agreed that (1) any increase in revenues that resulted from CPI reforms should be refunded to taxpayers through Social Security benefits and not be available to fund other forms of federal spending and (2) any incorporation of CPI reindexing would be carefully integrated into a comprehensive reform of outlays so that the net use of general revenues was *reduced*, not increased, relative to current law and relative to alternate reform proposals.

This bridged a key gap between negotiators. It also avoided the fiscal "sin" of simply committing projected revenues that the plan itself did not create. Politically, it seemed an attractive compromise. It meant that fewer restraints would be needed on the defined benefit side. Left-leaning Democrats could be shown that the plan was no longer a pure "carve-out" in the sense that the money in the OASDI system would be greater than 10.4 percent of payroll. Republicans could be shown that refunding the CPI money through Social Security benefits would mean that the CPI reforms would not result in a net tax increase. Fiscal conservatives could be shown that even with the CPI money included in the package, the net reliance on general revenues would still be significantly less than required under current law and less than the leading alternatives.

Congressmen Kolbe and Stenholm were the first to use this method in revising their previous legislation, referring to their revised plan as "Kolbe-Stenholm Lite." Their new plan retained most of the features of the NCRP bill, with a few modifications. They retained the provisions that would adjust the "bend-point factors," that is, changing the Social Security benefit formula to make it more progressive. They also retained the provisions to correct the actuarial adjustment for early and late retirement, as well as to repeal the earnings limit, and to guarantee a "minimum benefit" at the poverty level or higher for anyone who had worked a full lifetime.

Kolbe and Stenholm moved towards Moynihan in one other respect. They slowed their plan's increase in the early and normal retirement ages (NRAs). The plan would still effect an increase in one month every two years, once NRA reached 67 at the end of 2011. But instead of raising the retirement ages as aggressively as did the previous commission's bill, a portion of the fiscal work would be done by applying a "life expectancy index" to the benefit formula itself.

Backing off from raising the retirement age was one concession to politics that was made in every quarter in 1999. Even the most fiscally austere public servants were less willing in 1999 to level with the public about the cost of permitting everyone to continue to retire at age 62. The Senate bipartisan plan would not raise the normal retirement age or the early eligibility age at all, beyond current-law levels. The House bipartisan Kolbe-Stenholm plan would raise it much more slowly than in the previous year's legislation. Every other major plan on the table left the retirement age untouched.

The political judgment that raising the retirement age was off the table seemed to have been generally made with little substantive reflection. Polls seemingly indicated that the public strongly opposed raising the retirement age, but those same polls were extremely shoddy in their mode of asking the question. The organization Americans Discuss Social Security, for example, reported that a vast majority of respondents opposed raising the normal retirement age, but from the same poll also reported that a plurality favored increasing the early eligibility age. Taken together, naively, one would conclude that Americans favored gradually raising the early eligibility age until it hit normal retirement age—in other words, that they favored gradually eliminating early retirement. Other surveys, however, make clear that Americans do not favor eliminating early retirement. Most of the polls simply reflect a misunderstanding of the reality that "normal retirement age" does not actually determine when individuals are permitted to retire. When the questions were asked more carefully by the American Academy of Actuaries, raising the retirement age actually emerged as one of the *more* popular options to restore Social Security to solvency.

The new Kolbe-Stenholm plan was a more expensive plan than the previous year's bill, but in 1999 it was still the most fiscally conservative plan. The net cost of the Kolbe-Stenholm plan was estimated by the Social Security actuaries in a memo of May 12, 1999, and is shown in Table 20.1 as a percentage of national taxable payroll.[4]

In the near term, the Kolbe-Stenholm plan was similar to the Archer plan or any 2 percent plan in the immediate "cost" to the federal government. The difference between the two plans, however, comes in the later years, where the outlay restraints in the Kolbe-Stenholm plan begin to produce cost savings to the federal government. Under the previous assumption that all costs of transition are met by issuing more federal debt, the net effect on federal budget balance of the two plans (cumulatively) can be seen in Table 20.2.

As previously noted, one has to take these distantly projected figures with a grain of salt. They compare to an implausible baseline that assumes that every penny of projected surpluses would otherwise be saved. But the point is that even if the *entire* cost of Kolbe-Stenholm were paid for with new debt, it would exert an enormous net positive effect on federal budget balances within approximately three decades.

NOTES

1. Report of the Social Security and Medicare Trustees, 1999, Table III.A.2, p. 169.

2. Stephen Goss, Deputy Chief Actuary, memorandum, April 16, 1999, p. 4.

3. Ibid., April 29, 1999.

4. Stephen Goss, Deputy Chief Actuary, and Alice Wade, memorandum, May 12, 1999. OASDI costs given in memo are lower than those given here by 2 percent of payroll, the difference being that the table provided here includes the cost of required contributions to the personal accounts, whereas the actuaries only estimate the OASDI income and costs, which do not include personal-account contributions and withdrawals.

21

The Last, Best Hopes: The Senate Bipartisan Plan and Other Efforts

A description of the legislative proposal that emerged from the bipartisan Senate negotiations can best be organized with attention to the following criteria:

- Its long-term fiscal implications
- The reasoning behind each component of the proposal
- The anticipated effect on Social Security benefits

First, the fiscal implications. The Senate package nearly matched its House counterpart in terms of how much of the long-term fiscal problem it would solve. In Table 20.1 can be found the projected cost rates for the Senate plan as determined by the Social Security actuaries, as usual expressed as a percentage of national taxable payroll.[1]

As projected, the Senate plan would eliminate a significant portion of the projected growth in the nation's Social Security tax burden. By 2020, the annual cost of the program, including the investment in personal accounts, would be less than current law; by 2030, it would be significantly less, and dropping.

The Senate plan reflected several creative policy choices. One problem always faced by reformers is how to demonstrate that personal-account benefits will likely produce more income than a similar package of traditional fixes. Even though the NCRP, CRS, and other experts had repeatedly demonstrated this fact, people could simply choose not to believe it. What was needed was a way to show that the personal accounts themselves were not the "cause" of any reductions in defined benefits.

The best solution was found in a provision of a bill offered by Congressman Nick Smith of Michigan. This provision tied the adjustment of the current Social Security benefit to the tax refund into the personal account. The size of that tax refund would be compounded forward at the Trust Fund interest rate, and the resulting retirement benefit would be subtracted from the previously promised Social Security benefit.

In other words, if beneficiaries simply bought a Treasury bond with their personal accounts, one that received the 3 percent real interest rate earned by the Trust Fund, they would come out exactly even. The personal account could not thus be construed to "cause" a benefit reduction. If the beneficiaries chose to invest in a stock fund or any other fund that they felt would beat the Trust Fund interest rate, they had that right, but no one would be obliged to accept the risk of a lower benefit.

Note also that this approach does not have the policy drawbacks of the "clawback" plans. The government's liability is reduced up front, in proportion to the size of the tax refund given. All accumulations earned by the beneficiary are theirs, free and clear. There is no "clawing back" of their accumulations as they are earned, and thus the incentive to put in more money and to invest better is wholly preserved.

Moreover, proposing offsets in this fashion also solved some other nagging policy problems, such as what to do about carry-over effects upon disability benefits. The new proposal avoided that problem simply by not applying the personal account offsets to the disabled. If an individual stops working due to disability, then the tax refunds and contributions also stop, and thus so do the benefit offsets.

Individuals would not have access to their personal accounts until retirement age. Thus, disabled individuals continue to receive the previously promised defined benefit until retirement age, when they receive both the offsets and the proceeds from the retirement account. In other words, the new formalism would leave the disabled unaffected.

The negotiators believed that a 0.5 percent future change should still be made in CPI. (Kolbe-Stenholm used only 0.33 percent, to reflect recent changes made by BLS.) All agreed that the reforms should be made with methodological corrections rather than by simply legislating a reduction in CPI. The legislative language would require BLS to make the remaining reforms identified by the Boskin Commission to address upper-level substitution bias and product quality improvement, the latter particularly critical to the 0.5 percent assumption.

The most significant change, however, to the CPI provision was the decision to apply it only prospectively to benefits. Individuals already eligible for Social Security benefits would continue to have their benefits indexed under the old CPI formalism. This was done so that current retirees could be shown that they would be affected in no adverse way by the reform package. As it was the elderly who were often most concerned about the ramifications of reform, negotiators felt that there was a significant advantage in letting them know that they would not be affected.

Chairman Archer (R-TX) as well as others zeroed in on this as a "notch" at the Ways and Means hearings, because some birth years of beneficiaries would under the plan have their benefits indexed with one formula and others with a different one. He noted that this would produce powerful political pressure to ultimately bring everyone back up to the old CPI level. He had a point. The CPI "hold harmless" provision for current retirees was a result of negotiators dividing over the best possible way to present their package politically and showed the marks of several cooks seasoning the broth.

Negotiators agreed to adopt the Moynihan-Kerrey approach and to abandon the changes in the early eligibility age contained in the NCRP legislation. The current-law increase in the NRA would be accelerated to conclude by the end of 2011, and after that point, life-expectancy indexing would be applied to the primary insurance amount (PIA) formula, instead of raising the NRA, consistent with the proposal made by Senator Moynihan.

Negotiators also agreed to retain the provision that would correct the actuarial adjustments for early and late retirement, as well as other work-reward provisions such as eliminating the earnings test on Social Security benefits and counting all years of earnings in the numerator of the AIME formula (see previous descriptions of NCRP proposal).

Some negotiators balked at the "minimum benefit" provision that had been contained in the NCRP plan. All agreed on the need for additional progressivity in the basic benefit formula, to counter whatever reductions in the defined benefit guarantees for low-income individuals would result from the other provisions. The negotiators in the end approved an extremely progressive change in the Social Security bend-point factors, replacing the 90 percent, 32 percent, and 15 percent bend-point factors with a 90 percent, 70 percent, 20 percent, and 10 percent bend-point–factor system. The change would be phased in over 10 years and would greatly increase the size of the guaranteed benefits on the low-income end.

Negotiators also agreed not to include newly hired state and local workers and to avoid changes in the nonworking spouse benefit.

Certain negotiators felt that 2 percent accounts were too small for low-income individuals to be able to get appreciable gains from their personal accounts. Others were unwilling to cut more deeply into the defined benefit system in order to make room for larger accounts. Fiscal conservatives were unwilling to embrace an "add-on" contribution from general revenues to make the accounts larger. A compromise was eventually struck: a matching program would be created for low-income individuals whereby voluntary contributions would entitle them to additional matches from general revenues. By making the matching contributions contingent upon *new* saving, negotiators took a more fiscally responsible stance than simply creating the contributions as a "gift." By making the "trigger" for matching contributions very small, the match program was made extremely progressive.

The matching program would establish a cap of 1 percent of the maximum taxable wage amount, as the limit on contributions that the individual would receive from current taxes. Specifically, for example, in a year such as 1999 in which the maximum taxable wage amount was $72,600, the cap would be set at $726.

Consider the example of an individual with $20,000 in annual wages:

Total Cap: $726

Minus

Mandatory Personal Account Contribution = 2 percent of $20,000 = $400

Eligible for Remaining Match of: $726 - $400 = $326

The way that the individual could receive $326 in matching contributions would be to make the first $1 of voluntary contributions, which would produce a $100 "match." (This $100 "kicker" was a means of helping out those with little money to save.) After receiving $100, individuals are eligible for $326 minus $100 of additional matches, or $226, on a 1-for-1 match basis. Individuals were not limited in their contributions by the size of this cap. They could make up to $2,000 in voluntary contributions overall.

Note that the formula works to target matching assistance on individuals with incomes of half of the wage base or below. Someone with an income of $40,000 would have $800 in mandated contributions and thus be over the limit already.

In order to understand the plan's impact on benefits, consider the case of a "steady low-wage earner." This is defined by SSA as a worker who has earned 45 percent of the national average wage for his or her entire working career. In 1999, this annual amount would have been $13,380.

The initial benefit levels promised under current law to that low-wage worker, retiring at age 65, can be found for various retirement dates in Table 21.1. The benefits diminish in the year 2034 because that is the year that Social Security projects to have insufficient revenues to pay benefits.

The added progressivity in the Senate bipartisan plan would increase these individuals' total benefits whether they received only the Trust Fund's interest rate of return on their personal accounts or a higher rate of return such as the historic stock rate.

In addition, this individual would be eligible for the "match program" and thus with small additional contributions would receive much more. If

Table 21.1
Current-Law Benefit Promise, Low-Wage Worker, Retiring at Age 65, versus
Benefits in Senate Bipartisan Plan

Year	Monthly Benefit Promise	Senate Plan, Low Interest Assumption	Senate Plan, High Interest Assumption
2010	$624	$620	$624
2020	$673	$733	$754
2030	$690	$776	$843
2040	$536	$821	$993
2050	$582	$869	$1,100
2060	$611	$920	$1,168

Source: All figures for this section come from a Congressional Research Service memorandum
of June 8, 1999.

the individual retiring in 2040, for example, made annual contributions
equal to 1 percent of wages, the benefits would range from $981 to $1,115,
depending on the interest rate.

This is a favorable example, because the plan's progressivity increases
benefits on the low-income end. But medium-income and high-income individuals gain, too, albeit in different ways. Table 21.2 shows the benefit
levels that current law provides relative to the Senate bipartisan plan in the
year 2030. Again, the column on the left assumes that taxes have been *raised*
as is necessary to fund current-law promises. Let's look again at the size of
the tax burden faced by these workers five years before retirement, in the
year 2025. For current law, it's effectively 16.6 percent. For the bipartisan
plan, it's 15.4 percent.[2] For individuals working in 2030, it's 17.7 percent under current law. Under the bipartisan plan, it's 15.7 percent.

Where the tax savings would accrue is on the general revenue side of the
ledger. Payroll taxes would not need to go up either under current law by
2030 or under the bipartisan plan, but the general tax burdens are very different under the two plans. Under current law, it's equal to an increase of
3.61 points in the payroll tax in 2025. Under the bipartisan plan, this increase would be reduced to 2.17—a reduction of 39.8 percent. Under current law, in 2030, the general tax burden would be the equivalent of a 4.62
point increase in the payroll tax. Under the bipartisan plan, this would be
reduced to 2.38—a reduction of 48.5 percent.

Because these are general income tax burdens, rather than payroll tax
burdens, they would be progressively applied and would fall dispropor-

Table 21.2
Projected Monthly Benefits of Senate Bipartisan Plan at Various Wage Levels

Worker Income (1999 Dollars)	Current Law	Bipartisan Plan
$10,000	$597	$644-$694
$20,000	$872	$880-$980
$30,000	$1,146	$1,037-$1,187
$40,000	$1,407	$1,168-$1,368
$50,000	$1,536	$1,247-$1,497

tionately upon higher-income workers. Thus, what high-income workers have to gain from this reform is relief from these large tax increases.

Let's put it all together by considering the case low-average, and high-income workers. Let's pretend that they retire in 2040, and let's examine their changed tax burden as workers in 2030. What do they get out of reform? (All figures are in 1999 dollars.)

Low-Wage Worker

Tax burden in 2030: Reduced $150 annually below current law.

Benefits in 2040: Raised between $69 and $241 monthly above current law.

Average-Wage Worker

Tax burden in 2030: Reduced $533 annually below current law.

Benefits in 2040: Range between increasing $234 monthly and decreasing $149.

Maximum-Wage Worker

Tax burden in 2030: Reduced $2,439 annually below current law.

Benefits in 2040: Range between increasing $495 monthly and decreasing $481.

In summary, the low-wage worker gains on both the tax and the benefit end. The average-wage worker faces lower tax burdens and is more likely to gain benefits than to lose them. (If he's concerned about the possibility of losing benefits, he has a much greater opportunity to increase those benefits by contributing his tax savings to the accounts voluntarily than if the government had coercively taken his taxes to fund the current system.) The high-wage worker is as likely to lose benefits as to gain them, but that's the price of alleviating his tax burden.

The argument for the status quo and for the personal account plans that do not scale back defined-benefit increases essentially boils down to the argument that we should tax higher-income individuals more in order to give more benefits to those same high-income individuals. No political analyst would countenance the notion that taxing and giving more to the well-off is a political strategy that bodes well for the political future of the Social Security program.

The bipartisan plans received a record amount of support upon their introduction—between the Senate and House versions, 15 cosponsors came aboard. One particularly important cosponsor in the Senate was Iowa Senator Chuck Grassley, who helped to ensure that all CPI reforms were done through methodological improvements as opposed to legislative reductions. The senator also authored an expanded survivor benefit provision, to alleviate the concentration of elderly poverty among widowed women.

Chairman Archer's 1999 hearings brought forth a number of plans based on alternate approaches. Congressman Nadler's plan tracked the form of the president's, although combined with an aggressive increase in the cap on taxable wages. This tax increase was the only element of Nadler's plan that would have an actual impact on the financing challenge. Its remaining provisions—to redistribute existing savings returns through reinvestment of the Trust Fund in equities and transferring "credits" to the Trust Fund—would have no net substantive effect.

Congressman Stark came forth with a plan to simply transfer 2.07 percent from general revenues perpetually (2.07 percent being the average annual deficit over the valuation period) to the program. This was a somewhat tongue-in-cheek response to Archer's plan to create 2 percent accounts from general revenues, perpetually. Stark's point was that if we had to devote an additional 2 percent of payroll to this system forever to fund existing promises, then there was hardly any point in creating the artifice of personal accounts. Just raise the tax burden by 2 percent and be done with it.

Stark's point was somewhat undermined by his implication that the effects of his 2 percent plan and Archer's were economically similar. They weren't. There would be immediate effects on the federal budget of refunding 2 percent of payroll into personal accounts, whereas the 2 percent transfer proposed by Stark would have no budgetary effect until it came time to redeem the new debt created, at which point the cost would be larger than under the Archer plan.

But amid the tongue-in-cheek plans came forth another serious plan from Congressman Kasich. The Kasich plan was politically significant because Kasich, who retained credibility with House conservatives, attempted to develop a cost-reducing proposal. His was the first new Republican plan (Congressman Nick Smith had already done so in a previous Congress) to join the bipartisan efforts to pursue these objectives.

The Kasich plan can be summarized as follows:

Reforming Social Security

1. One simple, large reduction in long-term outlays
2. A highly progressive personal-account system of some complexity
3. Constructive movement in the direction of fiscal sustainability
4. Identification of the funding sources needed to fill in the plan's financing gaps

Taking these in turn:

The Kasich plan would do one simple thing to limit the growth of long-term Social Security outlays. It would index the program's initial benefit levels to inflation rather than to the growth in national wages. This would save an enormous amount of money over the long term, though these savings would be very gradual at first.

The virtue of this provision is that it produces its savings in a less politically volatile way. It does not yet embody the political flashpoint that raising the retirement age or changing the measurement of CPI does. From a policy perspective, it is entirely reasonable to postulate that initial benefit levels should rise with inflation, pursuant to the goal of maintaining a constant buying power over time.

That being said, the proposal is not quite a panacea. Outlays would slow gradually relative to current law before 2040, but on the other hand they would be reduced more than is strictly necessary in the distant years after 2060. Moreover, the benefit changes would take effect across all wage levels, reducing the defined benefit safety net on the low-income end. They are not beyond the realm of constructive adjustment, however. They could easily be improved by accelerating them and by making them more progressive.

The more significant difficulties with the Kasich plan lie with the construction of the personal accounts. The plan would create larger personal accounts proportionally for low-income individuals, ranging from 3.5 percent of taxable income at the bottom end of the wage scale to 1 percent of taxable income on the higher end. This formula does not result in a simple and gradual diminution of contribution rates as one goes higher in income. In some examples, even the *absolute value* of the personal-account contribution would be lowered as one's income increased, potentially distorting work incentives.

The Kasich plan would require additional borrowing authority for Social Security in order to make it through the transition years before outlay savings accumulate sufficiently. It's anticipated that this additional borrowing would be required from 2000 through 2045, under current projections. Later, when the advance funding enables the system to operate in surplus, the system would pay back the loans from the surplus revenues, commencing in 2061.

The net cost rates projected for the Kasich plan relative to current law can be found in Table 20.1. By 2030, the Kasich plan would reduce costs significantly relative to current law, though not as much as the bipartisan plans.

The Senate Bipartisan Plan

Benefit analysis of the Kasich plan produces the predictable results relative to the bipartisan plans—that the Kasich plan's benefits would likely be higher in the first 30–40 years, and the bipartisan plan's higher at the end of the valuation period.

The Kasich plan, even if adopted unamended, would be an enormously positive reform. Any amendment should be done without destroying its considerable virtues. One possibility includes the following:

- Replace the sliding-scale personal-account contributions with a simple 2 percent account for everyone, with the offset for the value of this contribution being that used by the Senate bipartisan plan.
- Combine the benefit reindexing with changes to the bend-point factors, phasing in four bend points of 90 percent, 70 percent, 20 percent, and 10 percent, over 20 years to eliminate any erosion of defined benefits on the low-income end.
- Increase the actuarial adjustment for early and late retirement so as to restore work incentives and to produce important additional savings before 2030.
- Provide additional widows' benefits as in the bipartisan plan, phased in over several decades, and repeal the earnings limit.

NOTES

1. In the case of the Senate plan, national taxable payroll would be slightly different than in each of the other plans, because the Senate plan would reindex the cap on taxable wages to keep it at its current level of 86 percent of total national wages. (Under current law, a decreasing share of national wages is projected to be subject to the Social Security tax.) Consequently, the tax burdens for the Senate plan given here should be increased, depending on the year, by between 1 and 2 percent in order to be comparable directly to the tax burdens associated with the plans previously reviewed.

2. It is important to recognize that these figures include the effects on income tax revenue of reindexing the Consumer Price Index. In other words, this income tax revenue is not an added cost in addition to the figures given here, but is included within it. Even with this inclusion, the total tax claims of the bipartisan plan are significantly less than in current law.

22

Where We Are and Whither We Are Tending

Responsible Social Security reform was treated like an unwanted stepchild in 1999. The president made a willful decision to abandon it. Prominent Republicans clung precariously to the dissonant mantras of personal accounts and of preserving all current-law defined benefits, heedless of internal contradiction. Substantive Social Security reform was pushed to the sidelines in favor of a distantly related partisan debate about the federal budget. The "lockbox" became the ground over which this battle was fought.

By 1999, the federal government was on the verge of balancing its books for the first time in recent memory *without* counting the Social Security surplus. As mentioned before, the government has no mechanism to "save" the Social Security surplus even it if runs a surplus of that magnitude and doesn't in any tangible way "spend" the money. If the government balanced the non–Social Security budget, overall public debt would be bought down with the Social Security surplus. While this would not produce any direct funding for future benefits, the government's overall fiscal position would be improved.

"Saving" the surplus can reduce an existing public debt. But if the debt is paid off, the government has no place to "save" and to accumulate such assets in a way that can be drawn down to pay future Social Security benefits. In order to do this, the government would need to accumulate a reserve of tens of trillions of dollars.

Republicans were in no mood to engage the president on Social Security reform, but they did want to position themselves as the true guardians of the Social Security surplus. Hence, they developed a proposal for a "lockbox"—a mechanism requiring that the government run a surplus equal in size at least to the size of the Social Security surplus and enforced by requiring that public debt be reduced to that extent.

The administration objected to the lockbox idea at first, claiming that tying the lockbox to public debt reduction would adversely impact the Treasury Department's ability to manage cash transactions, that the government might inadvertently default.

Republicans did start with something of a moral high ground in the lockbox debate. The Congressional Budget Office reaffirmed that even with the larger tax cuts that Republicans were embracing, the total amount of public debt would be less under the Republican budget than under the Clinton administration's submitted budget. But many Republicans were themselves confused into believing that the lockbox was itself a solution to Social Security's problems.

The currently projected insolvency date of Social Security, 2034, presumes that every penny of the Social Security surplus is saved in some way and earns interest and that these reserves can be drawn down from 2014 through 2034 to fund benefits. If the public debt were entirely eliminated by 2014, then when the government must produce an additional $7 trillion in general revenues to supplement payroll tax revenues through 2034, it would have a more realistic chance of doing it. But the lockbox itself doesn't produce any actual financing. Even if it did, the program would still be insolvent in 2034.

The administration found itself in a troublesome political place. It had been caught in the "double-counting" of its budget. Moreover, its budget proposed to spend more of the Social Security surplus than Congress's. It needed to retool its position.

It did so in the spring of 1999, proposing a new framework in which the government would not double-count projected surpluses, but instead run a surplus from 2000 to 2010 that would be used to reduce public debt. Beginning in 2011, instead of in the very beginning of the 2000–2014 period, additional transfers would be made to the Social Security system, of a size equal to the reduction in federal interest payments resulting from buying down debt from 2000 to 2010.

The new proposal contained marginally less chicanery than the previous one. The transfers of credits to the Social Security system still were not real financing and still represented a type of double count. They proposed to credit Social Security a second time with the interest savings supposedly arising from saving a Social Security surplus. It was still a form of double-counting, but of the annual interest alone, rather than the entire Social Security surplus.

Still, the administration proposal was not wholly without merit. At least in this form, it sought to relate Social Security solvency to some level of "good behavior" in reducing public debt. Consequently, bipartisan reformers began to look for choices other than simply saying "we won't," when the administration pushed for general revenue transfers.

One such idea we called the "shift for thrift" plan. This alternative would say to the president: "We are willing to consider paper transfers to the Social Security system that will extend projected solvency, contingent upon public debt reduction as in your proposal. But we will only agree to allow those if they are contingent upon real reductions in the system's actual unfunded liabilities. Only for every dollar of real action to reduce unfunded liabilities will we permit one dollar of paper cover-up of cash deficits." Such a posture would not only be good policy, it would elucidate the difference between accounting gimmickry and actual substantive action.

Though not an actual reform plan, it would do some substantive good and permit no harm. An appropriate measure of the system's unfunded liabilities are the cash flow deficits that begin to appear in 2014—the difference between the system's actual cash revenues, in payroll taxes and benefit taxation (and not counting intragovernmental transfers such as interest payments or other accounting changes) and its cash obligations. The actuaries could project the annual cash flow gap beginning in 2014 and beyond and permit additional transfers only to the extent that these are actually reduced relative to the 1999 trustees' report. If no substantive action is taken to reduce these, no transfers occur.

Such a negotiating posture would force lawmakers and administration officials to disallow transfers without serious reform, while at the same time it would signal that Congress's mind is open to the administration's framework.

We also met with individuals from both the administration and from Republican staff in an attempt to find ways to reach a responsible outcome that contained fewer of the political stumbling blocks in the bipartisan plans. Though each office was noncommittal about what they would accept, they did not discourage us from trying.

The following is an outline of a solution that might well be an appropriate compromise between the positions taken by other principals. As a gesture to the president, it would allow for some general revenue transfers based on public debt reduction. As a gesture to Chairman Archer, it would fund the personal accounts to an extent from general revenues in the near term and would eliminate any changes in CPI. As a gesture to Senator Gramm, it would create larger personal accounts from near-term unified surpluses, and thus more advance funding. As a gesture to the bipartisan reformers, it would ultimately turn these accounts into carve-outs, make no new open-ended commitments of general revenues, and provide for full ownership over personal account proceeds. Specifically, the revision would include:

Reforming Social Security

1. "Lockbox" and interest recapture, as in the president's proposal, require that Social Security surpluses pay down public debt from 2000–2010. Beginning in 2011, transfer approximately $80 billion annually from general revenues to the Social Security Trust Fund. This is a reasonable estimate of the interest savings that would come from paying down debt with the surplus remaining after creating personal accounts and would be a smaller commitment of general revenues than under current law and alternate plans.

2. Use the near-term surplus to establish 3 percent accounts, with benefit offsets as in the Senate bipartisan plan. From 2000 to 2014, the accounts would be funded 1.5 percent from general revenues, 1.5 percent from the payroll tax. By 2045, the accounts would be fully phased over to be wholly funded from the payroll tax.

3. Eliminate the earnings test (as in the bipartisan plans, the Moynihan plan, and the Archer plan).

4. Correct the actuarial adjustment for early and late retirement, phased in from 2006 to 2010.

5. Retain the current-law projected change in the normal retirement age to 67, but remove the current-law hiatus in getting there.

6. Create new progressivity in the PIA bend-point factors to offset the effects of other benefit changes for low-income individuals. Moving to 90 percent, 70 percent, 20 percent, and 10 percent bend points should work well, phased in over 20 years from 2006 to 2025.

7. Phase in a higher widows' benefit from 2001 to 2050 as in the Senate bipartisan bill.

8. Create life expectancy indexing in the PIA formula as in the Moynihan and bipartisan plans. Currently these indexing factors are often constructed to imitate a change in NRA to 68 by the year 2017, and then tracking projected life expectancy after that. It is smoother and provides fairer treatment across birth cohorts to apply the indexing more gradually, for example, a factor of 0.993, starting in 2012, when the NRA again remains fixed.[1]

The variable in such a plan is point 8, which can be adjusted as necessary to achieve the maximum possible equity of treatment between various cohorts of beneficiaries and taxpayers.

Such an agreement could enable all sides to claim victory. It would not achieve as much in terms of fiscal responsibility and cost restraints as, for example, the Kolbe-Stenholm plan, because of the additional revenue let into the system through the period of time when personal accounts are partially an add-on and also because of the additional interest-recapture revenue permitted in 2011. But it clearly would improve fiscal prospects relative to the current system, largely because of the increased advance funding that it would create. And by devoting a larger share of near-term surplus revenues to the Social Security accounts, there would be less left over for Congress and the president to "spend" on other appropriations and on other targeted tax breaks.

Moreover, this outline would stay away from the biggest political hot buttons on the table—raising the retirement age and adjusting the CPI. This is not necessarily the best policy. The Consumer Price Index does have various methodological problems that ought to be corrected, and only bureaucratic inertia prevents this from being done. Moreover, it is absurd to hold that our current retirement ages should remain fixed when so many of us are leading longer and healthier lives than previous generations. But as long as political judgment insists that we should assess the costs in other ways, instead of forthrightly raising the retirement age, we must recognize that political reality.

If Congress enacted such a plan, we would have achieved Social Security solvency without raising the payroll tax, with increased benefits for workers through personal accounts, with a reduction in future tax burdens, with increased protections against poverty, and without changing CPI or the retirement age. That's not a bad result.

The United States currently stands at a historic threshold. We are truly masters of our own destiny to a degree that we have not been in several years. We enjoy peace and prosperity simultaneously. We stand poised to reap the bounty of the first significant federal budget surpluses in more than a generation. We have a luxury rarely afforded to nations—the opportunity to plan for the future with excess resources.

We also have severe choices to make. We know that the beneficiaries of tomorrow's senior entitlement spending have already been born. We know how many there are and how many children they have. We know how much we have promised to them in benefits, and we know the approximate size of the tax burden that we would impose on future generations in order to pay what is currently promised.

We stand at a fork in the road. If we continue straight along the path that we are on, then we will require future generations of Americans to pay more to support senior entitlement programs than Americans have ever been required to pay for anything short of war. Economic growth will not change this. A Social Security "lockbox" will not change this.

The other road would lead us to reduce the proportion of the future retirement benefits that we currently stand to collect from future taxes and to assume some of the responsibility ourselves for funding our own retirement. We have the resources to do it. We could put some of today's surplus money into retirement income accounts and hold future generations' tax burdens to something closer to what we ourselves have been required to pay.

Taking the responsible course would require minimal sacrifice on our part. We would not have to raise taxes today. We would not have to cut benefits to current or near-term retirees. The only choice we would need to make would be to scale back some of the less realistic promises that we are making to ourselves, the retirees of the future.

It may well be the case that the United States does wish to travel the route of higher taxation, of moving to a United States in which people are induced to spend more and more of their lives in retirement, and in which the earnings of wage earners are taxed more than 50 percent more than they are today. I personally find this to be a troubling vision, but will happily concede to the majority if they wish it to be this way.

What I do advocate, however, is seeing the truth and telling the truth. Those who favor this vision of the United States have an obligation to acknowledge the costs of it and to persuade the U.S. public as to why those costs should be borne. It is clear from the arguments that are used for the status quo that many advocates of the status quo do not, in fact, believe the U.S. public to be with them, because they go to extraordinary lengths to obscure the realities.

An advocate of raising the tax burden effectively to 18 percent of national taxable payroll by 2030 to fund Social Security benefits may have a perfectly persuasive case. It is not information, but rather deception, that holds that the system will not have any difficulty paying benefits through 2034 without a massive increase in revenues. Those who publish papers and books saying there is "no crisis" until 2034, whreas they know perfectly well the cost of redeeming the Social Security Trust Fund through that date, are willfully denying the choices before us and depriving citizens of what they need to know to choose a course.

To these individuals, I simply ask, Speak the truth. Do not pretend that the Trust Fund can finance benefits without that money being taxed from working Americans. Make your case, advocate the assessment of the costs that you favor, but be truthful. If you wish to defend these costs, admit that they exist. If your recommendations are best, they can prevail with the truth being known.

Too many policymakers ask Americans to believe in a fantasy world in which we can all enjoy a longer retirement period than any previous generation of Americans, that we can live off the earnings of smaller proportion of workers relative to retirees, and that our benefits will magically appear by themselves without anyone being taxed to pay for them. The United States was built on dreams, but not on fantasies. We didn't rely on the transcontinental railroad to materialize from nowhere; we built it. And we must build the funding to provide for tomorrow's Social Security benefits, if we want them to exist.

As 1999 draws to a close, it is clear that the United States is not yet ready to seize its historic opportunity to turn the nation onto a sustainable fiscal course. Times are good, and many political leaders do not wish to acquaint Americans with the planning that must be done to ensure that tomorrow is also good. If a responsible Social Security reform proposal had been floated in 1999, it might well have been torn apart in political campaigns.

But we will not be ready, indeed will never be ready, until Americans are sufficiently cognizant of the choices before us, to be able to react appropriately and to ask the right questions when politicians address—or avoid—the subject. No one who refuses to address Social Security reform has any right to be in the Congress. Trillions are at stake, literally thousands of dollars per person in the annual tax burdens of future generations of Americans. Any politician who doesn't feel "ready" to deal with the issue should get out of town in a hurry.

This book has been an attempt to acquaint the reader with the choices before the United States as it stands poised to deal with Social Security reform. I am not in the least offended by any reader's disagreement with my policy prescriptions. This is why I provide hard numbers where many choose vague adjectives and descriptions. Prose does not suffice if the goal is to inform as much as to persuade.

Each month, it seems, someone publishes a new book about Social Security, and each month, it seems, public understanding of the issue is set back. Many of these books focus on emotion rather than facts. They discuss political activity rather than data. They spend many pages giving the political history of Social Security's "enemies" or disparage the term "crisis," as if winning a linguistic battle is the key to solving Social Security's projected problems.

It is often said that in the United States young people are indifferent to politics, that they do not participate. To American youth, I say, This battle is about you. It is not about the current elderly in the United States; they will be well taken care of, and can be affordably taken care of within current structures. This is about what kind of country you want to live in in 30 years.

To today's older adults and to senior citizens, I say, I know that most of you agree with me that the United States is more than the sum of everyone's narrow self-interests. We have a common lineage and a common interest in posterity. A strong and prosperous United States has been revealed to be the difference between triumph and defeat against the forces of fascism and communism. Social Security is solvent for you. Now let us ensure that it works for the next generation. This is no time to be "fighting the last war." Demographic change requires other types of change.

Social Security shouldn't remain as it is solely because young people have a poor voter turnout. We're responsible for doing the right thing by today's young adults, whether they vote or not. If the only result of U.S. politics is that powerful voter groups aggregate resources to themselves, then this nation has departed irretrievably from the basis that made it great.

Of course, it has not. Americans are as determined to attain their manifest destiny as they have ever been. They may be more cynical today about many institutions than they have been in the past, but this frustration reflects the political process's inconsistency with their hopes and dreams rather than the abandonment of those hopes and dreams.

Sustained by a comprehending and patriotic U.S. public, we can together preserve these hopes and dreams for future generations of Americans.

NOTE

1. There are a number of reasons why this form of indexing might be preferable to the style employed in Kasich's plan. One is that because it imitates a change in NRA, it is clear that it should not apply to the disabled, whereas reindexing the bend-point factors as in the Kasich plan produces the troublesome policy conundrum as to whether it should. Second, the timing of the savings is more targeted to the fiscal health of the system. The 0.993 factor could be applied for a span of 48 years (2012–2059) or perhaps 36 years (2012–2047) and then stopped. The savings accrue more rapidly and do not need to compound to a significantly larger level in the period after 2060.

Selected Bibliography

Aaron, Henry, and Robert Reischauer. *Countdown to Reform: The Great Social Security Debate*. New York: The Century Foundation, 1998.

Bipartisan Commission on Entitlement and Tax Reform. *Final Report to the President*. Washington, D.C.: GPO, 1995.

———. *Interim Report to the President*. Washington, D.C.: GPO, 1994.

Budget of the United States, FY2000. Submitted by President Clinton to Congress. Vol. 4, *Analytical Perspectives*.

Congressional Research Service (CRS). *Social Security Reform: Projected Contributions and Benefits Under Three Proposals*. Report for the U.S. Congress. December 3, 1998.

———. "Social Security Notch Debate." CRS Issue Brief IB92129.

Employee Benefits Research Institute. "Assessing Social Security Reform Alternatives." Washington, D.C.: 1997.

Ferrara, Peter, and Michael Tanner. *A New Deal for Social Security*. Washington, D.C.: Cato Institute, 1998.

National Commission on Retirement Policy (NCRP). *Can America Afford to Retire? The Retirement Security Challenge Facing You and the Nation*. Washington, D.C.: Center for Strategic and International Studies, 1998.

———. *The 21st Century Retirement Security Plan: Final Report of the National Commission on Retirement Policy*. Washington, D.C.: Center for Strategic and International Studies, 1999.

Neustadt, Richard, and Ernest May. *Thinking in Time: The Uses of History for Decision-makers*. New York: Free Press, 1986.

Peterson, Peter. *Facing Up: How to Rescue the Economy from Crushing Debt and Restore the American Dream*. New York: Simon and Schuster, 1993.

Selected Bibliography

———. *Gray Dawn: How the Coming Age Wave Will Transform America—and the World*. New York: Times Books, 1999.

Report of the 1994–96 Advisory Council on Social Security. Vols. 1 and 2.

Schieber, Sylvester, and John Shoven. *The Real Deal: The History and Future of Social Security*. New Haven, Conn.: Yale University Press, 1999.

Schlesinger, Arthur, Jr. *The Coming of the New Deal*. Boston: Houghton Mifflin, 1988.

Social Security Administration. *1999 Annual Report of the Board of Trustees of the Federal Old-Age and Survivors Insurance and Disability Insurance Trust Funds*. Washington, D.C.: GPO, 1999.

———. *1998 Annual Report of the Board of Trustees of the Federal Old-Age and Survivors Insurance and Disability Insurance Trust Funds*. Washington, D.C.: GPO, 1998.

Steuerle, Eugene, Edward M. Gramlich, Hugo Heclo, and Demetria Smith Nightinggale. *The Government We Deserve: Responsive Democracy and Changing Expectations*. Washington, D.C.: Urban Institute Press, 1998.

U.S. Senate. Hearing of the Senate Finance Subcommittee on Social Security and Family Policy, June 20, 1995. (Transcript).

World Bank. *Averting the Old Age Crisis: Policies to Protect the Old and Promote Growth*. New York: Oxford University Press, 1994.

Index

Index

Baby boomers, 56, 88, 110; retirement of, 3, 6, 61, 62, 111, 122, 127, 144, 178, 187, 192–93, 194, 197; Social Security benefits for, 170, 180–81, 198

Balanced budget amendment, 86, 87

Ball, Robert, reform plan of: actuarial solvency of, 106, 132, 147, 150, 208, 215; vs. personal account plans, 131, 132, 141, 204–5, 207–8; proposals in, 75, 99, 105–6, 129, 133, 138–39, 147, 157, 188, 201–2, 203. *See also* Government investment

Beard, Sam, 94

Belt, Brad, 95

Benefits: and AIME, 45–46, 118, 120, 174–75, 179, 191, 192, 207, 235; under Archer-Shaw plan, 226–27; for baby boomers, 170, 180–81, 198; cuts in, 1, 38, 57, 70, 74–75, 77, 111, 115–17, 119, 122, 128–29, 132, 135, 140, 141–43, 154, 169–71, 175, 179, 201, 203, 204, 206, 240, 247; as defined, 111, 127, 131–32, 147–49, 155–56, 157, 160, 190, 191–92, 193, 222, 223, 226, 230, 234, 235, 238–39, 240, 241, 243; vs. economic growth, 53, 56–57, 62–66, 108, 110, 111, 116–17, 144–46, 160; income groups receiving, 12–13; vs. individual contributions, 2–4, 22–24, 25–28, 29–30, 42–43, 44–48, 53, 64–67, 79, 97–98, 102, 103, 107, 110, 112–17, 118–19, 121, 203, 223; under Kasich plan, 240; under NCRP plan, 131, 171–73, 176, 179, 179–80, 191, 201, 205, 206, 207, 223, 231, 235; and PIA formula, 156, 191, 192–93, 194, 207, 228–29, 231, 235, 241, 246; and rates of return, 44, 112–17, 118–19, 120, 123, 124–25, 140, 148–49, 178, 179–80, 181; and replacement rates, 71, 112–13, 114, 176; under Senate bipartisan plan, 236–37, 238; taxes on, 2, 43, 50, 53, 108, 121, 190, 218, 230, 245; for widows, 239, 246. *See also* Taxes, payroll

Bipartisan Commission on Entitlement and Tax Reform. *See* Kerrey-Danforth Entitlement Commission

Bipartisanship, 21, 87, 93, 95, 245; in House, 6, 229, 231–32, 234, 239, 240, 246; in Senate, 6, 12, 20, 199, 214, 227, 229–30, 231, 233–39, 240, 241, 246. *See also* Kerrey-Danforth Entitlement Commission; National Commission on Retirement Policy (NCRP); Third Millennium

Borrowing, federal, 3, 52, 109, 224, 227, 232; and Social Security Surplus, 4, 23, 54–55, 76, 77, 134, 139

Boskin Commission, 234

Breaux, John, 92, 95, 184, 186, 229

Brookings Institute, 92

Budget, federal, 94, 188; appropriations spending, 3, 18, 22, 55, 146, 151, 246; balanced budget amendment, 86, 87; balancing of, 2, 4, 9–10, 13, 17–19, 22–23, 37, 142, 146, 215, 228, 232, 243–44; entitlement programs and deficits in, 11, 23, 37; relationship to Social Security surplus, 2, 4, 17–18, 23, 52, 54–55, 76, 95, 115, 134, 142, 161, 215, 218, 243–45; surpluses in, 162, 212, 218, 225–26, 227–28, 244–45, 246, 247

Bureau of Labor Statistics (BLS), 174, 207, 234

Bush, George, 11, 17, 18

Business Week, 110

Catastrophic health care insurance, 86

Cato Institute, 92, 94, 208–9

Census Bureau, 61–62, 175

Center on Budget and Policy Priorities, 37, 204–5

Center for Strategic and International Studies (CSIS), 95, 184, 185

Charles Schwab, 222

Christian Coalition, 82, 84

"Clawback" proposals, 147–49, 150, 222, 234

"Cliff effect": and actuarial solvency, 98, 111, 141, 147, 170, 187, 188, 189; in reform plans, 147, 187, 188, 189

Index

Index

About the Author and CSIS

Charles P. Blahous III is currently Executive Director of the Alliance for Worker Retirement Security. He served from 1996 to 2000 as Policy Director for U.S. Senator Judd Gregg, where he staffed the Senator's co-chairmanship of the National Commission on Retirement Policy. Dr. Blahous first came to Congress in 1989 upon being named the American Physical Society's Congressional Science Fellow. Through 1996 he served Senator Alan Simpson as his legislative director and as his liaison to the President's Commission on Entitlement and Tax Reform.

The Center for Strategic and International Studies (CSIS), established in 1962, is a private, tax-exempt institution focusing on international public policy issues. Its research is nonpartisan and nonproprietary.

CSIS is dedicated to policy impact. It seeks to inform and shape selected policy decisions in government and the private sector to meet the increasingly complex and difficult global challenges that leaders will confront in the next century. It achieves this mission in four ways: by generating strategic analysis that is anticipatory and interdisciplinary; by convening policymakers and other influential parties to assess key issues; by building structures for policy action; and by developing leaders.

CSIS does not take specific public policy positions. Accordingly, all views, positions, and conclusions expressed in this publication should be understood to be solely those of the author.